CROOME
A CREATION OF GENIUS

CROOME

A CREATION OF GENIUS

Catherine Gordon

SCALA

This book is dedicated to
George William Coventry,
13th Earl of Coventry,
and his family

This edition © Scala Arts & Heritage Publishers Ltd, 2017
Text by Catherine Gordon © Croome Heritage Trust, 2017
Illustrations © Croome Estate Trust, 2017, unless stated otherwise

First published in 2017 by
Scala Arts & Heritage Publishers Ltd
10 Lion Yard
Tremadoc Road
London SW4 7NQ, UK
www.scalapublishers.com

In association with
Croome Heritage Trust

ISBN 978-1-78551-115-8

Project manager and copy editor: Linda Schofield
Designed by Maggi Smith
Printed and bound in China

10 9 8 7 6 5 4 3 2 1

Frontispiece: Croome Court, south elevation from the river
Cover: *Croome c.1800*, by David Birtwhistle, 2016
Inside back cover: Design for a bridge, Croome, Adam office, 1771

ABBREVIATIONS

AA	The Archive at Antony House, Cornwall
BAM	Badminton Muniments at Badminton House, Gloucestershire
BL	British Library
HoP	History of Parliament online
SoL	Survey of London
WCRO	Warwickshire County Record Office, Warwick
WAAS	Worcestershire Archive and Archaeology Service at the Hive, Worcester

Please note that the Croome Collection
was accepted by HM Government in
Lieu of Inheritance Tax and allocated to
Worcestershire County Council in 2006.
The Collection was being re-catalogued at
the time of writing but updated references
can be obtained by written request to the
Worcestershire Archive and Archaeology
Service, The Hive, Sawmill Walk, The Butts,
Worcester WR1 3PD.

CONTENTS

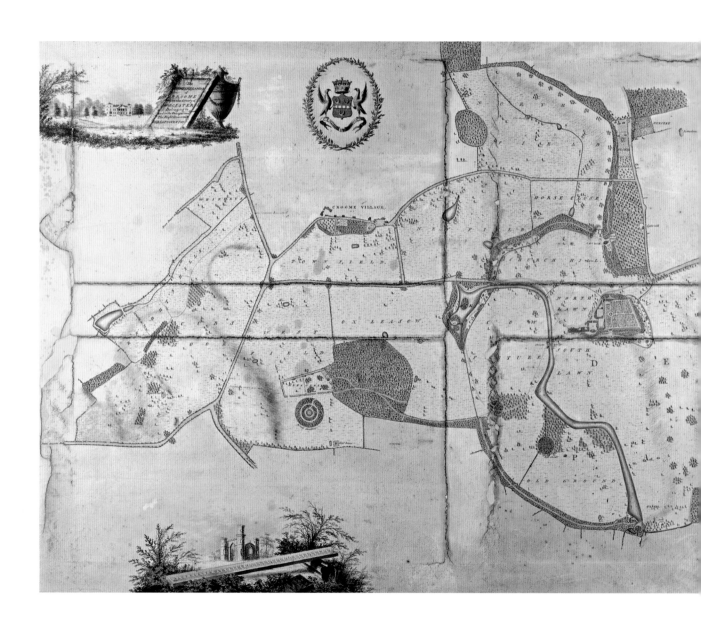

ACKNOWLEDGEMENTS

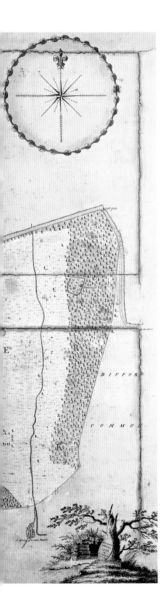

I am indebted to many individuals and organisations for their invaluable contribution to this book. I would like to make special mention of Peter Beresford and Peter Scott, who have steered the project with such vision and commitment from beginning to end, and also the Croome Heritage Trust, which has provided the means and support to make it possible. I am very grateful to the many members of staff and volunteers of the National Trust at Croome and to the Friends of Croome who have contributed so much to our understanding and appreciation of the house and park. Also I would like to thank the staff of the Badminton Muniments, Cornwall Record Office, the Library of Birmingham, Warwickshire Record Office, and especially the Worcestershire Archive and Archaeology Service for their help and advice. I am most grateful to Maggie Campbell-Culver, Mark Purcell, Christopher Rowell, Rosalind Savill and Helen Wyld for their support and expertise, to Jack Nelson for his excellent photography, and to Sarah Kay, whose research and involvement at the inception of the project was particularly welcome. Special thanks are also due to the following individuals: Katherine Alker, Jane Bradney, Nicholas Cooper, Robert Copley, James Finlay, Andrew Foster, John France, John Henderson, Simone Hill, Nick Joyce, Anne Owen, Tom Pimenta, Frances Sands, Lisa Snook, Charlene Taylor, Robert Thrift, Ric Tyler and John Wilton-Ely.

Finally, I would like to thank, in particular, Jeremy Musson, for the benefit of his extensive knowledge, support and advice; David Birtwhistle, whose superb watercolour recreations of the Croome landscape were commissioned specially for this book; Linda Schofield, who has edited the text so painstakingly and with great patience; Maggi Smith, for her wonderful design work; Pip Webster, who has resolved any management issue with such swift and unerring efficiency; and Jill Tovey, whose knowledge and insight will always be an essential component of any study of Croome and its history.

Catherine Gordon

Plan of Croome Park, by John Snape, 1796

FOREWORD

Croome Park has one of the most remarkable of great estate stories but the house in particular has been much overlooked after the all too typical disruptions of the late nineteenth and twentieth centuries when important interior elements found their way into museums in both Britain and America. That the house and its stately park are now in the hands of the National Trust, is a subject for celebration, as is the active contribution of the Friends of Croome and also the important work of the Croome Heritage Trust, who have made this fine publication possible.

Any works of restoration should always follow research and improved understanding, and Catherine Gordon's perceptive new history, covering both house and park, gives us a fresh scholarly view of the whole story. In particular, it provides new insight into the patronage of the 6th Earl of Coventry (whom Horace Walpole described as 'the remains of the Patriot breed'), and the outstanding and original contributions of both Lancelot 'Capability' Brown and Robert Adam: two of the greatest British designers of the Georgian age who both worked at Croome Park during the 1760s and 1770s.

Adam worked for Lord Coventry for over 30 years, designing many of the grand interiors of Croome Court as well as buildings in the park. Thankfully, the elegant Adam-designed ceiling of the Long Gallery 'finished in the Antique Taste' remains *in situ* to suggest the full glories of his work of this period (see p. 150). Catherine Gordon, adding to the foundation of her first book, *The Coventrys of Croome*, places the work of Adam and Brown in a wider contemporary context, and thus sharpens our accepted picture of the dynamic relationship of these three figures to the evolution of Croome in its fullest flowering in the eighteenth century.

Jeremy Musson

Croome Court, west elevation from the lake

PROLOGUE

Consult the Genius of the Place in all;
That tells the Waters or to rise, or fall,
Or helps th'ambitious Hill the heav'ns to scale,
Or scoops in circling theatres the Vale;
Calls in the Country, catches op'ning glades,
Joins willing woods, and varies shades from shades;
Now breaks, or now directs, th' intending Lines,
Paints as you plant, and as you work, designs.

Alexander Pope, *Of Taste* (1731)

On 20 May 1744 Thomas Henry Coventry, Viscount Deerhurst, eldest son and heir of William, 5th Earl of Coventry, died suddenly at the family home in Grosvenor Square. He was only 23, bright, popular, handsome and full of promise. On that dismal day in spring, the pleasant and privileged world of his younger brother, George William, was rent apart. Devastated, he wrote to his friend, the gentleman-architect Sanderson Miller:

> *I am so shocked that I know not what I say or do. If I could be severd [sic] into two and one part left alive and the other part taken away, the separation could be not greater. He was indeed the better half and therefore God thought fit the worthiest should be removed. O, may He grant that the remaining part may ever attain his perfection and then the sooner it is called away the less will be my portion of sorrow in this world.*[1]

The two eldest Coventry boys had been inseparable. They shared the same friends, the same education and the same ambitions. George William believed his future to be filled with opportunity and free from responsibility. Not just the shock, grief and loneliness overwhelmed him, but a sense of complete inadequacy and dread.

Croome Court, sphinx
on the south portico

This tragic loss proved the making of the new young viscount. Within months, he began to channel his grief and self-pity into a deepening desire to fulfil the ambitions he had shared with his elder brother for the family seat at Croome in Worcestershire. Slowly his resolve sharpened and when he inherited the earldom, aged 28, already his plans had begun to unfold. Tentatively at first, then with an all-consuming passion, he embarked on the total transformation of Croome and was soon acknowledged as one of the most exciting and influential patrons and collectors of his day. He had an unerring ability to recognise and nurture new talent, not least the creative genius of Lancelot 'Capability' Brown and Robert Adam. He also relished the pursuit of the rare, the new and the beautiful, and all this gave edge to his ambition, enabling him not merely to follow fashion but to dictate its course.

Croome is now widely acclaimed as Brown's first major commission. It is also renowned for its outstanding Adam interiors, for the treasures it housed, and for the exceptional collection of plants that thrived within the park and pleasure grounds. These have attracted much scholarly analysis, yet they do not tell the whole story.

The remodelling of the house itself has so far escaped close scrutiny, and there is good reason for this. Compared with the more spectacular architectural achievements of the neo-Palladian era, such as Wanstead, Wentworth Woodhouse, Houghton or Holkham, Croome Court was merely a modest farewell, a final nod to this triumphant proclamation of Whig supremacy. Designed for comfort rather than magnificence, it is the narrative concealed beneath its golden stone veneer that makes it special. The story of the substantial and progressive seventeenth-century house that determined its existing form and plan is still not fully understood. The extent of Sanderson Miller's influence on the new design remains unclear. Then there is Brown's formidable task as executant architect. He could not have picked a more difficult architectural project to demonstrate his worth and serve as the centrepiece of his designed landscape. Nor could he have found a more challenging flat and marshy terrain to enhance or a more demanding client to please. He and his patron were obliged to develop their roles and establish an effective working relationship as the project progressed, and in doing so they forged a close and enduring friendship.

The arrival of Robert Adam heralded a new and more daring phase. A slick performer by all accounts, he brought polish and sophistication to the interior with some of his earliest and most influential designs, and with equal elegance he embellished Brown's landscape, learning from the 6th Earl's informed eye and restraining hand. Together they built a mutual respect and loyalty that lasted a lifetime. Adam's work was completed by James Wyatt, whose contribution brought the Croome project full circle in a remarkable fashion that underlined Coventry's ability to remain at the vanguard of Georgian taste.

The creation of Croome was a collaborative exercise and an extra-ordinary experiment, where some of the greatest contemporary talents were nurtured and some of the most influential aesthetic ideas of the day were established. It was driven forward by its inspiring and enigmatic patron with relentless energy, commitment and vision for over 50 years.

This book was commissioned by the Croome Heritage Trust as a tribute to this achievement. As the first published study of its kind, its intention is to further our understanding of Croome and its history, of the part played by the 6th Earl in its transformation during the second half of the eighteenth century, of the special relationship that Lord Coventry shared with Brown and Adam, and of Croome's impact upon the cultural life of Georgian Britain.

AN ARISTOCRATIC AGE

Enlightened eighteenth-century Britain was a place of unprecedented opportunity, particularly for an aspiring young aristocrat. Under the new Hanoverian regime, the country was filled with a fresh sense of optimism. After decades of strife at home and abroad, relative stability had enabled a surge of enterprise and investment. This had reinvigorated the economy and instilled the nation with confidence and pride. Britain now benefited from an increasing religious tolerance, freedom of the press and trial by jury. Her naval strength was enhancing her reputation abroad, securing her overseas trade and reaping the rewards of an emerging colonial empire. Her horizons were expanding both literally and metaphorically. Relative peace and prosperity brought the freedom to travel and allowed curiosity and ingenuity to flourish, and slowly the great engines of industrial progress were set in motion that would soon transform the world.

George William Coventry could count his blessings that he belonged to the accomplished and articulate elite responsible for this enviable success, and that also claimed most of its benefits. Following years of civil upheaval, the Bill of Rights of 1689 had initiated the gradual shift in the balance of the constitution away from the Crown to the aristocracy, and the Act of Settlement of 1701 had secured a Protestant succession and stripped away any lingering delusions of divine right. The monarch could no longer be a Catholic, nor suspend the laws, and depended upon parliament for his or her income and army. Although parliament was still subject to the patronage and authority of the Crown, the new shifting dynamic between the monarchy and aristocracy had settled down with surprising ease due in part to George I's disinclination to exert such authority, let alone speak the native language. The reformed constitution was now held in high esteem elsewhere in Europe and was even relatively advanced compared with countries such as France.[1]

London now superseded Amsterdam as the leading financial centre. The wealthy staked out territories around Mayfair and Marylebone on the Grosvenor and Portland estates. Imposing new residences fringed

PAGES 14–15
Croome Court, Worcestershire,
by Richard Wilson, 1758

View of Whitehall, Adam office, 1759

St James's and Green Park, and the Thames was clogged with vessels ferrying novel and different kinds of merchandise from foreign ports to fuel the appetite of the emerging consumer society.[2] Shop windows tempted the rich, deals were made and debts compounded in the coffee houses, clubs and inns, while a range of diversions, musical entertainments, pleasure gardens, masquerades, assemblies and balls encouraged polite society to mingle and, more importantly, be seen to be mingling.

Surrounded by such visible evidence of their success, members of the ruling class flexed their muscles with increasing self-assurance, secure in the belief that their rank, status and education provided them with the necessary tools for leadership. This, they believed, was their duty to their country and to posterity, and the nation appeared willing to accept this, mainly as there was little option to do otherwise.[3] The poor could only suffer in silence. Often they endured appalling hardship. Infant mortality remained high, disease was rife, and migration to the growing provincial towns and cities usually meant a life of violence, drinking and utter squalor. The emerging and increasingly obstreperous middle classes fared better. They might grumble about the power of the aristocracy but they made no serious challenge to its supremacy until late in the eighteenth century. Incapable of offering any effective political resistance, many were content to reap the advantages of the nation's economic vitality. Maybe too, just as the aristocracy was convinced it was its duty to lead, there existed a mindset among the professional classes and artisans that the Whig aristocrats, with their noble breeding, education and values, were inevitable leaders.

Although the trauma of Charles I's execution and the English civil war was not easily forgotten, and the Jacobite uprising of 1715 had unsettled the new regime, political allegiances remained as complicated as ever. Certainly the distinction between Whig and Tory was far from clear. The Whig party became split into various factions, allied to the great aristocratic families and united primarily in their support of the Protestant Hanoverian succession.[4] They were held together under Sir Robert Walpole's (1676–1745) government, notably by prominent figures such as Thomas Pelham, 1st Duke of Newcastle (1693–1768), assisted where necessary by the shrewd distribution of honours. The Tories drew their support from the landed gentry and they upheld the values of the established Church of England, although their inherently conservative tendencies were inclined to be associated with the Jacobite cause, and sometimes with good reason.

During the 1720s, there had emerged a coalition of dissident Whigs and Tories opposed to Walpole's government and its abuse of patronage. Some were critical of foreign policy and objected to the idea of standing armies; many wanted annual elections of benefit to the landed interest, and from their ranks emerged the first effective parliamentary opposition. Although still a world away from the modern political system, this rising tide of resistance rallied around Frederick, the disgraced Prince of Wales, who was distrusted by his father, George II. This included many influential figures, especially those associated with the Temple dynasty of Stowe, who followed the lead of Richard Temple, 1st Viscount Cobham, among them an enthusiastic younger generation, notably Richard and George Grenville, William Pitt and George Lyttelton, known as the Boy Patriots (or more derogatorily Cobham's cubs) due to their youth and views on foreign policy. Yet despite its internal squabbling, the Whig aristocracy clung onto power with a steely determination and decades passed before any growing resentment took effective form, stalled by the unnerving excesses of the French Revolution of 1789–99.

Whig control was most deeply entrenched in rural Britain where the great country houses of the old and new aristocracy served as symbols of their authority and the focus of political, economic and cultural influence. Built to impress and intimidate, they formed the hub of vast estates, often of ten thousand acres or more: nerve centres that controlled the rhythm of rural life. Gordon Mingay estimated that there were only around four hundred families among the great landowners.[5] Some of the houses were well established, like those of the Earls of Pembroke or the Dukes of Devonshire, but many more were built for landowners who had acquired their wealth and titles more recently. Houghton Hall, Norfolk, created for Sir Robert Walpole, was an obvious case in point. Others included Wanstead House, Essex, built for a former governor of the East India Company; Harewood House, Yorkshire, for the Lascelles family, who were traders and sugar planters; and Stourhead, Wiltshire, and Cadland, Hampshire, the homes of the wealthy bankers, Henry Hoare and Robert Drummond.

The appearance of the countryside was altering too. Enclosure was redefining the landscape, imposing a structure on the former open fields and commons and enabling large areas of land to be improved, drained and cultivated. Secure grazing and improvements in crop yields and varieties supported new breeds of livestock. Farmsteads were built away from the traditional settlements and land was set aside for sporting pursuits. The Game Acts of 1707, 1723 and 1755 made shooting the privilege of the landed rich and revolutionised hunting. Copses and woodland belts provided habitats for breeding birds, which became easy prey for lighter and more accurate guns, and land was managed for the specific purpose of hunting hares and foxes. Today it is hard to appreciate how quickly this change occurred. William Hoskins observed that 'a villager who had played in the open fields as a boy, or watched sheep in the common pastures, would have lived to see the modern landscape of his parish completed and matured'.[6]

A key feature of the new landscape was the improved road network. The countryside became more accessible as the turnpike companies steadily upgraded the condition of the roads. Coaches became swifter

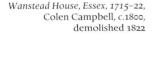

Wanstead House, Essex, 1715–22, Colen Campbell, c.1800, demolished 1822

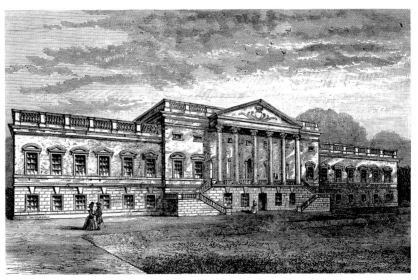

and less cumbersome. News could reach everyone faster, goods could be transported more quickly and people began to travel for pleasure. As distances shrank, attitudes and outlooks began to change, feeding the growing thirst for knowledge of the variety of natural scenery, and of different cultures and customs.

There was also time now for the curious to discover new worlds both on an infinite and a minute scale, with the introduction of improved telescopes and microscopes. A fourth dimension crept into the cultural imagination too, as it became clear that the origin of the world itself was much more remote than had been imagined previously, and that the landscape, the very rocks, valleys and mountains that shaped the world and formed the foundation of civilisation, were mutable.[7]

This age of broadening minds and expanding horizons demanded a new image that complemented its ambition. Under Stuart rule, the nation had turned to France and the Netherlands for aesthetic guidance but such associations were now deemed inappropriate and outdated. Georgian Britain wanted an image more compatible with its ideals of reasoned order, moderation and enlightened improvement. The answer was not hard to find. Informed by their classical education, the Hanoverians need look no further than the virtues and values of the classical world, the discipline and dignity of ancient Rome and the unadulterated splendours of Greece.

This new ideology also derived inspiration from the theories pro-pounded by Lord Shaftesbury (1671–1716) that traced a determined path through Georgian culture. As Christopher Hussey observed, Shaftesbury's proposal that 'beauty of life and beauty of form' were complemen-tary aspects of the humanist ideal, and that nature was the source of all perfection, accorded well with the contemporary preoccupation with classical ideals of beauty and proportion, together with the growing interest in the natural world.[8] During the 1750s, these ideas were fortified further by the influential writings of Edmund Burke and William Hogarth. Hogarth's *The Analysis of Beauty* (1753) had instilled the concept of the serpentine 'line of beauty' within the public imagination, a shape found in nature that was innately pleasing to the eye, while Burke's *A Philosophical Enquiry into the Origin of Our Ideas of the Sublime and Beautiful* (1757) had struck a particularly receptive chord. The idea of the Sublime was not new, but Burke had attempted to define the attributes of Sublimity and Beauty in the way the human mind perceived and responded to the natural landscape. He associated the former with the wild, the dramatic, the rugged and the irrational, and the latter with the smooth, the small, the gentle and the delicate. This reinforced the idea of the well-proportioned and orderly beauty of the classical world, but also introduced the seductive notion of a landscape that could thrill by inspiring the pleasurable excitement of possible but unlikely terror.

For the early Georgians, the Vitruvian principles of symmetry and harmonic proportion, particularly as interpreted in the architectural theories and designs of the Venetian architect, Andrea Palladio (1508–1580), appeared ideally suited to their cause. Palladio was an authority on the ruins of ancient Rome. He had published his *L'Antichità di Roma* in 1554, provided the illustrations for the 1556 edition of Vitruvius, followed by the publication of his celebrated *I Quattro Libri dell'Architettura* in 1570. English architecture was still reeling from the impact of giants like Christopher Wren (1632–1723), John Vanbrugh (1664–1726) and Nicholas Hawksmoor (1661–1736), masters of the English Baroque, whose work represented all the drama, sensation and complexity of Stuart rule. The Palladian style, or strictly speaking the neo-Palladian or Palladian Revival style, would dismiss this era of political and stylistic agitation and embody all the calm, order and reason of the Whig regime. As it derived its overall effect from the careful articulation of each separate part and the balance of each element within each part, it echoed Shaftesbury's observations of the natural world most satisfactorily. Palladio's villa designs, with their strong profiles and bold details, would prove particularly inspirational to the new generation of British architects. Another important influence was the great English architect, Inigo Jones (1573–1652), one of the earliest English advocates of the Palladian style. Jones had visited Italy in the entourage of the Earl of Arundel and had studied Palladio's designs at first hand. His work had demonstrated how Palladian forms, so well suited to strong light, might be adapted to the English taste and climate.

In 1715, the Scottish architect and writer, Colen Campbell (1676–1729), published his first volume of *Vitruvius Britannicus* (the second volume arrived in 1717 and the third in 1725), and the first volume of Giacomo Leoni's English translation of Palladio's *I Quattro Libri dell'Architettura* appeared. Both were of key importance in establishing the neo-Palladian style in Britain, and both were also dedicated to the monarch, George I. This was a well-judged ploy, for both George I and II were keenly aware of the advantages of securing a fresh identity for the Hanoverian dynasty, and their patronage of two of the leading proponents of the style, Richard Boyle, 3rd Earl of Burlington (1694–1753), and his friend, protégé and colleague, William Kent (1685–1748), was significant. Kent began his career as an artist but developed an exceptional talent as an architect, interior decorator, furniture and landscape designer. He brought breadth, scope and context to the new aesthetic. His work embodied all the spirit and grandeur of the classical world but it was also finely tuned to appeal to the tastes and preferences of his wealthy clients.

William Kent, by William Aikman, *c.*1723–25

Burlington had met Kent while in Italy on the Grand Tour. For many a young Georgian nobleman, aesthete and adventurer, Italy, and the awesome spectacle of Rome in particular, was their goal. Armed with commendable determination and a copy of Palladio's *L'Antichità di Roma*, the rewards of such an arduous journey across the Alps could be life-changing. They were lured by the sultry landscape and shimmering blue heat hazes painted by artists like Nicolas Poussin (1594–1665) and Claude Lorrain (1600–1682), while the artworks of Salvator Rosa (1615–1673) promised the drama of jagged mountains, deep ravines and lurking *banditti* to add a hint of danger and excitement to their exploits. Most importantly, many Tourists believed that to experience the classical world at first hand was the best way to acquire a discriminating eye and a true understanding of the ancients.[9] And there was also the thought of the sensual delights on offer in Rome and of the treasures waiting to be plundered as trophies of their rite of passage.[10]

Landscape with Aeneas at Delos,
by Claude Lorrain, 1672

That these Tourists enjoyed an elite camaraderie was not surprising. In 1734, a group of them founded the Society of Dilettanti. Despite the modern connotations of its title and that it functioned principally as a dining club, the Society was intended as a serious scholarly institution for the celebration and promotion of the study of classical art. Probably its most influential act was to sponsor James Stuart and Nicholas Revett's Athenian expedition in the 1750s, which resulted in the publication of *The Antiquities of Athens.* The first volume appeared in 1762 and was a work of seminal importance, revealing the pure and simple forms of Greek architecture as never before.

Over 200 country houses were built or remodelled during the early Georgian period. These were the perfect vehicle for the exposition of the new neo-Palladian style and elegant showcases for the spoils of the Tour. The work of Colen Campbell was a chief source of influence. His three designs for Wanstead House of 1715–22 inspired several later variations, including Henry Flitcroft's (1697–1769) Wentworth Woodhouse and James Paine's (1717–1789) Nostell Priory, both in Yorkshire, and John Wood's (1704–1754) Prior Park in Bath, all begun in the mid-1730s. Campbell's striking design for Houghton Hall of the 1720s, with its remarkable articulation of parts and prominent corner pavilions, was adapted from his third design for Wanstead. The pavilions were surmounted by pediments in his original design and looked back to Jones's towers at Wilton in

Houghton Hall, Norfolk, principal
elevation, Colen Campbell and
James Gibbs, begun 1722

Holkham Hall, Norfolk, principal
elevation, William Kent et al.,
begun 1734

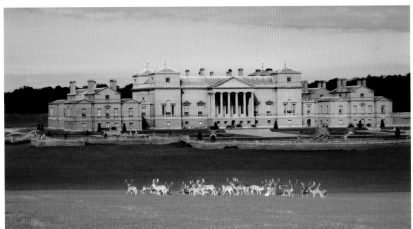

Chiswick House, principal
elevation, Lord Burlington,
begun 1725

Wiltshire. The design influenced a group of neo-Palladian houses of similar profile, among them Holkham Hall, nearby in Norfolk, and Hagley Hall and Croome Court in Worcestershire. Another important model was Campbell's design for Mereworth, Kent, again of the 1720s, derived from Palladio's Villa Capra, Vicenza, and the chief inspiration for Lord Burlington's iconic villa, Chiswick House, west London, begun in 1725, and adapted by Henry Hoare at Stourhead.

Alongside the work of these neo-Palladian architects was the idiosyncratic contribution of James Gibbs (1682–1754). His designs rejected the austere discipline of Campbell and the clever articulation of Burlington's work and instead incorporated Mannerist characteristics and Baroque expression that looked back to the achievements of Wren. Remembered chiefly as a church architect and for his eponymous door surrounds, Gibbs also designed impressive country houses, such as Ditchley House in Oxfordshire of 1722. His iconic design for the Radcliffe Camera in Oxford, completed in 1749, would be hard to ignore by contemporary young scholars, not least among them the Coventry boys from Croome.

Palladian principles persisted until around 1760, by which time the increasingly informed appreciation of classical antiquity had begun to dictate a pronounced shift towards the neoclassicism of Robert (1728–1792) and James Adam (1732–1794) and of their rival, Sir William Chambers (1723–1796), rising stars who dominated the architectural scene for the following 30 years.

The interiors of these great early Georgian houses were testament to the discerning and highly competitive nature of art collecting of this period. British collectors were among the most important and admired in Europe.[11] Prominent among them were men like Lord Burlington, Henry Hoare, Sir Francis Dashwood (a leading member of the Society of Dilettanti) and Thomas Coke (1697–1759; created Earl of Leicester in 1744). Coke had met Burlington and Kent in Italy and together they had conceived the outline design for Holkham. Although the detailed design was undertaken by Matthew Brettingham (1699–1769), the elaborate interiors were devised by Kent to include a fine sculpture gallery and a library to house Coke's collections. This extraordinary collaborative work set a benchmark for aspiring contemporary aesthetes and has been described as the 'purest example of a house created for its art collection and an art collection formed to fill a house'[12].

By the mid-eighteenth century, a new generation of collectors was emerging, among them the 1st Duke of Northumberland, the 6th Earl of Coventry and Sir Lawrence Dundas. They needed look no further than the grace and elegance of the Adam style, with its emphasis on movement, its inventive adaptation of classical precedent and its sense of theatre,

Holkham Hall, Norfolk, view of the Entrance Hall, William Kent, begun in 1734

to provide an infinite variety of beautiful and novel settings where they could display their collections to the best advantage.[13]

Designing an appropriate backdrop for these Georgian country houses was also crucial to the overall effect. Gone were the rigid geometry and high maintenance of garden designers such as George London and Henry Wise in favour of a more subtle informality. This originated in the appeal of influential figures like Shaftesbury and John Evelyn for a greater appreciation of the natural world, but it was also influenced by the ideas of the Whig journalist, Joseph Addison (1672–1719), and of Stephen Switzer (1682–1745), a writer, garden designer and former employee of London and Wise. As attitudes began to change towards the use and purpose of the landscape, Switzer had followed Addison's lead in his plea for a more economically viable approach to garden design that provided for both pleasure and profit. He favoured, in particular, the idea of a *ferme ornée*: a country estate that served aesthetic as well as agricultural purposes.

The new informality had been reinforced by Alexander Pope (1688–1744), poet and cultural hero of the day. In his famous *Epistle to Burlington* of 1731, he had exhorted his fellow gardening enthusiasts to consult 'the Genius of the Place', the *genius loci*, for their inspiration and guidance. It was a beguiling concept derived from the fifth book of Virgil's *Aeneid* and it had been taken up previously by Shaftesbury, but Pope had endowed it with a captivating charm. He created a magical garden full of incident at his small estate in Twickenham, a landscape garden in miniature, and his influence upon such creative minds as Lord Bathurst at Cirencester and Lord Cobham at Stowe, Buckinghamshire, helped to prove his point.

William Kent had captured the current mood quite brilliantly, not least for having 'leapt the fence' to embrace the surrounding countryside in his landscape designs.[14] Taking Pliny's garden at Tuscum as his precedent, he produced some of the most influential gardens of the early Georgian period, notably at Chiswick and Stowe, and at Rousham, Oxfordshire. Underpinned by their classical iconography, and rich in political and literary allusion, their lush pastoral beauty was contrived with great artistry to mimic the dreamlike quality of a Claude landscape: idyllic and secluded, but with framed views of the distant countryside.

Before long a growing band of enthusiastic gentleman-gardeners had evolved a variation on Kent's theme, most famously at places like Stourhead, Painswick in Gloucestershire, and Shugborough in Staffordshire.[15] Known as Rococo gardens, these followed Kent's lead in outline but were adorned with an exuberant combination of structures of Chinese, Turkish, classical and medieval inspiration, often brightly painted, that exhibited their owner's cultural breadth and dazzled with their inventive charm. It was perhaps not surprising that such bold eclecticism began to stimulate debate about matters of taste and aesthetics, prompted by the likes of Hogarth and Burke. There was, though, another factor underlying these adventurous new gardens, for while their sinuous paths, pools and picnic places may have still retained a certain intimacy of scale, they also represented a key stage in the move towards the natural landscape style made popular by Lancelot 'Capability' Brown (1716–1783). However, as Hussey has argued, it was more Hogarth's serpentine lines and Burke's aesthetic of sentiment that ultimately determined the peculiarly English character and widespread appeal of the Brownian landscape.[16]

Access to these great new houses of the Georgian era was not restricted to privileged guests. As increasing numbers of tourists and travellers began to explore the English countryside, visiting country houses became a growing pastime. It was not unusual for guidebooks to be published, as at Wilton House in 1731, at Stowe in 1744 and at Houghton in 1747, and there was even a hotel provided for visitors at Kedleston in Derbyshire. This intensified the competitive rivalry between patrons, as well as the designers and craftsmen who were involved with such projects, and this, in turn, proved beneficial to the quality and variety of the work produced.

However, such extravagant display and competitive rivalry was not without its risks, and it left many wealthy new patrons and collectors vulnerable to the scrutiny of the free press and contemporary arbiters of taste and moral judgement like Horace Walpole (1717–1797). As a celebrated collector himself, Walpole occupied precarious if well-defended territory. The items within his collections were also wide ranging and unusual, for he relished his status among the growing ranks of antiquarians eager to track down and accumulate relics from which to learn more about the history and traditions of their own country.

Interest in the past, in the virtues and libertarian values of Old England, had been particularly prevalent among the dissident Whigs in the first half of the century. It had manifested itself in their predilection

Painswick Rococo garden, Gloucestershire, created by Benjamin Hyett in the 1740s

for sham medieval ruins and similar structures ever since Lord Bathurst and Pope had created Alfred's Hall in Cirencester Park in 1732, and Gibbs had designed his triangular Gothic Temple at Stowe (see p. 85), completed in 1748. But this enthusiasm soon moved on from its patriotic roots to encompass a more widespread interest in fake castles and ruins, a favourite of Sanderson Miller and his friends and later a speciality of Robert Adam. It was accompanied by a tendency to accumulate medieval artefacts and a taste for Gothic novels, and it anticipated the sentiments of the Romantic era and the more informed and archaeological approach to the Gothic style that followed.

There was nothing new in the didactic purpose of these collectors and enthusiasts, but there was something different about their patriotic fervour and fascination with English history. It is tempting to associate this with a growing sense of unease, particularly among the ruling class, about their own roles and reputations, even a heightened awareness about their sense of duty and responsibility to their ancestors and to their own generation. Although these years of relative peace and prosperity had appeared to validate their leadership, it had also directed their thoughts to question their own place in history. Matters of lineage and pedigree suddenly seemed more important.

This was certainly the case with the 6th Earl of Coventry. His sense of duty to his ancestors, his commitment to his role and his obsessive attitude towards his legacy were nothing short of extreme and determined his every move and decision throughout his long and productive life.

AN ENVIABLE INHERITANCE

Confronted by the challenges of Stuart rule and the altered perspectives of the Hanoverian age, the Coventry family of Croome could take their place with pride among the well-established members of the ruling class. During the seventeenth century, the family had secured enviable power and influence as lawyers, diplomats and politicians, their success due largely to their sharp intellects, persuasive eloquence and not a small degree of luck.[1]

The family was descended from Sir Thomas Coventry (1547–1606), a London lawyer of considerable ability and diligence. Following his marriage to Margaret Jeffries (or Jeffrey) (b.1551) of Earl's Croome, he had purchased the adjacent estate at Croome in 1692 as an investment and a statement of his increasing stature. His achievements had provided a platform for the boundless ambition of his eldest son, also called Thomas (1578–1640), who was elected Recorder of London in 1616, became Solicitor-General the following spring and was knighted later that year. By January 1621 he had secured the role of Attorney-General and, on the accession of Charles I in 1625, he replaced the Bishop of Lincoln as Lord Keeper of the Great Seal.

Lord Keeper Coventry owed his rapid promotion to his particular gifts. His intellect was exceptional, and his integrity and impartiality were particularly welcome in the contemporary political climate. He was also a great orator and had, as Edward Hyde, 1st Earl of Clarendon, observed, a 'strange power of making himself believed'.[2] In 1628 he was created Baron Coventry of Aylesborough or Allesborough, part of the manor of Pershore and among a significant series of purchases of land and

Thomas, 1st Baron Coventry, Lord Keeper of the Great Seal of England, Follower of Cornelius Jonson, c.1630

property he made at this time. These were consolidated and extended by subsequent acquisitions that incorporated a vast swathe of south and central Worcestershire, including salt bulleries or phates in Droitwich, several key access points onto the River Severn, then the main artery of regional trade, and various desirable portions of Gloucestershire, Oxfordshire, Staffordshire, Lincolnshire, Warwickshire, Middlesex and Kent.[3] Despite his vast domain, Lord Keeper Coventry remained rooted in London, where he leased the principal part of the former episcopal palace of Durham House on the Strand. He died there on 14 January 1640, at a critical point in the constitutional crisis and a time when the impact of his passing would be felt most keenly, further elevating his admirable reputation.

Most of the Lord Keeper's ten children contributed to the family's prominent public profile. His eldest son, also Thomas (1606–1661), served briefly as MP for Droitwich and then for Worcestershire. He became a member of the Council of the Marches of Wales in 1633 and Compensation Commissioner for the Avon in 1637. He also developed a particular attachment to the family seat at Croome, which he improved at great expense, revealing a markedly informed appreciation of contemporary architectural developments in the capital.

Two of the Lord Keeper's younger sons, Henry and Sir William, became renowned politicians and statesmen, both of whom were skilled orators like their father, and the judicious marriages of his four daughters elevated the family's reputation still further. On 26 April 1697, in recognition of the family's support of the Stuart monarchy, Thomas (1629–1699), 5th Baron, the younger son of the 2nd Baron, was created Viscount Deerhurst and Earl of Coventry. Then, for a brief but unfortunate period, the luck of the Coventrys ran out.

Not that this was due to any lack of talent. Thomas, 2nd Earl of Coventry (1662–1710), was a distinguished mathematician, astronomer and a valued correspondent of the great physicist, astronomer and philosopher, Robert Hooke (1635–1703). He married Anne Somerset (1673–1763), the fourth daughter of Henry Somerset, 1st Duke of Beaufort, and his second wife, the botanist and gardener, Mary Capel (1630–1715). Anne was a woman of prodigious gifts, author of *Meditations and Reflections, Moral and Divine* (1707), and her impressive circle of friends included prominent figures like Sir Hans Sloane, Richard Jago and William Shenstone. Two sons were born and the marriage appeared full of promise. Tragically, the youngest son, John, survived no more than a year and died in 1706. Then, in 1710, the 2nd Earl also died, intestate and deep in debt, and, just two years later, the only surviving son, Thomas, (1702–1712), now 3rd Earl, died while at school at Eton. Distraught, Anne retreated back to their former home in Snitterfield in Warwickshire to unravel her husband's debts, leaving her husband's younger brother, Gilbert (1668–1719), in charge at Croome.

Wilful and artistic, Gilbert, now 4th Earl of Coventry, had spent much of his youth wasting his generous allowance in France and the Netherlands. In 1694 he married his first wife and second cousin, Dorothy Keyte (1671–1705), daughter of Sir William Keyte of Ebrington, and settled at her family home at Hidcote in Gloucestershire. Dorothy died in 1705, leaving one daughter, Anne (1795–c.1744), who married Sir William Carew (1690–1744) of Antony House in Cornwall in 1713.

As soon as he inherited the earldom in 1712, the 4th Earl embarked upon a major scheme of alteration and improvement at Croome, his funds boosted in 1715 by his second marriage to Anne Master (1691–1788) of Codnor Castle in Derbyshire. Had his scheme gone according to plan, Croome might have been remembered in a quite different light today, but Gilbert died in 1719, leaving no male heir and with his work at Croome still incomplete. This marked a critical point in the family history. The successes of the previous century were now clouded by doubt and uncertainty at a time when the nation itself was still adjusting to change and reeling in the wake of the Jacobite rising of 1715. The remaining family was sorely in need of sound leadership to rescue its finances and secure its position within the Hanoverian regime. As it happened, Gilbert's failure to produce a male heir proved the family's salvation. On his death, the baronry became extinct and the earldom, family estates and other honours reverted to a second cousin, William Coventry (bap. 1677–1751), then in his early 40s, a wealthy diplomat, a dissident Whig and a man of independent spirit and considerable common sense.

William was the son of a wealthy merchant, Walter Coventry (1634–1692), the second son of the Lord Keeper's younger brother, also called Walter. His mother, Anne Holcombe (1647–1728), was from a similar background, a merchant's daughter from St Andrew's, Holborn, and William was the oldest surviving son of their eight children.[4] His sister, Anne, was married to Sir Dewey Bulkeley (d.1735) of Nether Burgate in Hampshire, an estate later inherited by the Croome Coventrys, while his younger brother, Thomas, was a prosperous Russia merchant. His son, another Thomas (c.1713–1797), left substantial sums of money to the 6th Earl and his family, and one of his descendants, Thomas Darby (1776–1842), of Greenlands, near Henley-on-Thames, became benefactor to the 6th Earl's youngest son.[5]

William completed his education at Pembroke College, Oxford, and he became Whig MP for Bridport in 1708, a seat that he held until 1719 when he inherited the earldom. As 5th Earl of Coventry, he began to harbour doubts about Walpole's style of government and his sympathies were drawn increasingly towards the more conservative and dissident Whig faction. It came as no surprise to his political allies when his three sons all entered parliament as Tories.

William married Elizabeth Allen (c.1684–1738), the daughter of John Allen of Westminster, on 4 May 1719. Elizabeth was a courtesan and had been associated previously with the politician, Peregrine Bertie (c.1663–1711), the second son of the 3rd Earl of Lindsey, when she was known as 'Mrs Poltney'. Bertie and Elizabeth had two daughters, Diana and Isabelle, of whom only Diana (c.1708–1754) was brought into the Coventry household. When Bertie died of apoplexy in 1711, he left his estate in trust to Elizabeth, including his house in Great Marlborough Street, and made generous provision for their two daughters. So Elizabeth was a wealthy woman when she married William.[6]

Three sons were born in quick succession: Thomas Henry, Viscount Deerhurst (1721–1744), George William (1722–1809) and John Bulkeley (1724–1801). Thomas and George were treated like twins, and the 5th Earl's ambition for his two eldest sons is apparent from his choice of godfathers. Henry Clinton (1684–1728), 7th Earl of Lincoln and brother-in-law of the Duke of Newcastle, became godfather to Thomas Henry, while the Duke of Newcastle himself became godfather to George William.[7] They seem to have been a close family. Thomas and George were known to their family and friends as 'Deer' and 'Cov', while John was nicknamed 'Bunny', possibly as the Bulkeley name was often written as Bunckley. The group portrait by Charles Philips (bap. 1703–1747), painted in the early 1730s, shows the family posed within a wooded landscape, probably Croome, which is represented by the symbolic seat, just as Lord Deerhurst can be identified by the young deer he is fondling (see p. 32). Both older boys are dressed in scarlet and look towards their father, while John is dressed in green and stands close to his mother's chair, always, it appears, the outsider.

In 1725 William and his new family moved from their home in Margaret Street to 45 Brook Street, Mayfair (later demolished to make way for Claridge's Hotel). They remained there for ten years before settling at an even more prestigious address in nearby Grosvenor Square.[8] This was the second largest square in London. It had been built on land belonging to Sir Richard Grosvenor and surrounded a large garden with a central statue of George I by John van Nost the Elder (d.1729). Developed piecemeal on plots of varying sizes from 1725 to 1731, the Coventry family lived at No. 3 (demolished 1936), one of the more modest plots acquired for speculative development by John Simmons, a carpenter. Their friend and neighbour, Sir Edward Turner of Ambroseden, lived at No. 2 from

1743 to 1756, and on 17 December 1743 he wrote excitedly on moving in: 'I have Cornices in the House... which would draw your eyes out of their sockets. I have Proportions which would command your attention during the two courses, an House, on the glimpse of which you would pronounce – I'm satisfy'd.'[9] Evidently young George William's sensibilities were honed from a tender age and No. 3 remained his principal London home for almost 30 years.

From 1730 to 1737, the Coventry boys were educated at Winchester College, a decision intended no doubt to sharpen their competitive faculties and where the standardised classical curriculum would prepare them for a future role in society and government. Thomas was held back a year so that he and George could progress through their education together. The inspired teaching of the Headmaster, John Burton (1690–1774), was particularly effective in encouraging an interest in the antique, not least by staging performances of Greek and Roman drama.[10] Burton also established a custom whereby boys of noble birth had their portraits painted by Isaac Whood (1689–1752). As Christopher Rowell has observed, among the 12 portraits still hanging at Winchester, curiously the only one missing is of George William Coventry, painted in 1731.[11]

Thomas Henry and George William matriculated at University College, Oxford, on 6 July 1737 to complete their classical education.[12]

George William was then still only 15 years old. John Bulkeley followed on behind in 1740. The brothers would have had a private suite of rooms with their own servants in attendance, enjoyed the distractions on offer – the coffee houses and taverns, the dining and political clubs – and, as Gentleman Commoners, would have been allowed to dine at High Table with the Fellows. Over 20 of George's college notebooks survive, which are filled with scribbled copies of orations and notes on English, Scottish and French history.[13]

Correspondence from this period reveals an endearing sense of fun and a youthful delight in displaying their erudition. Thomas and George shared their letters or took it in turn to write to their friends, in particular their Winchester friend, Thomas Walter Younge (d.1785), of Little Durnford in Wiltshire. Younge was one of several of their friends who shared their growing enthusiasm for architecture and landscape gardening. Prominent among them was the gentleman-architect, Sanderson Miller (1716–1780), to whom they may have been introduced by their mutual friend, Sir Edward Turner. Miller played a significant part in the development of George William's interests as well as his initial plans for Croome. This happy period at Oxford was marred only by the death of the Countess Elizabeth on 23 November 1738.

All three Coventry boys were painted by the Scottish artist, Allan Ramsay (1713–1784), at this time. George William, good-looking and dressed in bright blue velvet and lashings of gold lace, adopts an arrogant stance that belies his somewhat bashful expression. A portrait of a young woman by Ramsay of a similar date may be of Diana Bertie, the

LEFT TO RIGHT
*Thomas Henry Coventry,
Viscount Deerhurst,*
by Allan Ramsay, c.1740

The Hon. George William Coventry,
by Allan Ramsay, c.1740

The Hon. John Bulkeley Coventry,
by Allan Ramsay, c.1740

Countess's daughter, as the sitter bears a close resemblance to John Bulkeley. In June 1751, Diana married George 'Gilly' Williams (1719–1805). Williams was a friend of Horace Walpole, the politician George Selwyn (1719–1791) and Richard Edgcumbe (1716–61), the gifted amateur poet and painter, who all met regularly at Walpole's house at Strawberry Hill or Selwyn's Thursday Club in Pall Mall for conversation, drinking and whist. It was an unlikely connection that threatened the privacy of Diana's family at Croome, but the marriage was brief. Diana died on 16 September 1754 while visiting Selwyn at his Gloucestershire home.

Following their graduation on 20 November 1739, the two older Coventry boys spent an indulgent few months at Grosvenor Square with their friends enjoying, according to Thomas: 'a London Life where … there is Time for nothing but to eat, drink, and play at Whist'.[14]

Portrait of a Woman. Believed to be Diana Bertie, by Allan Ramsay, *c.*1740

There was no suggestion of a Grand Tour. The 5th Earl was keen for them to follow him into politics and in 1740 Thomas Henry contested the Whig parliamentary seat for Worcestershire together with George Lyttelton of Hagley, on behalf of their respective fathers' joint interests. According to Walpole, their defeat infuriated the 5th Earl.[15] As a dissident Whig, he felt snubbed by his Tory supporters, so the following year he opted for more blatant tactics and successfully secured the Tory seat at Bridport for Deerhurst. The young viscount's agreeable disposition and engaging personality earned him considerable popularity despite his inclination to vote with the opposition in 1742 and 1744. Sadly, he never had the chance to prove his worth as he died in May 1744, after a brief illness, most probably typhoid fever.

His death sent shock waves through his close circle of friends. Thomas Lennard Barrett (later 17th Baron Dacre, 1717–1786) wrote to Sanderson Miller, 'how very few are left behind like him; so good, so virtuous, so sweetly tempered'.[16] *The London Evening Post* praised the sincerity and impartiality that had marked Deerhurst's brief political career, adding that he had 'adhered to neither party knowing that this enabled him to displease both'.[17] More likely he had no inclination to displease either.

The tragic loss prompted a steady deterioration in the 5th Earl's health and he retreated from his official responsibilities. On 12 November 1744 he wrote to his friend, Richard Coote, 3rd Earl of Bellamont, that his son's death had rendered the rest of his life 'uncomfortable as all my endeavours will not Remove it from my Mind, tho' thank God [I] have two very dutiful sons left'.[18] Equally devastated, George William wrote to Miller that summer: 'never can I sign the name without a fresh torrent of grief for the late possessor of it and a bitter remorse that the present one falls so short of his perfections'.[19] That he was obliged to adopt his brother's role, his title and responsibilities, his very identity, made him feel the loss all the more keenly. Comparisons were inevitable and particularly painful to him as he tormented himself with feelings of inadequacy.

It was a small consolation that he was returned unopposed as Tory MP for Bridport that year and his correspondence suggests that, during this brief but painful period of his life, politics and the startling events surrounding the Jacobite rising of 1745 provided a welcome distraction. He spent an increasing amount of time at Croome, healing his grief and making plans for the future and, by 1747, he was braced for the task ahead. This was the year that his father settled the estate upon him. It was also the year he was elected MP for Worcestershire, the seat his elder brother had lost and the one most valuable to his future influence.[20] He could now step out from behind his brother's shadow and demonstrate his commitment to the county and to Croome, and by the time his father died on 18 March 1751, his grand design was already taking shape.

EARL OF CREATION

In 1764 the 6th Earl of Coventry was painted for the second time by Allan Ramsay to mark the occasion of his second marriage, to Barbara St John. It was a flattering and striking image, so much so that Ramsay reproduced it all bar the head for another of his clients.[1] This was probably how the Earl would want to be remembered: a man at the height of his powers, a handsome figure, clad in glowing crimson velvet, posing beside a pile of books and a classical urn, appearing every inch the patron, scholar and fashionable man of taste. The portrait was set within a frame carved by Sefferin Alken (1717–1782) after a design by Robert Adam to hang above the chimney piece in his new Library at Croome (see p. 151). It served as a welcome reminder to a doubtful man of what he had achieved.

Although the Earl was probably a difficult man to get to know, it would have been well worth the effort. Sensitive to criticism, he prized his privacy highly and much of his personal correspondence was unsparingly edited by himself and his family. He was accused of appearing proud, arrogant, intolerant and irascible by the free press, and his serious manner and steadfast commitment to his duties made him an ideal target for malicious rumour and cruel caricature. Certainly some of the criticism was justified. This was a Georgian aristocrat who performed his role with an unusual seriousness, tenacity and finesse. Famously described by Horace Walpole as 'a grave young Lord, of the remains of the Patriot breed', the Earl believed he owed a duty to his family, his county, his country and his monarch, and the prospect of failure stalked his every move.[2] Consequently his dedication to his role bordered on obsessive, and he could be single-minded to the point of ruthlessness, but when duty combined with pleasure he was at his very best, and at Croome it almost always did.

The Private Man

Blessed with good looks, Coventry cultivated his fashionable public image with great care. His clothing bills provide ample evidence of this.[3] This was a man who purchased his finest clothes in Paris; a man who

George William, 6th Earl of Coventry, by Allan Ramsay, 1764

cared deeply about the quality and variety of his waistcoats, which he acquired in impressively large quantities in embroidered silk, cashmere, 'fancy striped swansdown' and fashionable Marseilles quilting; a man whose Parisian wedding attire was richly embroidered, sparkled with gold sequins and shone with flowers of *lamé d'or* and gold *bouillon*. It was not so much that he was conceited. Rather that, as the surviving evidence suggests, his haughty demeanour and stylish image were all part of an act, designed to intimidate, to ward off ready criticism and close scrutiny and, like the testing goals he set himself, his personal insurance against the failure he feared.

Beneath this gilded mask was a man of wit and scholarship, someone to be watched and imitated, but also someone from whom one could learn. He could be loyal and supportive to his friends, who came from a wide range of backgrounds. Among them were the Lords Temple and Strafford, and talented gentleman like Sanderson Miller, Warren Hastings, Arthur Young, Richard Sheridan, Judge Perrot and Lancelot Brown, but he was equally content in the company of his steward, his blacksmith or his carpenter when rank could be forgotten in the enjoyment of shared enthusiasms. He was also reputed to be an entertaining host. One of his friends remarked that: 'Coventry has given us one dinner in Margaret Street and has been most excellent in his old way of disputation.[4]

Lord Coventry was very much the enlightened aristocrat. A fierce curiosity underlined his intelligence. He was fascinated by novelty, by new discoveries and by the scientific and technological advances of the age. This was not just for show or status, but fuelled by a compulsion to stand in the vanguard of progress. His regular purchases of contemporary scientific instruments, including one reflecting and two achromatic telescopes and a microscope between 1762 and 1763 alone, suggest more than a passing interest in the natural world. He updated his carriages regularly to keep pace with improvements in speed and comfort, and he brought the latest devices into his homes from stoves and cooking apparatus to pumps and hydraulic systems, not least of which was a huge underground water pump installed at Croome in 1764 to supply the closets of the private suite. As a large landowner, he enjoyed the usual country pursuits. His stables were stocked with fine horses and he added to his collection of guns and fishing rods at frequent intervals. More significantly, his informed interest in agricultural innovations was exemplary, and he bred his own herds of Holderness and Alderney cattle at Croome and carried out cross-breeding of Leicester sheep.[5] His horticultural expertise was even more outstanding, and he brought together an astonishing and extensive plant collection at Croome. But it was as a patron of the arts that he truly made his mark. As an ardent

Maria Gunning, Countess of Coventry,
by Francis Cotes, c.1755

Francophile with a passion for French decorative art, the high quality of his collections of furniture, porcelain and tapestries soon secured him an enviable reputation as a man of precocious and sophisticated taste.

The Earl married twice. Much has been written, not all of it flattering, about his first wife, the celebrated beauty, Maria Gunning (1732–1760). The marriage did little to build Lord Coventry's brittle public image, for Maria's vanity and foolish self-regard caused her to fall victim to the emerging cult of fame.

Maria was the daughter of John Gunning, an Irish country gentleman, and the Hon. Bridget Bourke, daughter of the 6th Viscount Mayo.[6] During 1751, she and her sister, Elizabeth, had caused a sensation among London society and Lord Coventry became infatuated with her. Following Elizabeth's impromptu marriage to the Duke of Hamilton, Coventry was under increasing pressure to follow suit and he married Maria a few weeks later on 5 March at St George's, Hanover Square. On their honeymoon Lord Coventry and Maria travelled through Belgium, Holland and Germany to Paris where they were entertained by the French aristocracy. Maria's social ineptitude was cruelly exposed and caused her husband continual irritation and embarrassment.

The couple returned to England in haste, where the new Countess provided the county with a source of welcome glamour and gossip.[7] However, Lord Coventry was not a tolerant man. His impatience at her social inadequacies began to dull the natural vivacity that had made her so appealing. Constant child-bearing weakened Maria's constitution and, susceptible to consumption and suffering from the toxic effects of the white lead in her cosmetics, her health deteriorated significantly during 1759. She rallied the following spring, but retreated to Croome that summer, her appearance ravaged by her condition. By the autumn, wraith-like, she shrank into the shadows of her bed curtains and withered away.[8] She died on 1 October 1760, aged just 28.

Maria was the dainty Rococo shepherdess who had embellished Coventry's early Arcadian ideals. His second wife, Barbara St John, was a different proposition altogether. Her intelligence and tolerance were a refreshing relief from Maria's immature wiles and capricious whims. A competent society hostess, she brought order and calm to his world, a dignity and charm that attuned with Lord Coventry's increasing stature and reputation. She also provided the essential support and reassurance needed to ward off his irascible moods and lingering depression. More important still, she shared his love of Croome.

Barbara St John (1737–1800) was five years younger than Maria, and the daughter of John St John, 11th Baron St John (d.1757) of Bletso, in Bedfordshire, and his wife, Elizabeth Crowley of Greenwich.[9] She had four brothers, one of whom, Ambrose, died young in 1775. John became 12th Baron; Andrew was Dean of Worcester Cathedral; and Henry (d.1780) became a Captain in the Royal Navy. She wrote frequently to her family, especially her sisters Jane, Anne and Elizabeth, and their correspondence is lively and affectionate.

According to gossip among Lord Coventry's friends, he was introduced to Barbara at a local function by her brother, the Dean, just months after Maria's death.[10] On 14 February 1763 he purchased a diamond ring for a staggering £280 from Charles Billiard, a London jeweller, and with his engagement now official, he set off to Paris that summer in search of furnishings for Croome, where not just his taste but his conduct raised a few eyebrows.[11] According to George Selwyn: 'His preparation here [for his forthcoming marriage] has been the most extraordinary that ever was made for any sacrament whatever'.[12] The following summer he was back in Paris again to make further purchases, order his wedding suit and, much to his friend Lord Temple's amusement, to continue his preparations.[13]

Barbara St John, Countess of Coventry,
by Angelica Kauffman, c.1770

Not until 27 September 1764 did he marry Barbara St John, in the small village of Bengeo, in Hertfordshire. With alterations already in progress at Croome to welcome his bride, the search was also on for a new townhouse. He continued to indulge Barbara with every possible luxury for the next 40 years, from the finest jewellery to the asses' milk in which she bathed. A note that he sent to her from Maidenhead Bridge on his way to London suggests theirs was for the most part a strong and happy marriage. It begins:

My Dearest Life
Tho I only slept at the Devizes to breakfast for Half an Hour, I did not reach this place till, ½ past six, an Hour too late to think of traversing Houndslow Heath, so I determined to take up my Quarters here, & to be stirring with the dark tomorrow – I repent already of having made this Journey, it appears already an Age since we parted. I think I can finish all my Business so as to return to you on Sunday Night, & I certainly shall not stay in Town an Hour longer than is necessary.[14]

Bill for fireworks supplied by Mr Clanfield of Holborn, Artist in Fireworks to the Royal Family, dated 26 July 1796

Unlike Maria, Barbara thrived at Croome. She loved animals. She kept dogs and bred exotic birds; a Menagerie was built for her where she kept 'red parrowquets', 'Turkish ducks', a 'snowbird' and even a flying squirrel.[15] Her interest in plants was of particular benefit to her husband's collection. Her brother, the sailor, brought her seeds from his travels, as did her friend, Captain Williams, who wrote to express his disappointment in 'the seeds he expected from Botany Bay', but promised to send her 'as many plants as she wants' from his trip to the West Indies the following year.[16] She also gave many gifts of seeds and plants to her friends and relatives, including her sister, Jane, who claimed enthusiastically: 'you have made mine the best furnished Greenhouse in this country'.[17] Under Barbara's supervision, Croome provided a memorable setting for many special events, boating parties, balls and grand firework displays. Several large bills for fireworks dating from the 1790s survive from Barbara's favourite firework artist in Holborn, which hint at the spectacular nature of these occasions.[18]

There were three surviving children from the Earl's first marriage, and two from his second. Maria had three daughters: Maria Alicia, who was born on 9 December 1754, Elizabeth Ann, who died in infancy in 1756, and Anne Margaret, born on 18 March 1757.[19] Finally, a son was born, George William, who arrived on 25 April 1758. With his second wife, Barbara, Lord Coventry had two sons and one daughter. John, the eldest, was born on 20 June 1765 and was Coventry's favourite child. Thomas William was born more than a decade later in 1778, and a daughter, Barbara, was born the following year, although she did not survive. One source also claims to have identified an illegitimate child, Emilie, born in the 1750s. She married Joseph Bouchier Smith, the Westminster school friend of her half-brother, George William, Viscount Deerhurst.[20] Quite possibly there were other children too.

The boys were educated at Winchester and Oxford, while the girls shared innumerable private tutors. Family correspondence suggests that the 6th Earl was an affectionate and dutiful father. Neither did he forget his children on his shopping expeditions. After one memorable spree in February 1767, he returned home with a rocking horse, a set of 'Draftsmen' and a toy cat.[21] As they grew older, there were gifts of jewellery and harpsichords for the girls, ponies and fishing rods for the boys. Perhaps they were too much indulged. Whatever the case, it was not long before Lord Coventry's unreasonably high expectations tore the family apart and all his children, with the exception of John, rebelled.

The eldest daughter, Maria Alicia, married Andrew Bayntun Rolt on 28 June 1777, the fourth and only legitimate son of Sir Edward Bayntun

Rolt (d.1800). The couple went to live at Battle House, Bromham, and had two daughters, of whom only the youngest, Maria Barbara (1780–1870), survived. Maria Alicia had an affair with her husband's nephew, John Allen Cooper, a young officer in the 20th Foot Regiment, who mistreated her. There followed a very public trial, which ended in a divorce by Act of Parliament on 15 February 1783, and less than a year later Maria Alicia died from self-neglect on 18 January 1784.

The youngest daughter, Anne Margaret, as shown in her portrait attributed to Sir Joshua Reynolds, appears to have been at least as beautiful as her mother. She married Edward Foley (1747–1803) on 27 October 1777, the second son of the 1st Lord Foley of Stoke Edith, of the important Midlands family of iron founders. It was a favourable connection, but the marriage failed due largely to Anne's infidelity and it was dissolved by Act of Parliament in 1787. The following year, on 15 July 1788, she married Samuel Wright (1754–1839), who came from a Nottinghamshire banking family and was a Captain in the 15th Hussars. Her journal, kept from 1811 until her death in 1822, tells the sad tale of the steady decline of a chastened hypochondriac.

Lady Anne Margaret Coventry, attributed to Sir Joshua Reynolds, *c.*1780

His son George William, Lord Deerhurst, proved the greatest disappointment to the 6th Earl, mainly as he had the highest expectations of him. In the autumn of 1776, he eloped to Gretna Green with Lady Catherine Henley, daughter of the Earl of Northington. He returned to Worcestershire in disgrace, where he and Catherine were married again in a more dignified fashion, but thereafter Deerhurst became estranged from his father. On 7 May 1776 he had enlisted as an ensign in the 64th Regiment of Foot, and in January of the following year he was made a lieutenant in the 17th Regiment of Light Dragoons and travelled to America to fight in the War of Independence (1775–83). Before he left for America he wrote to Barbara from his ship, full of regret for his rash and inconsiderate behaviour. He ends the letter: 'I must live a Victim to my own Indiscretions but shall ever retain a sense of that Affection which I have so imprudently squandered.'[22] Within weeks of his arrival, he sold his commission for £500 and returned to England to clear his debts and seek his father's forgiveness, but it never came, despite repeated pleas to the Countess to intervene on his behalf.

Following Catherine's death in childbirth in 1779, Deerhurst suffered further misfortune when he fell from his horse while out hunting and was blinded. With his future prospects erased, quite literally, he sullied his reputation further by staying with his friend, Sir Richard Worsley (1751–1805), the politician and antiquarian, at his home on the Isle of Wight, and became involved with his scandalous wife, her elopement with George Bisset and the subsequent trial. A chance introduction to Margaret 'Peggy' Pitches (*c.*1760–1840), the daughter of a wealthy

Streatham brandy merchant, proved his salvation. They were married in 1783 and together they had ten children, eventually settling in Streatham around 1800, where Deerhurst purchased a small country estate.

John, the Earl's eldest son from his second marriage, had married Anne Clayton in 1788. They had two sons and two daughters and moved into Springhill House on the Broadway estate, left vacant by John Bulkeley. The Earl's youngest son, Thomas William, was 13 years younger than his brother John, and a generation younger than his sisters and George William. In July 1800, aged 21, he married in secret a young girl from Clapham called Catherine Clarke, probably a family servant and also a minor. She gave birth to their first son, also called Thomas William, a week after the wedding on 23 July and from this time onwards he was estranged from his father and relied mainly on the support of his cousins.

To such a highly creative and motivated man as Lord Coventry, his children's lives appeared wasted and were a public rejection of the rigid rules of duty and responsibility that governed his own. Their refusal to conform contributed much to his persistent 'dark moods and depressions'.[23] It was an unfortunate situation, which would serve only to heighten Coventry's resolve to set an example and to make Croome, something over which he had absolute control, as perfect as possible.

Patron and Public Figure

The first family historian, the Earl's head gardener William Dean (d.1831), observed that Lord Coventry devoted 'much of his time and his thoughts to the public service'.[24]

His portrait by Nathaniel Dance-Holland of 1774 for the worthy citizens of Worcester was less about flattery and more about power, duty and commitment. Here we see the patriot and public figure: a man upon whom the weight of responsibility hung as heavily as his robes.

In truth, Lord Coventry derived considerable satisfaction from performing these duties, and his royal duties were probably for the most part a genuine pleasure. From 1752 to 1770, he served as a Lord of the Bedchamber to both George II and III. In a letter of 1753 to his friend, Sanderson Miller, he says of his appointment: 'Great as the honour is I shou'd not have accepted it without the best opinion of my Royal Master ... I never saw a greater Assemblance of Virtue than in the Person I have the Happiness to serve'.[25]

He admired both monarchs and seems to have enjoyed George III's company in particular. Unfortunately his integrity forced his resignation in 1770, allegedly due to his views on the unfolding crisis in America. Although his decision to resign was contrary to George III's wishes, it did at least earn him the respect of the monarch, who regarded him as

George William, 6th Earl of Coventry,
by Nathaniel Dance-Holland, 1774

'the wisest, handsomest, prudentest [*sic*] of his subjects'.[26] Their friendship continued and in July 1788 George III visited Croome. A contemporary source noted that Lord Coventry appeared on excellent form and 'laughed and joked with the king'.[27] Coventry was no doubt proud and delighted to show him an early masterpiece by their mutual friend, the late Royal Gardener, Lancelot Brown.

But there were rumours of less noble reasons for his resignation. Walpole believed it followed an incorrect assumption that he was to be made a Groom of the Stole.[28] Also, a few years previously, in 1765, a cruel trick had been played on him by George Selwyn, who sent him a letter on which he had forged the Duke of Grafton's signature informing him that the King had no further use of his services.[29] Lord Coventry discovered the truth before any harm was done but the incident must have unsettled him. Ever susceptible to criticism, he may have cited matters of integrity as an excuse to pre-empt further humiliation and fear of rejection by the King. Such acute sensitivities may explain why he never developed a taste for fierce political debate. Not a natural orator or statesman like his forebears, the only time he made any impact in the House of Lords was his speech in 1782 concerning his opposition to the American War of Independence.

Lord Coventry performed most effectively within the county he served.[30] In his capacity as Lord Lieutenant he organised and raised the Worcestershire Regiment of Militia between 1758 and 1770.[31] More significant still, according to his friend, Judge George Perrot, of Craycombe House, Fladbury, was his achievement in bringing 'a million of money into the county by his exertions in the improvements of public roads and buildings, by his encouragement of all its useful public institutions, and by his constant attention, directed to every object connected with its general order and prosperity.'[32] His interest in public transport also extended to the navigation of the River Severn and its connection to the new canal system, and although there was an element of self-interest in this, it was also typical of his foresight and enterprise. His contribution to the work of the new Worcester Royal Infirmary was particularly important. Founded in the 1740s, the hospital had been built in the 1760s to the design of the local architect, Anthony Keck.[33] The patronage of leading noblemen in attracting funds and organising support was crucial to such projects and Lord Coventry was prominent among the subscribers and personally chaired the majority of annual board meetings for over 50 years. He also gave £21 annually to the hospital and in his will left £200 towards its upkeep.

He derived his greatest fulfilment, however, as a patron of the arts and as a collector. This was his privilege and his greatest indulgence but, as Lord Shaftesbury had also furnished his generation with moral justification for their aesthetic ambition, it would not have been difficult for the Earl to perceive his principal passion as just another part of his duty to society should it be convenient to do so. With his great wealth and exceptional taste, he spent over 50 years perfecting the patron's art, cultivating his reputation with considerable care and living long enough to witness its impact.

His wealth was not in the league of, for example, the Pembrokes or the Devonshires, but it was more than ample. Although he spent large amounts annually for around half a century, his accounts reveal how carefully this was regulated. Contemporary sources reckon that he spent around £400,000 in total on Croome, approaching £45 million today.[34] However, this figure is likely to be inaccurate as it was based on rumour rather than fact and it would not account for the huge difference in labour costs in the eighteenth century. In truth, the 6th Earl probably spent at least £500,000 on Croome, something in the region of £50 million pounds in today's money, if the initial works, constant drainage issues, repairs, and the almost continual redecoration and alteration work are added to the equation. Of course, Croome was only one of his projects. During the late 1750s and early 1760s he repaired and refurbished the family home in Grosvenor Square. Then there was his new townhouse in Piccadilly, which he purchased for 10,000 guineas in 1764 and which absorbed a significant proportion of his expenditure during the 1760s when it was refurbished by Robert Adam. An insurance valuation carried out in 1799 estimated the contents to be worth around £8,000, of which the wine in the cellars alone was worth £1,319 19s. The construction of Springhill House on his Broadway estate was funded by his brother, John Bulkeley, but work on the estate and later projects such as the Panorama Tower and Broadway Tower were evidence that his ambition remained undimmed and his resources ever plentiful.

Labour may have been relatively cheap, but skilled craftsmen and men of the calibre of Brown and Adam were certainly not. Brown was paid around £5,000 in fees for his work at Croome, over half a million pounds today, of which £3,450 was paid into his account at Drummond's in the 1750s.[35] Adam also banked at Drummonds and it has been estimated that he was paid in the region of £750 just for his designs at Croome.[36] Add to this Lord Coventry's bills for materials, maintenance, wages, transport, household expenses and his regular shopping expeditions and it is clear that his annual expenditure ran into tens of thousands of pounds.

Much of this was paid for from the estate income. Since the 1730s this had shown a modest but dependable annual increase, thanks to his father's efforts and those of a sequence of prudent and conscientious agents that

Part of a bill for French wine, dated 1776

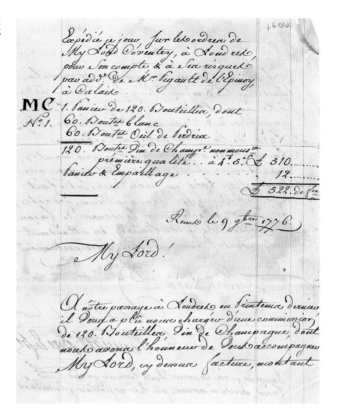

included Thomas Harbutt, Joseph Hurdman and William Phelps. In 1751, the average rental income was £11,000, or well over a million pounds today, and each subsequent decade this figure increased and had doubled by the end of the century.[37] A significant proportion of this, sometimes even up to a half, was spent on repairs, allowances, wages, levies, etc., but these funds were supplemented by income from elsewhere, including substantial investments in stocks and salaries from his official appointments. Recent calculations suggest the Earl's royal salary would have been worth around £1.6 million per annum at 2016 prices and this was for little more than six weeks' work.[38] Lord Coventry had also inherited great wealth from both his parents and received an ample dowry from his second wife.

Despite this, Coventry spent his money with care. His innate thrift, competitive zeal and sound business sense ensured that he regulated his expenditure most effectively, planning each phase of the project at Croome with precision in order to balance his accounts with predictable ease. Indeed, the balance was often so finely tuned that one suspects this element of control, of permitted extravagance, was a source of immense satisfaction to him in itself. He also took pride in his reputation for securing the best possible quality and value for his money. He scrutinised many of the bills personally, sometimes scribbling notes on them, and even Robert Adam learnt early on that he was not immune to his patron's scrupulous attention to his expenditure.

But it was Lord Coventry's taste that marked him out. Admittedly, it had been shaped in the typical fashion of his day, by his classical education, by the paintings of Claude Lorrain, Nicolas Poussin and Salvator Rosa, by contemporary cultural heroes like Alexander Pope, by the buildings of Oxford and London, by the designs of William Kent, Lord Burlington and James Gibbs, and by his friends, not least among them Sanderson Miller, who had encouraged his interest in landscape design and antiquarianism. Of key importance, too, was that he had never set foot in Italy. Neither did he show any inclination to do so. This was not particularly unusual. Not every young nobleman and gentleman was fortunate or wealthy enough to embark on a Grand Tour, but for someone of Lord Coventry's tendencies it is surprising. Possibly the deaths of his mother and elder brother deterred him, perhaps the 5th Earl did not approve of the idea, or maybe the discomfort and heat did not appeal. Whatever the reason, it might explain why Brown's approach to the transformation of Croome, more airbrushed Worcestershire than sunlit Arcadia, seemed quite so agreeable to him.

But although neo-Palladian disciplines had formed the foundation of his youth and the design of Croome Court was a late flowering of these early ideals, he began to seek something more original and challenging as the project developed. Neoclassical references began to be introduced into the interior of Croome from the late 1750s and Coventry's interest in current developments in the decorative arts in France increased significantly. Rome may have remained a distant legend to the Earl, but Paris was another matter. Despite the embarrassment of his visit there with Maria, the city had left an indelible impression. French designers were considered the best in Europe by this time and he loved the sophistication, refinement and ingenuity of their distinctive creations and soon played an important part in their promotion. In particular, he was drawn to French neoclassicism, *le goût grec*. This appealed to his scholarly interests and his desire to be different and daring and, with its bold new profiles and decorative details, it offered a striking and stylish contrast to the extravagance of the Rococo.

Following the Treaty of Paris on 10 February 1763, the 6th Earl was one of the first English noblemen to visit the French capital that summer. It seems this was the start of reciprocal shopping expeditions across the Channel. According to Walpole: 'Our passion for everything French is nothing to theirs [the French] for everything English. The two nations are crossing over'.[39] The Earl soon acquired a reputation among the leading Parisian *marchands-merciers*, particularly the fashionable and outlandish cabinetmaker, Simon-Philippe Poirier (c.1720–1785), based at 85 rue Saint Honoré. His patronage of Poirier, and of the London dealer Peter Langlois, and his major purchases of early French neoclassical items during the 1760s were of considerable significance to the dissemination of the new French style. Similarly, his magnificent French Tapestry Room and his exceptional collection of Vincennes and Sèvres porcelain all bear witness to his influential and adventurous taste and appreciation of French quality and design. Lord Coventry was one among only an important few of Robert Adam's clients, notably Sir Henry Bridgeman and Sir Lawrence Dundas, who shared and nurtured Adam's own enthusiasm for French design so that it became an important component of his repertoire. In a letter of 1766, Gilly Williams wrote: 'I told Coventry that he and Count Caylus were joined together as the standard of taste, and he made me repeat it ten times'.[40] It was intended as a light-hearted gibe but, for Lord Coventry, to be mentioned in the same sentence as the Comte de Caylus (1692–1765), the great French antiquarian and leading man of taste, with a reputation as edgy as it was erudite, was the ultimate compliment.

Not just Lord Coventry's taste marked him out as an exceptional patron. His charisma, informed approach and controlling personality ensured that he acquired a strong and loyal team of designers and craftsmen around him and also enabled him to command the respect of his workforce. As a loyal employer, with a reputation for quality and good contacts, craftsmen knew he could help to secure their future and consequently would be more inclined to give of their best.

Most important was the Earl's ability to recognise and foster new talent. There was a slight element of risk in taking on Lancelot Brown and Robert Adam so early in their careers, for their special abilities were evident but not yet renowned. But the Earl was quick to sense their potential and the self-confidence that lay beneath their raw ambition. It helped, too, that Brown had irresistible connections with Stowe and came with Miller's recommendation, while Adam had pedigree and panache and the crumbling glory of ancient ruins still dusted his shoes. Both were also good communicators and not intimidated by title and wealth. They had commitment, passion and good business sense, and Lord Coventry liked that. So, it was a well-calculated risk.

Croome became a testing ground and advertisement for their genius: a place to develop their ideas in conjunction with a sympathetic and inspiring patron with whom they could build a close relationship based on loyalty, mutual respect and a shared understanding of each other's aesthetic goals.

An impression of the north elevation of the 1640s'
house at Croome, by David Birtwhistle, 2014

THE HIDDEN HOUSE

Even at first glance, Croome Court betrays its seventeenth-century core. The huge ridge stacks are the first clue. Down in the basement the evidence is everywhere, but the greatest surprise is in the roof space. Here the Georgian mansion becomes little more than an illusion, an elegant veneer beneath which the massive hulk of the seventeenth-century house remains pretty much intact.

In Tudor times, the site was occupied by a modest manor house. Built from local clay and timber with a multi-gabled roof, it would have formed a pleasing group with the little grey stone church. Around it the village of Croome D'Abitot straggled out across the marshy land to the north and east, a typical example of the many small settlements strewn along the Severn and Avon valleys in southern Worcestershire.

An early eighteenth-century account of the Coventrys of Croome D'Abitot, the first history of the family, informs us that the manor house was burnt down once in 'the time' of Thomas, 1st Baron Coventry, and again in 'the time' of his eldest son, Thomas, the 2nd Baron.[1] Whether this refers to their lifetime or period of ownership is unclear, but the latter seems more likely and would imply that the house was rebuilt between 1606 and 1627 and then between 1627 and 1661. No records survive among the Lord Keeper's papers that relate to the earlier rebuilding, but a reference of 1624 to new glazing and ironwork in the accounts may pertain to the construction of this Jacobean house.

Lord Keeper Coventry visited the place infrequently and in 1627 the estate was settled on his son, Thomas. Thomas had architectural ambitions, and began at once to make improvements to the grounds and outbuildings. These confirm the view that the house had been rebuilt only recently, as they included a new gatehouse, front and rear courts and a chapel that was added onto the south side of the parish church. A few years later, in 1632, he built a new barn and bakehouse too, and it is possible that the outbuilding immediately to the north-east of the house may be the bakehouse. Work to the garden and grounds was also undertaken at this time, and probably included the small, octagonal Evidence

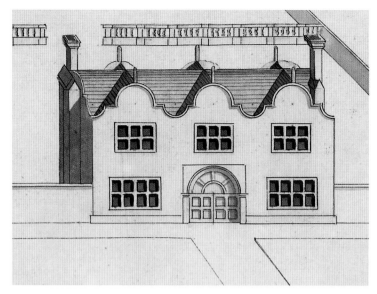

House in the south garden and the large, square kitchen garden on the flank of the ridge north-east of the house, both of which were shown in the survey undertaken by the Worcester surveyor, John Doherty or Dougharty (1709–1773), in c.1751 (see p. 74).

Brick walling and paving, timber beams, a leaded-glass window and perhaps much more survives from this time, including the great spine wall that defines the interior layout of the existing house. The footings of the south elevation have been discovered recently to be less than half a metre in depth, which suggests that they are likely to be Jacobean or even earlier. So it would seem that this former Jacobean house was a large, double-pile structure and the new gatehouse probably reflected the design of the main building not just in plan but also in its symmetrical façades, shaped gables and stone detailing.

Documents in the Badminton Muniments confirm that the second rebuilding of Crombe House took place from 1640 to 1642, so the fire probably occurred just prior to this.[2] In view of the 2nd Baron's major improvements, this fire must have been a severe blow – or maybe not. Perhaps it presented an ideal opportunity that coincided conveniently with the recent death of his father. Certainly it seems the mounting political crisis did little to dampen his enthusiasm.

The 2nd Baron Coventry was among an increasing number of seventeenth-century noblemen and gentlemen eager to try their hand at architectural statement, spurred on by such new publications as

Croome Court, leaded-glass window in the south elevation of the basement

Jacobean gatehouse: detail from a bird's-eye view of the north elevation, Crombe House, c.1750, by an unidentified draughtsman

Sir Henry Wotton's *Elements of Architecture* (1624), which provided an invaluable grounding for the uninitiated. During the 1630s, Thomas had bought a new London home, Dorchester House in Covent Garden, at the heart of the capital's most architecturally progressive developments. He then proceeded to build himself a house nearby in Portugal Row, Lincoln's Inn, known as Pine Apple Gates.[3] His brother-in-law, the Earl of Craven, lived close by at Craven House in Drury Lane, and further east in Aldersgate Street was Thanet House, the new home of John Tufton, 2nd Earl of Thanet, whose daughter, Margaret, married Thomas's son, George, in 1653.

In this convivial and fashionable part of London, the design of these houses looked to Inigo Jones's startling new brand of classicism for their inspiration, as well as to the pattern books filtering in from the Netherlands and more scholarly sources like the first English edition of Sebastiano Serlio of 1611. They incorporated exuberant shaped gables, chunky cornices, pilasters, rusticated plinths and balconies in their design, advertising the wealth and status of their occupants to the passing world.[4]

Many of their owners tempted these talented London builders and craftsman back to their country seats. Among the worthy team that Thomas Coventry brought back to Croome was Matthew Browne, a master-bricklayer from St Martin-in-the-Fields, who shared his name with the man who rebuilt the house a century later. There was also William West, a master-carpenter who was working with Browne in the Covent Garden area at this time.[5] The other principal members of the team were Thomas Usher, a master-mason from Winchcombe in Gloucestershire, then part of the Coventry estate, and the metalworkers Richard Wells and William Bromwell, who recast much of the old leadwork for the downpipes and guttering.

The various Articles of Agreement among the Badminton documents provide a useful guide to the schedule of work and also the appearance of the new 1640s' house.[6] The main works were to be completed by midsummer 1641 and the tiling by 1 April 1642, so the shell was probably complete before the outbreak of the Civil War on 22 August. Although the Articles relating to Edmund Johnson, the principal painter and decorator, are dated 8 and 10 May 1649, the 2nd Baron and his two sons are recorded to have been living at Crombe House between 1642 and 1649, so the house must have been habitable during this period. A staunch Royalist, the 2nd Baron was prepared to endure any inconvenience to ensure that his new home survived the war unscathed.

His remarkably progressive approach was evident from the start. The Articles refer to 'Models' of the house, perhaps just plans and elevations but more likely proper scale models, which were still fairly unusual at this time. As a substantial part of the Jacobean house seems to have survived the second fire, and as the new work was built from a similar local brick and tile, determining the separate phases of work of the 1720s and 1740s is not straightforward. The new house was of roughly the same size as before and was also finished with stone dressings, but there the similarities end, for the Caroline building was a more fashionable affair altogether. The Badminton documents state that its stone dressings were to be made 'Hansome and smoote' with 'close and fyne jointes', and included a modillion cornice, a cornice comprised of small brackets supporting the upper member, chamfered quoins or blocks at the angles of the building and openings, moulded architraves and 'watertables', or cornices, above the windows. The Articles also refer to carving 'cartoses', or cartouches, used to embellish the façades.

Croome Court, seventeenth-century roof structure encased within the existing roof, central range looking east

Ample evidence survives of the form and profile of the house, not least the giant framework of the old roof. Built to an E-shaped plan, it had two principal storeys raised upon a semi-basement. The roof was hipped and incorporated an attic storey lit by 24 dormer windows, or 'lucarnes'. Right across the central roof ridge ran the massive ridge stacks that survive today, which were probably adapted from their predecessors at this time. The main façades were symmetrical. Early images, reused openings and straight joints in the brickwork all imply that the south elevation was of 11 bays and had an entrance in the central bay with steps down to the garden and a balcony above it. The north entrance elevation was of only nine bays, composed of shallow two-bay wings flanking a five-bay centre with a central porch and perron, a platform approached by steps outside the entrance door. Giant pairs of external chimney breasts were located on the side elevations, possibly flanked by openings, some of which appear to have been reused in the mid-eighteenth-century remodelling. The windows themselves would have been of the oak mullion and transom type with wrought-iron casements typical for this date but steadily abandoned in favour of sash windows towards the end of the century.

The idea of two main storeys of equal height set above a generous basement had been imported from Europe. Combined with a hipped roof and classical detailing, it was already in evidence in several influential new houses of the 1620s in London and south-east England, among them Chevening in Kent and Forty Hall in Enfield, but such a form and profile

Crombe House, bird's-eye view of the north elevation, by an unidentified draughtsman, c.1750. The detail of the drawing suggests it was executed at an earlier date and subsequently altered by a different hand.

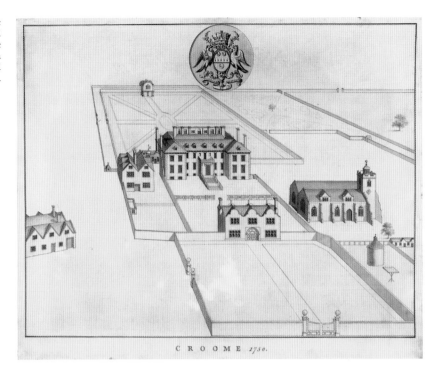

C R O O M E 1750.

would have appeared astonishingly different in rural Worcestershire at this time. The generous semi-basement had distinct advantages in that it raised the principal accommodation above the marshy site and it also had important implications for the social organisation of the household, enabling the servants' quarters to be tucked away below stairs, together with the associated noise and smells. The arrangement gained popularity as the century progressed and had the effect of downgrading the status of the servants, a process of separation that would become increasingly pronounced during the Georgian and Victorian eras.

Crombe House had inherited its double-pile plan. However, it was a type that grew in popularity during the seventeenth century and may have originated in the design of town houses where space was limited. Its compact form made it cheaper to build and easier to heat, and it could improve access within a house and provide better privacy, particularly when the junction between the ranges was flanked by a passageway. In the case of larger house there were important aesthetic benefits, too, as the building could be double-fronted, with the main elevations of equal stature. Crombe House was actually triple pile in that it had an additional small central roof built across the breadth of the massive central wall around the base of the chimney stacks.

The heft and bulk of the central spine wall anchored the building to its soggy site and continues to assert its presence throughout the building to this day (see p. 95). As it split the house down the middle, crucial clues to the house's complex evolution still remain embedded deep within it. The rooms in each range were linked by access passages of probable Jacobean origin, some of which survive and were arranged in tiers. One tier lies east of the existing Entrance Hall and Saloon. At basement level, the passageway is of notable width and the huge iron pintles, or hinge pins, on which the massive door was hung are still *in situ.* On the first floor above, the route was blocked in the eighteenth century to create a cupboard accessed via a jib, or gib, door, a concealed door flush with the wall surface and decorated to match, from the existing Chinese Bedroom. Another important tier of passages was at the western end of the wall, which may relate to the location of the former Great Stair. The route between the Entrance Hall and Saloon is of probable Jacobean origin too, as it would have created an important central axis through the building that ran from the gatehouse to the south garden. Although the Entrance Hall was entered on this central axis, the structural evidence suggests that the external symmetry was abandoned within and that it extended westwards from the centre of the house. On the attic storey, the central wall was shorter in length to accommodate the slope of the hipped roof and, for structural reasons, was also narrower in width and honeycombed with openings and recesses.

Various old chimney flues wind their way up through this wall. The pair of fireplaces in the present Saloon is known to have existed in the 1640s house, although the westernmost flue is likely to be earlier in origin. This tapers outwards into a spacious gather area (the area at the base of the flue in which smoke collects before it passes up the flue shaft) that probably once served a very large inglenook, possibly in the Entrance Hall in Jacobean times. The flue for the present Drawing Room fireplace shares similar characteristics, although it is smaller overall, and may have once served a fireplace slightly east of its present location, as suggested by a curious straight joint identified in the adjacent brickwork.[7]

The Badminton documents that relate to the work of William West, the master-carpenter, and Edmond Johnson, the principal painter, provide a fascinating insight into the accommodation on each floor as well as evidence of three staircases: the Great Stair, which had 83 steps, the Back or Lesser Stair, which had 81 steps, and a small service staircase with 14 steps. It seems likely that the Great Stair was at the western end of the Entrance Hall in view of the adjacent tier of arched openings in the central wall, and the big archway on the first floor may have housed the large door at the head of the Great Stair referred to by William West. As it was becoming the preferred option to locate the principal staircase in the rear range by this time, in this case the south range, the architectural historian, Nicholas Cooper, has proposed two other possible alternative locations, either west of the central south room or in the south-western corner of the house.[8] However, as this would compromise the south-facing accommodation on both floors, the north range does appear a more logical option, especially if a precedent existed in Jacobean times. The location of the Back Stair is recorded to have been in the eastern half of the house adjacent to the pantry. Just east of the existing Entrance Hall, opposite the tier of access routes through the central wall, an early wide doorway with a chamfered surround faces the lowest access route in this tier. On the upper floors, a narrow space has always been present opposite these tiered access routes so this would seem the most likely place for the Back Stair. As the third short staircase is recorded to have had only 14 steps, it probably just led down to the basement, possibly at the western end of the building for the use of the butler.

Beneath the existing floors, some huge principal and secondary floor beams remain from the seventeenth-century house. These provide further clues to the building's appearance, and the layered floor in the Lord's Dressing Room, or Alcove Bedroom, is particularly interesting. There are also some early timber-framed partitions that survive, notably one located between the Saloon and Drawing Room. In the eighteenth century, another timber-framed partition was constructed about a metre to the east of this to support the new vault. The earlier partition still retains its lath and plaster infill panels, which were well finished only on the upper east side of the partition where they would have been exposed in the Caroline house.

The two principal storeys included the private rooms for the family and public rooms for entertaining. On the ground floor, in addition to the porch, Entrance Hall and Great Stair within the north range, the Badminton documents refer to a 'Passage between the Hall and Parlour' and to the east of the Entrance Hall, Back Stair, pantry and a 'Room within the Pantry'. There was also a 'Little Room at the Upper End of the Hall', perhaps in the north-west wing.

In the south range there seem to have been three large rooms, as West, the master-carpenter, was instructed to make, frame and set up a 'seeling floore' of timber with ornate mouldings and corbel works 'in the three lower rooms on the south side of the house lying on the same floor as the hall'.[9] These included a panelled Little Parlour with three windows, the Great Dining Room, also panelled with four windows, and the Great Parlour, with four windows, one of which must have been in the side elevation. Johnson, the painter, refers to the coffering, or sunken

Crombe House, detail of the proposed south elevation, Henry Beighton, from his bird's-eye view of 1714

panels, and mouldings of the Great Dining Room ceiling and to painting two large chimneys to simulate white marble in this room. He also mentions a balcony, which may relate to the platform from which steps led down to the south garden as shown in the early eighteenth-century view by the Warwickshire surveyor, Henry Beighton (1687–1743).

On the first floor, Johnson's Articles refer to a Great Balcony Room, probably the room that provided access to the balcony set above the north porch (see p. 57). This was adjoined by the Floure Pott Chamber, by another small chamber, and by the 'Room next the Stair'. Then, in the south range, was the Lord's Chamber, which had east and west closets and an adjoining Dressing Room. Later bills support the view that the Lord's Chamber and Dressing Room were at the western end of the house, which again set a precedent for the eighteenth-century remodelling. Beyond was 'the Balcony Room towards the Great Garden', which had 'Little Rooms' on its east and west sides. Also listed are the 'Passage at the Lesser Stairs', the 'Blew Chamber' and two further rooms, quite possibly another closet and dressing room. Evidence of various seventeenth-century openings has been found along the south wall of the first-floor central corridor. Three of these were incorporated within the Georgian house: the large archway to the Lord's Dressing Room, the narrow archway that leads into an adjoining closet and the passageway into the Chinese Bedroom.

The attic floor was used primarily for servants' accommodation and storage and no room names are recorded in the Badminton documents. This floor has retained much of its seventeenth-century proportions, character and layout, particularly in the south range. The central corridor is flanked by ranks of doors from the earlier house, many altered but still swinging from sturdy strap hinges. Three seventeenth-century stone chimney pieces of high quality, one lugged, one finely moulded and one with shapely volutes, were likely to have been relocated up here in the Georgian period, as were some sections of salvaged Jacobean panelling.

The basement is more puzzling. Although it harbours a wealth of evidence, it has been much altered to fulfil changing social, domestic and technical requirements. The Badminton documents provide a list of rooms as follows: 'Common (Servants') Hall, Pastry Room, Kitchen, an Entry Tower to the Kitchen, Spicery, Larder, Meal Rooms, Cook's Chamber, Butler's Chamber, a Cellar, a Passage into the Cellar, and a Scullery'. Additional offices would have been located in the adjacent outbuilding. A reasonable assumption is that the cook's quarters, the kitchen and the pastry room were grouped together at the eastern end of the house, while the wine cellar and the butler's chamber or pantry were within the western half of the building. Both the chambers for the butler and cook had been moved into the outbuilding by the time of the 1719 inventory.

Frustratingly, the precise location of the original kitchen remains a mystery. If it was within the main house, as the documents imply, it would have required a space that provided adequate height and ventilation. Recent investigations in the existing strong room adjoining

Croome Court, seventeenth-century chimney piece on the second floor

the eighteenth-century butler's pantry have exposed two broad archways within the eastern wall, both of which are probably former fireplaces that made use of the external north-east chimney. If this was the original kitchen it must have occupied the entire north-eastern wing of the basement and ground floor, and also part of the central passageway, as the blocked arch of the southernmost fireplace extends into this area. Matthew Browne, the master-builder, also refers to constructing a drain across the kitchen court, which must have been located on the east side of the house.

As you entered Crombe House, it would have appeared surprisingly light and bright despite its double-pile plan. The painter's documents state that the wainscoting, columns, chimney piece and cornice in the Entrance Hall were all painted to simulate white marble, as were the chimney pieces in the main rooms.[10] Much of the ground floor, the grand rooms along the south front and the Great Stair, also known as the White Staircase, were painted white too, and even the timber balconies and balustrades were similarly treated. This would have given the house an impressively grand and classical feel, and would have provided an ideal backdrop for the rich hues and textures of the furnishings and fabrics. Not all the rooms were so bright and formal though. The 'Little Room at the Upper End of the Hall' was of snug proportions and walnut-grained, and upstairs the palette became more muted and intimate in feel. The Great Balcony Room, the Balcony Room 'towards the Great Garden' and also most of the smaller rooms were wholly or partly walnut-grained, as was the Back Stair. Then there was the Blew Chamber, but most memorable of all were the Lord's Bedchamber and Dressing Room, enriched with ornate architraves, friezes and cornices and painted a distinctive light purple, probably a pale mauve, an expensive colour suggestive of its occupant's high status and wealth.[11] The descent into the dimly-lit basement from the marbled magnificence of the principal ground-floor rooms would have made the division in the domestic arrangements of the household all the more pronounced.

Crombe House would have looked strikingly different from the traditional gabled Worcestershire manor houses in the vicinity: a bold and progressive statement that reflected contemporary architectural developments in London and south-east England. Although the classical style was seeping out of London into the neighbouring counties throughout

Croome Court, blocked seventeenth-century fireplace on the east wall of the butler's strong room

View of the South Aspect of Belton House, Lincolnshire, with the House Porter, by British (English) School, 1710–20

the first half of the seventeenth century, it became fully established and widespread only after the Restoration influenced by the work of Sir Roger Pratt (1620–1684) and Hugh May (1621–1684) of the 1650s and 1660s. Crombe House appears to be among a series of experimental and transitional dwellings that were built in the regions in the mid-seventeenth century, constructed by aspiring noblemen and gentlemen and their informed teams of craftsmen. Most combined fashionable details with traditional elements that were largely determined by any surviving fabric or were retained for reasons of habit and convenience.[12]

Nicholas Cooper has identified a number of houses that bear certain similarities to Crombe House. Among the earliest and most significant of these was West Woodhay House in Berkshire, of 1636, built for Sir Benjamin Rudyard (1572–1658), which had an even more progressive design with a layout that was notably advanced and included a rear staircase.[13] Crombe House seems to have had more in common with a group of houses built in the 1650s, such as High Meadow and Highnam Court in Gloucestershire, Moyles Court in Hampshire, Tyttenhanger in Hertfordshire and Yotes Court in Kent. These retain certain traditional elements but their refinement of detail anticipated the achievements of the post-Restoration period, exemplified by such outstanding designs as Belton House in Lincolnshire of the 1680s. A more local comparison might be made with Norgrove Court, a few miles away in Feckenham, built around 1749 for William Cookes (d.1672). This unusual brick house had a hipped roof and balconies, and was also similar to Crombe House in terms of its ambition, although its overall design and layout was otherwise too idiosyncratic for inclusion within any specific group. The true significance of Crombe House has yet to be evaluated, but it does appear to have been impressively advanced for its date and location, adding another exciting dimension to our understanding of the early house prior to its transformation into the neo-Palladian mansion known as Croome Court in the mid-eighteenth century.

The Thwarted Plans of the Snitterfield Coventrys

Thomas, the architect-baron, died in 1661 and during the time of his eldest son, George, and his grandson, John, who became 3rd and 4th Baron Coventry respectively, Crombe House was renowned for its hospitality. Thomas, 5th Baron and 1st Earl of Coventry, made modest repairs to the garden walls, and purchased 200 plants and a large order of seeds for the garden, but he was otherwise content to take pleasure in his retirement from politics and spent the last years of his life enjoying his good fortune.[14]

The 5th Baron's two sons had more ambition. Thomas, 2nd Earl, the astronomer and mathematician, and his equally accomplished wife, Anne Somerset, had been making some significant improvements to the family home in Snitterfield, Warwickshire, and his youngest son, Gilbert, 4th Earl, had also made changes at his home at Hidcote, Gloucestershire. By 1700 it would have been apparent that the old-fashioned layout of Crombe House was in need of alteration, particularly as it lacked a suite of state rooms appropriate to the family's new status. But if the 2nd Earl and his wife intended to correct this omission, there is no evidence of it, despite the fact that they are recorded to have spent £2,000 to £3,000 on Snitterfield and Croome D'Abitot. Some of this must have been on refurnishing Crombe House, as his father had remarried and left the contents of the house to his new young wife, Elizabeth. The 1719 inventory gives some idea of the quality and quantity of the furnishings and fittings they acquired, which included gilt-leather hangings in the Great Parlour, tapestries, marble tables, and a wealth of pictures and plate.

But Thomas and Anne's plans for Croome appear to have been otherwise confined to the garden, not least a large and rather grand greenhouse, or hothouse, for Anne where she could pursue her botanical interests. Almost certainly this stood at the upper east end of the kitchen garden as seen in Doherty's plan of c.1751 (see p. 74, far right). A bill for this survives that suggests it was intended for recreational as well as practical purposes for it had one main room flanked by smaller

Gilbert Coventry, 4th Earl of Coventry (c.1668–1719), by Michael Dahl (Stockholm 1656/9–London 1743), 1714

rooms, 13 windows, each 2.4 metres high, and an upper window, perhaps set within a central gable or pediment.[15]

On his death in 1710, the 2nd Earl left debts amounting to almost £8,000. Anne retreated back to Snitterfield, and by 1712 it was recorded that 'Crombe House, Gardens and Out Houses were neglected and gone to Decay'.[16] When the 2nd Earl's only surviving son died in 1712, his brother Gilbert became 4th Earl and wasted little time. He had his own investments in salt and coal and his late first wife had been left £1,000 on the death of her father, Sir William Keyte, in 1702, so funds were to hand. His account books survive at Antony House in Cornwall and record the development of his plans with admirable precision.

During the summer of 1712 he began to make monthly visits to Croome from Hidcote and probably moved in later that year. His initial intention seems to have been primarily to update the old stone mullion and transom windows and carry out essential repairs and redecoration. Payments were made for '76 foot of finished and 28 feet of unfinished Crown glass' as well as '140 Dutch tiles', and a further load of '200 squares of Bristol Crown glass' arrived later that summer. Roof repairs started in June, and a Mr Atkinson began painting the new sash windows, the 24 'Luthorn' or dormer windows, and part of the interior, including the Entrance Hall, staircases, pantry, cellars and butler's pantry.[17]

That autumn and winter, huge quantities of building materials were brought onto site; one load included 8,900 tiles, 20,000 clamp bricks and 1,000 gutter tiles. In 1713, payments were made for repairs to the house gutters, for mending the windows in the house with old glass (so not all the windows were replaced) and mending the glass in the hotbed frames, and that October the still house, porter's lodge and church gate received a fresh coat of paint too.[18] Work also began on the new apartment on the first floor. A reference to brass locks for 'ye new rooms' appears on 10 October 1713, and three days later a payment was made for a 2.4-metre hearth stone for the Red Room, the name given to the existing Lord's Dressing Room at this time, which may have formed part of this apartment. That winter, further payments were made to a Mr Stone, an upholsterer, for looking glasses, quilts and curtains, possibly to furnish the new apartment.

Then, around 1714, the 4th Earl appointed the prominent architect and master-builder, Francis Smith of Warwick (1672–1738), to supervise the work.[19] It is possible he was involved even earlier than this. As most of the craftsmen referred to in the bills were from Warwickshire, they were probably part of Smith's team or had been employed previously by the family at Snitterfield, perhaps on Smith's behalf. Among them was George Chine, the joiner, who charged over £40 for 128 yards of

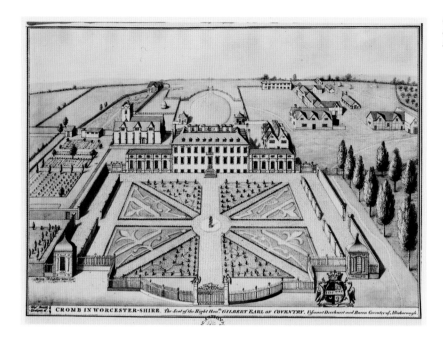

wainscoting and new flooring for the apartment in 1714 and for putting on the brass locks bought the previous year, and in August 1715 a new marble chimney piece was installed.

Also, on 4 November 1714, Smith was paid for a design for a stable. The contract book for that year records that 100,000 bricks were made at Seggy Mere, gouging a pit big enough to shape into the existing lake. These were intended either for the new stable or for additions to the house that Smith may have proposed.[20] That year Beighton produced his impressive drawing of these proposed alterations.[21] His bird's-eye view shows ornate new five-bay wings with tall windows flanking the south elevation, creating a much grander and more fashionable façade altogether. It also provides a detailed idea of the proposed south garden, with its quartered parterre, holly and yew topiary, central statue and flanking *allées* that were to lead to a pair of corner pavilions. Adding necessary splendour to the whole composition was a great pair of iron entrance gates with gilded Coventry eagles almost 90 centimetres tall perched upon the gateposts.

Work seems to have started on the eastern wing, the more important of the two as it screened the kitchen court and other outbuildings from the south garden. The tall lias plinth on the south elevation of the existing service wing certainly looks to be of this date, yet it extends the entire length of the elevation only to be cut off abruptly round the eastern corner. It must have been even longer before its western end was demolished to make way for the east wing of the Palladian mansion. This can only be explained by its subsequent extension and alteration, and this view is supported by the recent discovery of a straight internal joint just beyond the fourth bay and other structural anomalies that are visible within, particularly those associated with the fenestration of the westernmost bays along the south elevation.

The improvements to the formal garden seem to have proceeded less hesitantly. Mr Cooper, the new gardener, was sent to Bristol and Oxfordshire to purchase large quantities of plants and seeds in October 1712, including hollies, pyramid yews and carnations from George Adams, a Bristol nurseryman, who also offered to redesign the garden. There were deliveries of walnut and cherry stocks that winter and four deliveries of trees arrived the following spring.[22] The park was extended to the south of the house and a new contract was drawn up with William Thorneloe, the Park Keeper. More yew trees were purchased in 1714 and around 400 metres of bordering stone was laid in the garden.

Then there was a major change of plan. This coincided with Gilbert's second marriage in the spring of 1715. Although the marriage brought a welcome £10,000 to the project, the new Countess seems to have held strong views about the work in progress.[23] Probably the apartment was completed as intended, as a memorandum of 14 April 1716 from the

Croome Court, the first-floor corridor of the south range of the Red Wing, prior to its restoration by the National Trust. The straight vertical joints of the blocked openings of the tall early eighteenth-century windows are just visible beneath the sills.

joiner, George Chine of Warwick, refers to laying an oak floor in the Red Room similar to the one he had laid in the adjacent room and to wainscoting the walls with white English oak.[24] He also signed an agreement to make and hang new sashes in 'as many windows as his Lordship will be pleased to have sashes', but just how far this progressed is not known. The biggest issue seems to have concerned the general inadequacy of the service accommodation. If the 4th Earl still hoped to build one or both of the formal pair of wings shown in Beighton's view, the idea was abandoned entirely. The intention now seems to have been to adapt the initial work on the east wing to provide additional offices. This necessitated blocking the lower part of the recesses of the five tall and elegant south windows to screen the view of the south garden from within. The new wing may have been linked to the old brick outbuilding at this point as shown in a c.1750 view of the north elevation of the house (see p. 57).[25] Francis Smith was also obliged to alter his design for the stables for which payment was made on 29 October 1715.[26]

Exactly what was to be accommodated in the new wing is an interesting question. In 1714 repairs had been made to 'ye new and ye old cistern in the Kitchen'. However, on 30 October 1717, the accounts refer to a payment of two shillings and sixpence for giving a drink to 'ye stonemasons … who paved ye new Kitchen'.[27] As no kitchen is listed in the 1719 inventory in either the main house or the Jacobean outbuilding, it remains a possibility that the kitchen was moved out of the house into the new east wing at this point.[28] Certainly the advantages of placing the kitchen away from the main building to reduce the risk of fire and further remove noise and smells from the living accommodation was becoming more widely recognised by this time. It would have the additional benefit of making space for more rooms in the main house at ground-floor level, something that would tally with the increased number of ground-floor rooms recorded in the 1719 inventory.

The accounts for 5 February 1717 also note a payment to a Mr Chinn for 'Drawing a new Ground Plot' of 'ye new scullery Larder & stables' and another payment in September 1718 was made to Smith's stonemasons for laying a floor in the new scullery.[29] Further payments were made to Smith in March 1718, and April and June 1719, and to Smith's stonemasons and joiners in April, May and June 1719, and it does appear that work was proceeding at a steady pace on the new offices and stables.

Work also progressed in the garden. The central statue of Hercules was supplied by John van Nost the Elder on 21 April 1715 and the 1719 inventory describes it as being 'Gilt with Gold'. Benjamin Taylor, another Warwickshire craftsman, made the great gates and a payment for their installation is recorded in the accounts for 25 June 1717.[30] However, whether the pavilions and *allées* were ever built is unknown, especially as the actual layout may have been revised. Another new gardener, Mr Davison, appears around 1717, who was paid five shillings 'for his draught of my garden' and, in August of the following year, a payment was made for a drawing of the Evidence House, perhaps prior to its proposed alteration. During 1719 work continued in the garden on walling and at the new bowling alley.[31]

The 4th Earl suffered from recurrent severe attacks of gout and he died on 27 October 1719. Probably much of the internal work on the main house was complete but not much else. The Little Inventory of 1719 (a supplement to the main inventory of the same year) records quantities of building materials and scaffolding stored on site at the time of Gilbert's death, including numerous sash windows and piles of wainscoting stacked in the wood house and Evidence House. What happened to the offices from this moment until Lancelot Brown's arrival is a mystery. At some point the east wing was extended eastwards for the mid-eighteenth-century brick facing conceals extensive evidence of the phased construction within. Some of the 4th Earl's sash windows are even embedded in the fabric at the eastern end of the south wall, still unpainted internally.

It seems unlikely that Smith of Warwick was responsible for the somewhat haphazard workmanship. Equally unlikely is that they were caused by Brown's workmen in the early 1750s, whose task it was to present the muddled mess as a coherent whole. So something happened in between. No clues appear in the accounts. The 5th Earl must have completed Gilbert's work and made later alterations to it. Or could the bodged alterations to the wing have been a preliminary project undertaken by his keen and inexperienced son: the start of a much bigger experiment altogether?

THE PRIMARY AUTHOR

When William, 5th Earl of Coventry, arrived at Croome in the winter of 1719 to inspect his inheritance it was unlikely to have been an encouraging prospect. Smoke from the village hearths mingled with the rising mist from the dank and marshy fields. Farm buildings and dwellings lay scattered about. Beside the squat stone church was an impressive little gatehouse and then, looming up behind it all, was a huge and handsome brick house. But all was not well. Building materials lay in heaps in the courtyards, there was probably scaffolding still clamped around the offices and stables, and even the impressive formal gardens were being altered. Inside was little better. There was the smell of new joinery and fresh paint, and some of the furnishings were missing, removed prior to his arrival or put into store. It was a work in progress.

William returned to London to make plans. Within months the on-going work would have been patched up to an acceptable standard. The bills and accounts reveal little, but we can only assume that the scaffolding and building materials were tidied away, new furnishings were brought up from London and the garden was finished off as neatly as possible. William then embarked on the complex task of unravelling the legal and financial problems that accompanied his inheritance, not least the demands of the 4th Earl's widow and issues relating to the 2nd Earl's debts. But by the 1730s he was free at last to focus on the major overhaul of the estate and in doing so he proved an exemplary landlord.

With admirable speed the estate was restored to robust health and an effective system of management installed. Its debts were cleared and from the 1730s the accounts chart a steady and substantial increase in income that lasted for the rest of the century. Over a period of 20 years or so, considerable sums were invested in agricultural buildings, drainage and planting. Land was exchanged and enclosed, and in 1738 the parkland was extended westwards towards Severn Stoke. It is just possible that William added a new feature to the park too. A mysterious domed garden building is shown in the family portrait by Charles Philips (see p. 32). If this stood on the site of the existing Rotunda, it

Sanderson Miller (1717–1780),
attributed to Thomas Hudson
(Devonshire 1701–Twickenham 1779),
c.1750

might explain why the adjacent ha-ha is earlier in date than those built by Lancelot Brown elsewhere in the pleasure grounds. It would be the obvious location for a new park building as it would have terminated the view along the great avenue that ran south of the house from Seggy Mere in the west up to the eastern ridge.

Following the death of his eldest son, Thomas Henry, in 1744, the 5th Earl's health began to fail and his interest and enthusiasm in his estate at Croome diminished. It was left to his second son, George William, now Lord Deerhurst, to fill his brother's place. The estate was settled on him in 1747 when he was 25, by which time he had already revealed a remarkable aptitude for the task ahead.

Although determined to fulfil his elder brother's role and execute their shared plans for Croome to the best of his abilities, Deerhurst was insecure and uncertain how to proceed. During this time, he relied heavily on his college friend, Sanderson Miller. For a while their friendship was close, only to fade in the late 1750s, as Deerhurst's confidence and talent began to assert themselves and Miller's advice was sought elsewhere. Brief their friendship may have been, but it was of crucial importance. It brought Deerhurst back from a depression, which returned to haunt him from time to time throughout his life; it helped to ignite in him a sense of purpose that burned fiercely within him thereafter; and it brought about his auspicious introduction to Lancelot Brown.

Sanderson Miller was a keen amateur-architect and landscape designer whose informed opinion and inspiring ideas proved invaluable among his wide circle of influential friends. His life and work have been studied in detail, notably by William Hawkes and Jennifer Meir, and this has underlined his role in the evolution of the natural landscape style and as one of the leading exponents of Georgian Gothic architecture.[1]

Born in 1716, Miller was an exact contemporary of Lancelot Brown. He was the son of a successful Banbury merchant who had invested his wealth in an estate at Radway in Warwickshire. Miller's family also owned property adjacent to Stowe and, by fortunate coincidence, the Temple-Grenville family of Stowe were owners of land at Burton Dassett, not very far from Miller's residence at Radway. The association was further reinforced by Miller's marriage to Susannah Trotman in 1746, the grand-daughter of Elizabeth Temple. This enabled Miller to socialise among the members of the political and literary circle who gathered at Stowe, prominent among whom were William Pitt, George and Henry Grenville, and George Lyttelton.

At Oxford, Miller befriended Deane Swift, cousin of the satirist, Jonathan Swift, and William King, the college principal and prominent Jacobite, who encouraged his interest in the classics. He also became a member of a close-knit group who shared a competitive zeal for the improvement of their country estates that included the Coventry family's London neighbour, Sir Edward Turner of Ambroseden, Oxfordshire, Sir Roger Newdigate of Arbury, Warwickshire, and Thomas Lennard Barrett, later 17th Baron Dacre of Belhus, near Aveley, in Essex.[2] Other important contacts established during this period were Roger Nugent of Gosfield, created 1st Earl Nugent in 1776, a friend of the Prince of Wales and part of the Stowe set, and Francis, Lord North, created 1st Earl of Guildford in 1752, who lived not far from Miller at Wroxton, near Banbury. The two elder Coventry boys were probably introduced to Miller by Turner, and Miller's correspondence suggests that they were soon welcomed into his circle of friends.[3]

Miller remained at Oxford from 1734 to 1740 but was never awarded a degree. He simply enjoyed the convivial lifestyle, the scholarly atmosphere and the opportunity to develop his keen interest in architecture and antiquarian matters. He admired in particular the work of Inigo Jones and he also succeeded in acquiring an impressive knowledge of medieval architecture to rival that of Horace Walpole, much to the latter's irritation. As an undergraduate, he made his first visits to Stowe and he began to amass an impressive library.

Miller had inherited the Radway estate in 1737 and, inspired by his visits to Stowe, he began to drain and landscape the grounds and alter the house. From around 1738 he took on a similar project nearby at Farnborough Hall for William Holbech, and during the mid-1740s he began to advise his friends on their improvements. Encouraged by William Kent's example, his work marks an important step towards a greater informality guided by the local topography, with winding paths and with clumps and belts of trees to define ridges and boundaries, and his designs also reflect the increasing tendency to incorporate the wider landscape.[4] However, Miller had moved on from Kent, adopting a more eclectic or Rococo style in his park buildings, integrating them skilfully within his landscapes using his sound aesthetic judgement and his knowledge of estate management and hydraulic engineering. This rare ability to recognise and reap a site's potential was taken to a new level by his protégé, Lancelot Brown.

Miller concentrated increasingly on architectural projects after 1750. As Hawkes has demonstrated, Oxford provided him with a rich and varied architectural reference source. Initially, his antiquarian interests drew him to the romantic and picturesque qualities of medieval buildings, mock castle ruins becoming his speciality. Radway's location, on the site of the Battle of Edgehill of 1642, proved an irresistible stimulant to his interests and he experimented first with a thatched cottage, Egge Cottage of

The Ruined Castle, Hagley Park,
Worcestershire

1743–44, which appeared to incorporate a medieval ruin, and from 1745 to 1747 he built a mock medieval tower based on Guy's Tower at Warwick Castle. Similar structures soon followed for his friends, not least his famous ruined castle for George Lyttelton of 1747–48, set high on the wooded slopes of the Clent Hills, Worcestershire; his octagonal Gothic tower of 1749 at Ingestre in Staffordshire for Viscount Chetwynde; and the sham ruin at Wimpole Hall in Cambridgeshire that he designed in 1749–50 for Lord Hardwicke and which was built eventually by Brown in 1772.[5]

Miller combined this antiquarianism with an interest in Palladianism and the work of Inigo Jones. His stables and coach house at Hagley of c.1750 and the quadrangular stables with corner towers at Packington, designed in 1749 and built from 1756 to 1758, were both simple essays in Palladian proportion and detail. But it was Croome Court of 1751–58 and especially his two most important designs, Hagley Hall of c.1752–60, and the Shire Hall, Warwick, designed in 1753 and built 1754–c.1770, that demonstrated his accomplished handling of the style. Even some of his most memorable Gothic designs, such as the Great Hall at Lacock Abbey, designed in 1753 for his friend, John Ivory Talbot, were based on classical proportions and symmetry.

During the mid-1740s, Deerhurst was one of several of Miller's friends to seek his advice. In 1744, Francis North had consulted him on his plans for a new serpentine river, lake and grand cascade at Wroxton and from 1747 to 1748 Miller altered the Abbey chapel and advised on the rebuilding of the church tower.[6] Miller also began to advise Edward Turner in 1744 on the remodelling and decoration of Ambroseden House, and, from 1747 to 1749, the design of various park buildings, including a 'Gothic barn', a mock ruin, and a new gate and entrance lodge. He was also in Essex at this time, helping Barrett rebuild the south and west fronts of Belhus and landscape the grounds. In January 1748, Barrett wrote to Miller: 'I must tell you that I have made my River as wide as Lord North's ... I have planted above 200 Elms ye least of them above 20ft high and many of them 30ft. These I have put in ye grove behind my house'.[7] These extensive works were completed by Brown from 1753 to 1763. At Packington, prior to designing the new stables, Miller provided advice to Lord Guernsey on new dams, pools, a cascade and a Gothic building in the mid-1740s and again Brown was taken on in 1750 to implement these improvements. Lord Guernsey continued to seek Miller's advice after Brown's appointment, much as occurred later at Croome.

So Deerhurst embarked on his first few experiments at Croome at a similar time as his new friends. The General Account records the supply of trees and plants, and a pedestal was acquired for the Hercules statue – so possibly it was still in store until this point. By 1747 further land exchanges had taken place and John Doherty began his survey of the park. John Phipps had also been taken on to supervise the early stage of extensive tree felling and planting as well as the first phase of the drainage works, and a new road was under construction north of the house too. This is almost certainly when the felling of a section of the

Detail of a plan of Croome D'Abitot, John Doherty, c.1751

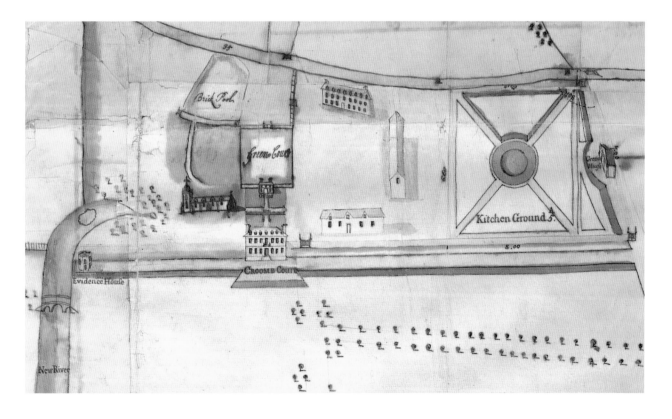

south avenue took place to open up the views on this side of the house, something that Miller is likely to have proposed. It can be seen from Doherty's plan of *c.*1751 how its truncated eastern end was softened by small clumps of trees, much as Barrett was attempting at Belhus.

With so much going on that summer, Deerhurst was in need of advice and reassurance. He wrote to Miller on 17 July 1747 with news of some painted glass he had acquired for him and to remind him of a promised 'Anniversary visit here having various Projects in my Head to embellish this untoward place, which I wou'd not execute without your Taste'.[8] In his reply of 3 August, Miller told him that rumours were spreading among their friends that his 'spirit of improvement' had begun to exert itself, and he urged Deerhurst to visit Hagley and Wroxton, stressing that if he were 'to see them but once you would return with Ideas as much enlarged as a Poet's would be the first time he reads Homer or Virgil'.[9] His concern that Deerhurst was charging ahead without fully developed ideas or a coherent plan was probably justified, and he agreed to visit Croome later that month and offered to take Deerhurst around the park at Hagley then to gather ideas.

Whether Deerhurst took up this offer is unknown: probably not. Several interesting similarities between the two projects would support the view that a rivalry became established between the Lords Coventry and Lyttelton. Living just a few miles apart, their families had known each other for some time. However, a certain animosity had arisen between the 5th Earl and Sir Thomas since their respective sons' failure to win the Whig seat for Worcestershire in 1740, and the dearth of correspondence between the two families is marked.

Both Sir George and the 6th Earl began to improve their country seats simultaneously and for both it helped assuage their grief: for Deerhurst from his elder brother's death in 1744, and for Lyttelton from the death of his first wife, Lucy, in 1747. Both turned to Miller for advice and assistance. Both came into their inheritance in 1751 and built substantial late neo-Palladian houses, each of which was set within an important designed landscape. It would be strange if they took no interest in each other's plans. Lyttelton, who became Sir George in 1751 and was created Baron Lyttelton of Frankley in 1756, presented a formidable rival. A successful politician, he later became secretary to Frederick, Prince of Wales, and served briefly as Chancellor of the Exchequer in 1755. He had enjoyed an instructive Grand Tour, was an amateur poet, a man of letters who also patronised other writers, and his friends included Alexander Pope, William Shenstone and Henry Fielding. Not that Lord Coventry lacked talent and titles, but in the late 1740s his special abilities had yet to manifest themselves.

Throughout 1748, Deerhurst persisted in pursuing his plans in an arbitrary manner, which Miller found increasingly disconcerting. Over the next couple of years, part of the formal gardens disappeared, possibly the old outbuilding immediately north-east of the house too, and he may have begun his abortive attempts to alter the east service wing. The most significant change of all was the construction of the new artificial river. This extended directly south from the house in a canal-like fashion, with its stumpy northern end hooked around towards the west elevation of the house and fringed with a grove of trees.

It was a bold step. Miller was busy with projects elsewhere. Maybe he was even keeping a tactful distance. On 17 July Deerhurst wrote anxiously to him from Croome: 'I was in hopes my Dear Miller to have seen you here long ago, where I much want your Assistance, independent of the pleasure your Company always affords me.'[10] Instead Edward Turner called upon him and was able to report back to Miller that Deerhurst had 'conducted his river well', but the absence of detail was telling.[11] Roger Nugent wrote from Gosfield on 20 September to wish him 'joy of your new Occupation, your Place will now be your own, and you will be your own master', but his courteous tone was rather spoilt by his precise instructions on how he should make the river watertight, ramming the clay down and treading it with horses and suchlike.[12] Poor Deerhurst must have rushed off to check for leaks right away. On 20 October Lord Stamford of Enville Hall proffered an equally dubious compliment, reassuring Deerhurst that 'by what you have already done you must convince everyone that you are able'.[13]

That winter, Deerhurst was still chasing Miller, writing to him from Grosvenor Square: 'I shall be glad to hear you are coming to Town, having some things of importance to confer with you upon relating to my Water.'[14] During 1749, Miller or no Miller, he pressed on. Richard Bateman (1705–1773) of Shobdon wrote to him on 17 April 1750 full of praise: 'I dare say Croomb is in great Beauty … You have made a River where no water ever ran before. No one but you could perfect such works as these'.[15] To add the finishing flourish, Deerhurst commissioned the accomplished architect and builder, William Halfpenny (active 1723–1755), to design him a Chinese Bridge.[16] Reinstated in 2016 by the National Trust, the bridge served a key function within the intended Rococo layout. Set amid new planting beside the old Evidence House, it was positioned in line with the remaining part of the avenue of trees south of the house that led up to the eastern ridge. This suggests that it was intended at this stage to combine old and new features within the new layout, which was a prudent strategy. The little octagonal Evidence House would have enhanced the eclectic mix and its historic associations would have appealed to Deerhurst's and Miller's antiquarian tastes.

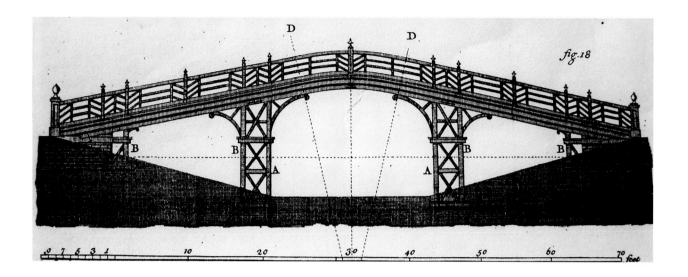

Design for the Chinese Bridge at Croome, from W. Halfpenny and J. Halfpenny, *Rural Architecture in the Chinese Taste: New Designs for Chinese Temples*, plate VIII, fig. 18

All appeared to be progressing satisfactorily but Doherty's plan served only to underline Deerhurst's impetuosity and inexperience. Admittedly work was still in progress but already the lack of coherence was worrying. A good start had been made on the drainage, the site had been transformed by the tree felling and the new river, but north of the house not much had changed. The parish church, Jacobean gatehouse and much of the village remained, and, to the east, the 2nd Baron's huge kitchen garden continued to dominate the ridge, complete with Anne Somerset's greenhouse. Interestingly, Doherty's plan shows no trace of the east service wing, although it does appear on the only other historic image of around this date (see p. 66). As Doherty's plan records details of the house inaccurately and the layout in general is shown somewhat schematically, it may be unwise to take his plan too literally.

What is certain is that Deerhurst had reached a point towards the end of 1749 when he had to make a big decision about the house and the remaining earlier structures surrounding it. The Chinese Bridge provided a welcome distraction and he procrastinated further by building some new hothouses. These were filled with pineapple plants presented to him by another kind friend, Lord Strafford of Wentworth Castle, who assured him they would be 'ready to fruit the following year as I conclude you will be impatient to have some effects from your expence in Hot Houses'.[17] The plant bills imply that the 6th Earl was particularly partial to pineapples and this was an important early horticultural venture that whetted his appetite for further experiment.

Deerhurst had good reason to dither. With his father still alive but ailing, he could do little else. The immensity of the task before him and the huge responsibilities he faced were becoming all too real, such that he began to plot his escape. On 14 February 1750 he wrote to Miller about a plan for a Gothic lodge on the Broadway estate as a retreat from Croome.[18] At this time he may have had a whimsical mock castle in mind, not unlike those at Stowe or Hagley. In his reply, regrettably missing, Miller must have expressed concern about the idea of a retreat, as when Deerhurst wrote back to him on 27 February he was obliged to explain that 'the Hospitality my Ancestors exercised for some generations at Croomb makes it impossible for me to effect any privacy or retirement there. It has always been an Inn and always must remain so.'[19]

The Gothic lodge idea was just another diversion from the big issue: the future of Crombe House. Although the house stood barely above the water table, the idea of demolishing it and building something more suitable on higher ground was never part of Deerhurst's vision. There is certainly no mention of it in his correspondence with Miller, despite the fact that, as his head gardener, William Dean, later pointed out in his 1824 guidebook: 'A more elevated situation might have been desired – and would, if sought, easily have been found'.[20] It might also have been simpler and cheaper, and it would have allowed far greater aesthetic freedom, a chance to make a bolder statement. But it was not the preferred option.

So why did Deerhurst not build a new house? Perhaps pride in his lineage prevented him, a sense of duty to his ancestry and a respect for the past. There were other associations too. He had spent his child-hood there with his beloved brother, and it was for old Crombe House that they had made their plans together. Pragmatism may also have played its part. The house was well built and the interior might readily be adapted to entertain his guests in style. He was not after a grand statement by a prestigious architect. Even if he had been, the timing was not ideal. Kent had died in 1748; Lord Burlington and James Gibbs were gone by the early 1750s. Talents like James Paine (c.1716–1789) and Robert Taylor (1714–1788) and others were filling the void, but the age of great Palladian palaces had nearly run its course and it would be a decade before Robert Adam appeared as the obvious choice. In any case, Deerhurst was quite content to have Miller. Miller had dealt with damp sites before, at Ambroseden and elsewhere, and the new drain-age was resolving the worst problems. Indeed, the site was not without some advantages. Sheltered on its shallow saucer of land, encircled by distant hills, the house lay at the very heart of the parkland. As Brown was quick to recognise, it could also control its territory and draw together all the principal viewpoints within the park, turning its central location on the flat terrain to good advantage. More important still, the house was never the primary concern. It simply required updating, internally and externally, so that Deerhurst might maintain his ancestors' reputation for hospitality in style and so that it would complement its new surroundings. It was part of the whole and never an end in itself, and so it remained.

The question of how to update the house was not difficult. That Deerhurst was thinking of a 'Gothic' design for his Cotswold bolthole suggests he was after a more formal classical design for his country seat. He even remarked to Miller in February 1750 that the 'Gothic' style of his proposed lodge, 'will give me frequent opportunity of speaking of the Architect in other parts of his character besides his Vitruvian'.[21] There can be only one reason why he anticipated speaking of Miller's Vitruvian expertise.

Neither can it be coincidental that, over the winter, Miller had been researching Palladian design principles. In November 1749 he noted in his diary that he had been 'reading Vitruvius', and on 6 January 1750 he was 'at Worcester to see Jones' designs', a reference to the large collection of Inigo Jones's designs, including his annotated copy of *Quattro Libri*, that were bequeathed to Worcester College, Oxford, in 1736.[22] Maybe this was just a pleasant diversion to occupy the winter months? It is more likely that he had a specific project in mind, and the only two major projects under consideration at this time were Croome and Hagley.[23]

The design of Hagley became a drawn-out and complicated affair.[24] The old house was in a dilapidated state and, according to Miller's diaries, Lyttelton and Miller had settled on a new site but were still deliberating about a Gothic design in 1751.[25] Lyttelton's new wife, Elizabeth Rich, disliked this idea and so in 1752 Lyttelton embarked on consultations with the architect John Chute (1701–1776), a friend of Walpole's and a cousin of Barrett's. Unhappy with Chute's efforts, Miller was requested to 'Transfer some of the beauties' from Chute's Italian Renaissance proposal into his own classical design, and only after further amendments by Thomas Prowse in 1753 and additional contributions to the interior by John Sanderson was the splendid Palladian mansion finally completed in 1760.[26] So Croome was Miller's only pressing major project at this time and the implication in Deerhurst's letter is that Miller was exercising his Vitruvian skills on Deerhurst's own behalf.[27]

On Friday 2 March, just a week or so after Miller received the letter from Deerhurst about his lack of privacy at Croome, he began to work on a drawing for him that took until the following Tuesday to complete.[28] Meir has observed that Miller rarely refers to spending so long over a plan. It cannot have been for the Broadway lodge as Lord Coventry was still nagging him for this design in February 1756.[29] Neither is it likely to have been for the Rotunda as it is clear from the Croome accounts that it was not built until the mid-1750s, and under Brown's supervision and most probably to his design.

The likelihood is that Miller was working on the outline design for Croome Court in early 1750. This took four or five days to complete and he sent it to Deerhurst for his consideration. Miller notes in his diary that he received a letter from Deerhurst on 13 March, but provides no details of the contents. That summer, the search began for a suitable person to supervise the task and it seems that Miller already had someone in mind.

On 13 September 1749, Lord Cobham of Stowe had died and he had been succeeded by his sister, Hester Temple of Wootton Underwood, as Countess Temple in her own right.[30] That November, Miller and Lyttelton had travelled together to Stowe to pay their respects to the Countess. Accompanied by a local clergyman named Dorrell, Miller was shown round the recent alterations to the landscape by the head gardener, Lancelot Brown.[31] This was not the first time Miller had met Brown. It seems likely they met at Newnham Paddox in Warwickshire as early as 1746, but on this occasion Brown must have been giving serious thought to his future. The gardens would have prompted a lively discussion and the tour took five hours.[32] Brown would have admired Miller's versatility as a landscape designer, as a hydraulic engineer and as an architect. He would have respected his practical knowledge and approach to design, which accorded well with his own outlook, and he would have noted, too, his social mobility and the freedoms and benefits this brought.

Miller recognised in Brown an extraordinary talent. On 15 June 1750, he wrote again to Deerhurst.[33] Possibly this contained a proposal, as just a few weeks later, on 9 August, Brown visited Miller at Radway. By this time Miller and Brown were on excellent terms and there seems little doubt that Miller was assisting him in setting up in private practice. Brown had already acquired several commissions in Warwickshire, at Packington and Warwick Castle, and he had also been approached by George Lucy at Charlecote. The former two commissions were probably on Miller's recommendation, and it has already been noted that Miller continued to influence Brown's work and business connections throughout the 1750s, and Brown continued to seek Miller's advice, as occurred at Burghley, in Lincolnshire.

Despite the wet weather that August, Miller gave Brown a tour of his estate and they rode across to Farnborough. Less than two weeks later, on 21 August, Miller met Deerhurst again at Croome. The timing of Brown's trip to Radway may well have been pertinent to this meeting. Next day, on 22 August, Deerhurst took Miller for a long walk to the top of Fish Hill above Broadway. Maybe this was to consider a suitable site for the lodge? Maybe it was to take in the view? It would certainly have been an opportunity to discuss the merits of Lancelot Brown. Things were definitely moving forward purposefully as, only a few days later, Miller noted in his diary that he had made a drawing of 'Stables &c' for Ld D'. These could have been an adaptation of Francis Smith's design, or possibly a new proposal altogether.[34]

Miller had helped Deerhurst visualise his ambition and, as a practical man, he understood how it might be realised. He was also aware that his friend's impatience masked a burgeoning creativity and curiosity that were becoming hard to contain. His plans were in urgent need of careful development and professional supervision, and they presented an ideal opportunity for Brown. The time was now ripe for Miller to make that momentous introduction.

But he did not abandon his friend or his protégé. As with his other projects, he continued to give advice as long as it was needed, at least until the mid-1750s at Croome. One particular request for assistance from Coventry in November 1752 was accompanied by the telling remark: 'whatever Merit it [Croome] may in future time boast it will be ungrateful not to acknowledge you the primary author'.[35] He was expressing not only his genuine gratitude for Miller's initial contribution to the design of Croome but, as Brown began to exert his influence on the project, he was also acknowledging that it had already moved on to a new phase.

THE EMERGING GENIUS

Lo, he comes!
Th'omnipotent magician, Brown, appears! ...
He speaks. The lake in front becomes a lawn;
Woods vanish, hills subside, and vallies rise:
And streams, as if created for his use,
Pursue the track of his directing wand ...

William Cowper, *The Task* (1785), Book III

Lancelot Brown was 36 in 1752 with a newly established business. Croome was just the kind of major commission he was after to help launch his practice and extend the range of skills he had to offer.

The story of his extraordinary career has become a familiar tale thanks to Dorothy Stroud's memorable account of his life and work, first published in 1950, and the many subsequent studies, including those that marked Brown's tercentenary in 2016. These have all underlined his astonishing achievement as the creator of the English Landscape Garden, deemed to be the nation's most important contribution to the visual arts.

The son of a land steward, Brown was born in Kirkharle, Northumberland, and baptised on 30 August 1716. Educated in Cambo until he was 16, he went to work as a gardener for the local land-owner, Sir William Lorraine, at Kirkharle Hall, where he learnt the principles of his trade. Brown's brother married Sir William's youngest daughter, so Brown's background was far from humble, and with his natural self-assurance he would have envisaged no likely impediment to the progress of his chosen career.

OPPOSITE
Entrance Hall looking south towards
the entrance into the Saloon

Lancelot Brown, by Nathaniel Dance, c.1773

Stowe, Buckinghamshire,
the Grecian Valley

In 1739 Brown moved south. According to most sources, he went first to Lincolnshire, where he gained practical experience of water engineering in the fenlands around Boston. Then, aged only 24, he received his first landscape commission at Kiddington Hall in Oxfordshire for Sir Charles Browne, and by 1740 he had moved to Stowe, securing the enviable appointment of head gardener the following year.

Caring for this idealised Augustan landscape, rich in contemporary political and literary allusion, and learning from the example of William Kent and James Gibbs and also from his inspiring patron, Lord Cobham, his talents were honed to an exceptional level. Kent had left Stowe by the time Brown arrived, but his Elysian Fields, laid out to exquisite pictorial effect with a chain of little pools formed from a dammed river, made a deep impression on Brown. He may have considered Stowe's complex iconography too contrived and abstruse for his practical tastes, but Kent's careful placing of buildings and structures within the landscape was a valuable lesson he would not forget. Under Lord Cobham's direction, Brown softened the outlines of the lake and of the maturing planting, and created the grand but naturalistic Grecian Valley. Begun in 1746 and flanked by belts of trees, its graceful contours reveal Brown's instinctive feel for form and perspective, incorporating just one strategically placed temple as its focus.[1] Its design anticipated the third and final phase of the Stowe landscape undertaken by Lord Temple.

During Brown's period at Stowe, Gibbs was working on the new large temples in Hawkwell Field, which had been laid out as a *ferme ornée*. The

Temple of Friendship, with its busts of Cobham and his patriot friends, had been completed in 1739, but Brown acted as clerk of works on the later projects. He was involved in building earthworks and supervising the completion of the Palladian Bridge, based on that at Wilton, in the early 1740s. He also supervised the construction of the Lady's Temple of 1742–48 (later altered and renamed the Queen's Temple) and of the Gothic Temple or Temple of Liberty built from 1744 to 1748, working with Gibbs's team of craftsmen, some of whom had also worked for Francis Smith of Warwick. Brown would regard this as an essential extension of his skills. In a letter to Humphry Repton (1752–1818), the poet William Mason (1724–1797) wrote: 'Brown ... was ridiculed for turning architect, but I always thought he did it from a kind of necessity having found the great difficulty ... in forming a picturesque whole'.[2] Jane Brown has shown how he was influenced by Gibbs's professional working methods, and he would have been familiar with his publications, such as *Rules for Drawing ...* (1732, reissued 1788) and *The Builder's Dictionary: or, Gentleman and Architect's Companion* (1734), from which he would have gleaned essential background knowledge.[3] Lord Cobham also encouraged him to gain experience elsewhere; for example, from 1746 he worked for Lord and Lady Denbigh at Newnham Paddox, where he may have first met Sanderson Miller, and also for Lord Cobham's nephew, Richard Grenville (later Earl Temple), at Wotton Underwood, nearby in Buckinghamshire.

On 22 November 1744, Brown married Bridget Wayett, who came from a respectable Lincolnshire family, and the couple had five children

Stowe, Buckinghamshire, the Gothic Temple, designed in 1741 by James Gibbs and completed in 1748

who survived to adulthood: two daughters, Bridget and Margaret, and three sons, Lancelot, John and Thomas. Lancelot became an MP, while John joined the Navy and became an admiral, and Thomas entered the Church. Following the death of Lord Cobham in 1749, Brown resolved to set up an independent practice but it was not until the summer of 1751 that he moved his family from Stowe to his new base in Hammersmith.

Sanderson Miller's friendship and recommendation was already proving of great benefit to Brown, and the move to Hammersmith resulted in another important connection, this time with the Holland family. Henry Holland (1712–1785) was from a successful family of builders, who undertook projects for many well-established architects. Holland encouraged Brown to pursue his architectural interests and worked with him on several commissions, including Croome Court.[4] His son, Henry Holland the Younger (1745–1806), established a leading architectural practice later in the century and was taken on by Brown as his business partner in 1771. This was an astute move by Brown that provided him with invaluable architectural backup and assurance when required, which eased further the smooth passage of his charmed career. The marriage of Holland's son, Henry, to his daughter, Bridget, in 1773 sealed this close personal and professional bond most agreeably.

Although Brown started work at Croome officially in 1752, the evidence suggests he made his first visit with Miller the previous year when he was introduced to the new 6th Earl. Some demolition and ground works had already begun by this time, and building was under way on the stables and offices. As Lord Coventry spent rather too much of 1751 lingering around the home of Maria Gunning's family in Brook Street, it was not until he returned in haste from his honeymoon in Paris in the summer of 1752 that he was able to give his full attention once more to the ongoing improvements.

The earliest record of Brown's involvement at Croome does not appear in the account books until Michaelmas of that year, and Brown's surviving account book in the RHS Lindley Library does not begin early enough to include details of the contract. By 1753, regular payments were being made to Brown from Lord Coventry, usually of £100 but often several multiples of that figure. The sum of £3,450 was paid eventually into his bank account at Drummonds, with a probable total of around £5,000 for work at Croome.[5] Only a few months after he started work, the Earl was full of praise for his efforts, writing to Miller with a little self-deprecating wit: 'I shall expect a positive Promise of a Visit next Summer, for I have many things to consult you upon. Mr Brown has done very well by me, & indeed I think has studied both my Place & my Pocket, which are not always conjunctively the Objects of Prospectors.'[6]

That Brown continued to seek Miller's advice has been noted already and only to be expected in this transitional period when Miller's outline design was being adapted to accommodate the existing fabric and fulfil Lord Coventry's practical requirements. It is generally assumed that Brown was taken on as executant architect to supervise the work on the house, offices and stables, while John Phipps continued to manage the landscaping works until 1753. However, it was probably always Miller's intention that Brown would supervise the entire project, aware that the Earl would need little persuading once he had gauged Brown's talent and warmed to his personable manner, and Phipps was just kept on until his contract ran out. Brown would have observed straight away that the Earl's initial efforts lacked cohesion, that the design of the house and the park could not be considered separately, and that they failed to embrace fully the wider landscape.

In the meantime, Brown could focus on the more pressing matters associated with the remodelling of the house. Despite his limited architectural experience, Brown had already proved himself a competent clerk of works. Even so, it was a risk on Lord Coventry's part for such a major and complex architectural commission. He must have been content to trust Miller's recommendation, and Brown's connections with Stowe had furnished him with irresistible credentials.

Croome Park, Croome D'Abitot, Worcestershire, a drainage culvert in the Evergreen Shrubbery

Brown's work at Croome fell into two main phases: the first belonged to the early and mid-1750s and the second to the early and mid-1760s. The remodelling of the house was part of the initial phase, which also included the first major phase of landscaping works in the vicinity of the house. This involved the planting of clumps and belts of trees and shrubberies in the pleasure grounds, the building of the Rotunda and ice house, the rebuilding and extension of the vast seventeenth-century walled garden, the completion of the massive brick culverts to drain the site, and the naturalising and extension of the river to meet the new lake formed out of the old brick pit at Seggy Mere. There was still an intimate Rococo flavour to this phase. The second phase coincided with Robert Adam's arrival at Croome. This related to a contract of 1760–65 recorded in Brown's account book, and encompassed the wider landscape and related landscape features. There was also a third intensive phase during the 1770s that included the major expansion of the drainage network.[7] It is a reasonable assumption that after this time Brown continued to provide advice right up until the early 1780s, probably even during the very hours prior to his death.

During the early 1750s, the more complex building and drainage works were taking place. The house would have been encased in scaffolding, with building materials stacked all around, and there would have been heaps of mud, spoil and rubble in every direction as the main culverts were established. Not that this kept Lord Coventry away. The correspondence implies that he was enticed up from Grosvenor Square even in the depths of winter to check on progress. In January 1754 he made the cold and uncomfortable journey, accompanied by his brother, John Bulkeley, and Brown, to inspect the completion of the structural work on the main part of the house. At least the conversation would have been invigorating.

Brown would have been pleased to find in Lord Coventry a patron as eager to learn as to contribute his own creative and constructive ideas. According to an article in *The Morning Post* of 30 July 1774, it was as a result of Lord Coventry's ready wit that Brown earned his soubriquet, 'Capability'. When asked by his patron for his opinion of Croome, Brown is said to have replied: 'Why my Lord, the place has its capabilities'. It is a nice story. It is also the type of cunning ruse that Brown might well have repeated to secure work, employing his practical good sense and his personable and persuasive manner to raise hopes while underlining the complexities of the task. This was how he marketed his magic.

The Team

Such a huge project required an impressive team of master craftsmen and labourers, whose disparate trades and skills were bound together by a common purpose, much as back in the days of the medieval guilds. As his reputation spread, Brown's workload became enormous, and was made possible only by highly efficient working procedures and by securing a loyal and talented team that could provide the quality and consistency of work he demanded.

His services ranged from a basic site visit to a simple survey and design, to a complete remodelling, such as at Croome, where he would be supported by a tiered structure of expertise, delegating his supervisory role to the more experienced members of the team when necessary so that problems could be resolved as they arose and work could be properly monitored in his absence. Brown would make regular visits to check on progress, during which he would instruct his team on any matters that did not meet with his approval. In this way he managed to maintain a tight control of proceedings, examining bills closely prior to their submission and insisting, on several occasions, that they were rechecked due to overcharging. Working on a project on the scale of Croome would be of particular benefit for the younger craftsmen at the start of their careers, as it provided an opportunity to refine their skills, develop new ones and make useful contacts to advance their careers.

Many of the skilled tradesmen at Croome were among Brown's, and later Adam's, own trusted teams. They were involved with a number

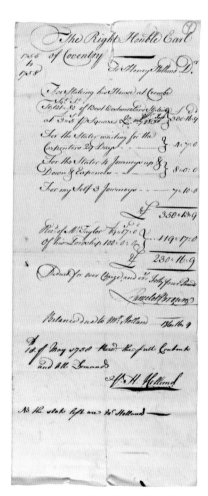

Bill from Henry Holland for work on Croome Court from 1755 to 1758, with an instruction from Lancelot Brown to deduct £44 for overcharging

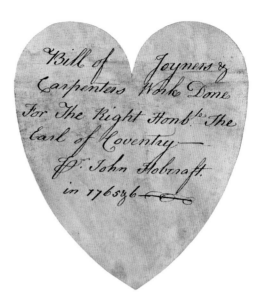

John Hobcraft's curious heart-shaped bill for joinery and carpentry for the interior of Croome Court from 1765 to 1766

of their major projects and some went on to work on Lord Coventry's new home in Piccadilly. A few worked for Miller too. Others operated independently, notably several of the more experienced craftsmen who were paid directly by Coventry and employed their own workmen.[8]

Prominent among the building and landscaping team was Benjamin Read, the landscape foreman, who worked with Brown for around 20 years and was left to supervise work in his absence. There was also William Donn, Brown's draughtsman and surveyor, who served as his associate rather than his principal assistant until 1764, when he went into business on his own and was replaced by John Spyers and Samuel Lapidge. Henry Holland, Brown's friend and neighbour, was of key importance on the structural side. He brought his own trusted workforce and he supervised the roofing works and was put in charge of the more complex structural alterations. Then there was William Eltonhead, the master-bricklayer, who began work in 1752, and Robert Newman, the master-mason, who started in 1753. Both men would have provided their own estimates and drawings, and both remained at Croome throughout the main phases of the project and also worked for Brown on other commissions. William Hiorn also appears in the accounts from around 1756. William and David Hiorn had taken over Francis Smith's Warwick business following the death of Smith's son, William, in 1747. The family worked for Miller, for example, at Arbury, the home of Sir Roger Newdigate, and were probably also known to Brown from his work in Warwickshire.

Other leading craftsmen included the stone carver, Robert Chambers; the master-carpenter and joiner, John Hobcraft, or Hobcroft; the plasterer, William Davis; and the master-blacksmith, Thomas Blockley. Hobcraft is of particular interest. He was also a builder and occasionally worked as an architect too. He knew Brown from Stowe and undertook a wide variety of tasks. By the 1760s he was signing documents on Brown's behalf, probably adopting a supervisory role on the internal building works. He also worked at Piccadilly and, like several other craftsmen of his calibre, he was paid by Lord Coventry directly and went on to work with Brown at Newnham Paddox, Corsham, Castle Ashby, Claremont and Broadlands.

Among the leading craftsmen who were involved on the interior of the house was the specialist carver in wood and stone, Sefferin Alken. He was already well established when he was first employed by Lord Coventry at Grosvenor Square in 1761, and he also worked at places like Blenheim and Stourhead. He began work at Croome for Adam on the new church interior around 1762, and provided much of the finishing touches and fine detail to Adam's interior decoration and furnishings within the house.

Other expert carvers included William Linnell (c.1703–1763), John Wildsmith (active 1757–1769) and James Lovell (d.1818); Lovell had links with Miller and was a protégé of Horace Walpole, but became bankrupt in 1768 and in 1777 was again declared insolvent. Both he and Wildsmith worked at Wroxton and Hagley, possibly as a result of Miller's influence but also due to high demand for their skills. The leading sculptor, Joseph Wilton (1722–1803), also worked at both Croome and Hagley. Wilton had met Adam in Italy, and Wilton worked for him on projects like Syon and Osterley, in Middlesex; in 1764, George III appointed Wilton as Sculptor to his Majesty. Finally there were the skilled *stuccatores* (plasterworkers): Francesco Vassalli (d.1763), who worked in England from 1724, and Joseph Rose Jnr (1745–1799), whose craftsmanship is such a distinguishing characteristic of so many fine Georgian houses. Croome was one of Vassalli's last commissions. He had already worked at places like Castle Howard, Ditchley Park and Petworth House, before he arrived at Croome around 1755. Rose Jnr, a key figure in the family business, Joseph Rose & Co., worked for Adam at Croome in the early 1760s with a small team of five plasterers, and later at Piccadilly. He was involved with many of Adam's other major ventures, including Harewood, Kedleston, Nostell Priory and Osterley, as well as projects for William Chambers and James Wyatt.

This complex structure of specialist teams and supervisors not only enabled jobs to be prioritised and managed very effectively, but also established an effective network of contacts through which opportunities for advancement and employment could flourish, creative influences could be disseminated and patronage could thrive.

The Proposal

The house at Croome needed a cosmetic overhaul. It also had to assert its presence as the chief embellishment of the landscape, determine the viewpoints and articulate the whole. Internally, an impression of symmetry had to be imparted to the former layout and a new circuit of reception rooms was required for dining, dancing, and cards, appropriate to the current more informal, free-flowing approach to entertaining.

Miller's solution appeared deceptively straightforward. Demolish the north porch, infill the north front, conceal the sturdy seventeenth-century brick house beneath a carapace of Bath stone, and add wings at each end with corner towers to elongate its proportions and punctuate the composition. The north entrance was to be distinguished by a central pediment containing the Coventry coat of arms and approached via a dignified double flight of stairs, while an impressive tetrastyle portico, one with four frontal columns, and single flight of steps gave equal distinction to the south front (see pp. 50–51). The hipped roof could be tucked away beneath a canopy of lead and slate behind a balustraded parapet. More of a problem were the old chimney stacks, so much part of the old house's identity, which would intrude into the new profile. But they would have to remain.

Croome Court, north elevation

This solution was neither novel nor daring, nor was it intended to be. Instead it traced a respectable and convincing lineage back from William Kent to Colen Campbell to Inigo Jones at Wilton House.[9] The great central portico was the essential key feature of the Palladian composition, while the Venetian windows in the corner towers echoed those of earlier influential designs like Houghton and Holkham. Campbell's design for Houghton had placed pediments on the corner towers, as had occurred at Wilton, but these were replaced by domed towers as executed by Gibbs (see p. 23).[10] However, at Holkham, the towers were surmounted by shallow pyramidal roofs, following the lead of Andrea Palladio's Villa Pisani at Bagnolo. This created a precedent for a small but distinct group of neo-Palladian houses that included Lydiard House, Wiltshire, remodelled 1742–43 for the 2nd Viscount St John, as well as Miller's designs for Croome Court and Hagley Hall of the 1750s.[11]

The plan of Houghton had resolved the dilemma of the layout. In fact this plan was deemed so admirable that it became a Palladian standard. Based on a double-pile form, it adopted the idea of a central axis leading from the Hall to the Saloon, with flanking drawing and eating rooms, and with end wings terminating in corner towers. This combined elements from the work of Jones and Christopher Wren with the popular post-Restoration layout, exemplified at Ragley Hall, Warwickshire, and Belton House, Lincolnshire, of the 1680s, and it was widely imitated, notably at Shobdon Court in Herefordshire of a similar date, the home of Lord Coventry's friend Richard Batemen. It was also a plan form that was developed to dramatic effect at Holkham, with its apsidal Hall and majestic flight of colonnaded stairs up to the Saloon. Better still, it was particularly

Lydiard House, Lydiard Tregoze, Wiltshire

well suited to the existing layout of old Crombe House. The end wings also allowed for an impressive *enfilade* of rooms along the south elevation, as well as a new west gallery and additional accommodation elsewhere.

So Miller endowed Croome Court with a most respectable lineage, linking it closely with several seminal works of the neo-Palladian movement, in particular Holkham, with its enviable pool of talent. No wonder Lord Coventry fell for the idea so readily. It appeared to suit Sir George Lyttelton too. However, although Croome and Hagley bear obvious similarities, in that both were designed by Miller, employed some of the same craftsmen, and were built roughly at the same time and within a few miles of each other, it is important that their similarities are not over-stressed.

Their overall theme derived from the same sources, but at Croome this was restricted by the constraints of the existing house. At Hagley, which was a new building, Miller was able to develop it with greater freedom and finesse, employing the Houghton-type layout to its full benefit, so that its theatrical central Hall, sculptural chimney piece and flanking staircases were able to play a prominent role in the overall composition. Croome was also more modest in conception and the emphasis was on comfort rather than spectacle. There simply was no space for an impressive Entrance Hall or for the staircases to play a primary role within the layout, although both houses were equipped with fine west galleries in the wings. The sites were dissimilar too. The landscape at Croome is fairly flat and open, while Hagley Hall sits at the foot of a steep wooded hillside. By the time Hagley was complete in the early 1760s, it would have niggled Lord Coventry far more that Lord Lyttelton had such a wonderful sham ruin, such a splendid tapestry room and, most of all, that he was constructing a remarkable Doric temple designed by James 'Athenian' Stuart (1713–1788) built under Miller's supervision from 1758 to 1762. This was simply too cutting edge as far as Coventry was concerned, and not to be tolerated for long.

In the meantime, Lord Coventry was content to have Brown at his side. That Brown was not taken on at Hagley is interesting, especially as he would have known Lyttelton from their Stowe connections. Michael Cousins has suggested that a possible explanation may lie in Thomas, 2nd Lord Lyttelton's scathing comment that 'Brown's landscaping style was not suitable for Hagley, or for anywhere else for that matter'.[12] Certainly Brown's appeal was not universal, not that he was ever short of work.

Back at Croome in 1752, Brown had plenty of obstacles to overcome. Although the site had been partially cleared, a few remaining domestic and agricultural buildings still had to go. Like many big landowners of his day, Lord Coventry believed it was his right to act in such a manner. Arguably, he was equally deserving of Oliver Goldsmith's famous attack on Lord Guernsey:

> ... The man of wealth and pride
> Takes up a space that many poor supplied;
> Space for his lake, his park's extended bounds,
> Space for his horses, equipage, and hounds;

Oliver Goldsmith, *The Deserted Village* (1770), lines 275–78

Coventry would consider it ignorant, old-fashioned and lacking in vision and imagination to act otherwise. However, the idea that he uprooted an entire village in order to create a new designed landscape around his house is an exaggeration. Croome D'Abitot was a fairly minor settlement. Its parish church had become little more than a family chapel and changing farming practices and population fluctuations had limited its growth over the preceding centuries. The required demolitions had nothing of the impact of those at, for example, Packington or Houghton, and Brown did build a replacement settlement nearby at High Green. There is a hint of hypocrisy here though, for his evident interest in history and ancestry did not prevent him from demolishing the church. At least protocol gave dignity to the proceedings, for it was not until 1758 that the necessary Faculty and Deeds of Exchange were put in place for the demolition and rebuilding of the church, and its replacement was not consecrated until 1763. Richard Wilson's (1714–1782) iconic view of Croome of 1758, therefore, was intended more to flatter the Earl's vision rather than an accurate record of his recent accomplishments (see p. 127).

The Strategy

That work proceeded steadily, if not speedily, is all credit to Brown and his team. The old house was well built and still sound, although some initial settlement of its northern range due to the waterlogged site had to be accommodated, as is evident along the corridor of the attic storey. By now the great central wall had grown accustomed to the whims of architectural fashion and remained a strong and steadfast backbone to this latest metamorphosis.

Although the proposal appeared simple enough, in truth it must have tested Brown's ingenuity and Lord Coventry's patience to the absolute limit. Holland's expertise and moral support must have been crucial.

Croome Court, ground-floor plan, 2016, showing the mid-eighteenth-century additions and alterations. The probable seventeenth-century layout is shown in the top left-hand corner.

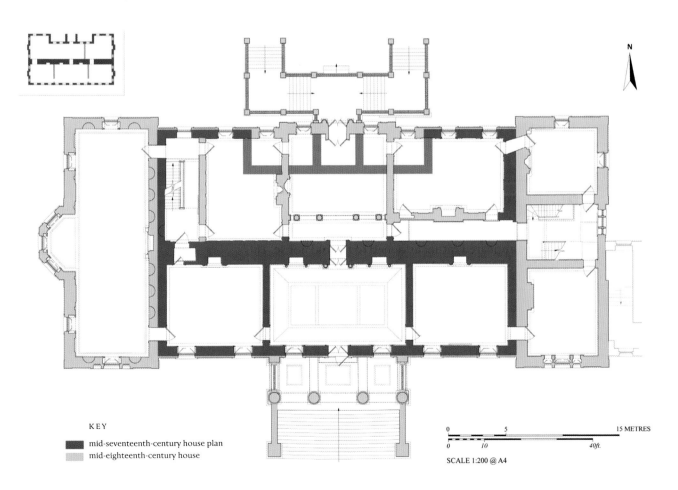

KEY

■ mid-seventeenth-century house plan
■ mid-eighteenth-century house

0   5   15 METRES
0   10   40ft.

SCALE 1:200 @ A4

Most difficult was the demolition of the north front together with the associated basement works. This could be done only when the new north wall was in place to provide the necessary structural support and protection. The central first-floor rooms on the south elevation had also to be removed to accommodate the great double-height vault above the new Saloon, and partitions needed to be built to support it. Another problem was that the Palladian façades had fewer, larger sash windows. Including the new wings, there were nine rather than 11 bays to the south, so the old brickwork had to be ruthlessly patched and perforated and consequently weakened. The floor heights on the principal storeys required some adjustment too. In several areas the new floor was simply laid over the top of the original, and included massive beams laid diagonally, a common practice at this time and a cautious means of reinforcing the floor structure. At least the framework of the old hipped roof could remain intact to help maintain the building's structural integrity. The end wings were completed last of all, treated almost as independent entities that were just bolted onto the former end walls.

There was also an urgent need to deal with the offices. Whatever state the service wing had reached at this point, there would have to be provision made for feeding and housing many of the workmen, and adequate stabling and storage for the transport of materials. The inevitable delays and losses due to bad weather, pot holes and broken wagons may well have instigated Lord Coventry's commitment to the improvement of the county's road network.

Added to all Brown's problems was that his patron wanted to be involved as much as possible. He needed to provide accommodation within the house for Coventry while work was in progress, and for his wife, Countess Maria, when she could be persuaded to leave London. It would also become clear to Brown early on that his patron did not like to waste his money and appeared rather attached to the old house. This was going to be a game of tact and tolerance and it was fortunate that Brown had both.

No bills survive within the Croome archive for building works from 1751 to 1757, only Brown's monthly bills without detail. This is frustrating, particularly in view of the wealth of fascinating bills after this date. It is also curious in view of Lord Coventry's scrupulous attention to such matters. Could they have been lost in the upheaval? It seems unlikely that they were destroyed deliberately as the later ones survive. Fortunately, the general progress of the build may be established from the account books, although it should be noted that some of the entries, for example for pantiles, that is, tiles curved to form an S-section, must refer to structural work elsewhere on site.[13]

1752 Scaffolding poles and cording. Hauling 53,456 bricks and 338,000 bricks. Payments to Wm Eltonhead, the master-bricklayer, and Robert Newman, master-mason. Also payment for boarding to Mr Brown.

1753 Payments made for bricks with separate entries for 12,800 bricks, for 4,000 rubbing bricks, for 6,600 rubbing bricks, for 1,500 bricks, and for three smaller loads of brick. Payments for nine and a half tons and a further 21 tons of alabaster and also for hair [for the plaster]. Payments for deal and for lath and nails. First regular payment to Brown (5 March 1753) and further payments to Newman and Eltonhead and also to Doherty for surveying.

1754 Payments for Bath stone, reeds for plasterers, more alabaster (27 and 14 tons and four further payments). Additional hair. Payments to ironmonger, glazier and plasterer. Payments for sawing and squaring boards. Also 2,500 pantiles from Gloucester, 27 tons of pebbles and for carriage of slate. Completion of main alterations to central block.

1755 Several payments for Bath stone, for Painswick and Bredon stone, for reeds, pantiles, for a freight of deal from Bristol, for discharging slate from a ship, and for brick, nails and pebbles. Further payments to Newman and Eltonhead. Payment to Henry Holland. Payment to Robert Chambers for two Ionic capitals and trusses. Refacing and roofing started.

1756 Further payments for large amounts of Bath stone and some Painswick stone. For brick making and for more deals, nails and hair. Payments to the plasterer, plumber, glazier and painter. Large payments to Newman and Eltonhead. The first payments to Vassalli. Also items for providing accommodation for Vassalli, Brown, Hobcraft and Donn. More work to façades. Roofing of main block probably complete as interior decoration started.

1757 Payment to George Rawlinson for weathervanes and for turning the ball finials on the towers. Payment to Robert Chambers for carving capitals and trusses. Payment for 1,335 feet of boards for floors and large quantity of deals. Payment for additional Bath stone, Cleeve and Painswick stone. Payment for Forrest stone [from Forest of Dean]. Payment for 900 pantiles, alabaster, nails and for turning banisters. Individual payments to Newman, Eltonhead, Henry Holland's man, to Hobcraft, Vassalli and others. Structural work to wings completed. Refacing and roofing continues. Interior fittings and decoration in progress.

Although the building bills survive from this point, the bills for materials are not included among them so it is still necessary to continue to rely on entries within the accounts for this information. As the bulk of the structural work on the house was almost complete by this date, the relevant entries for 1758–60 are considerably reduced in number and from 1760 they must relate to other building works.

1758 More Painswick and Bibury stone, alabaster and oak boards. Payments to Newman and Robert Chambers. Final payment to Holland. Payment to Hobcraft. Payment to Lovell for carving, including seven chimney pieces. Roofing and structural work complete.

1759 Payment for a massive 3 tons of alabaster. Further payments to Vassalli, Newman and Eltonhead. Another payment to Hobcraft [substantial payments to Hobcraft continued into the 1760s]. Interior work continues.

Taking the initial ground works into consideration, it may be deduced that the main structural works on the house were undertaken between 1751 and 1758. By 1755, the refacing of the building in Bath stone was in progress, although not complete for at least another couple of years. Many of the windows had been installed by this date too, as indicated by a massive order of 907 feet 3 inches (276.5 metres) of crown glass from William Cobbett, the glazier. The roofing work had also begun, but the main part of house was not fully watertight until 1756 when work on the interior fittings and decoration could go ahead.

That January, with the tricky work to the main block completed, and Brown's work on the landscape maturing and softening at the edges, the 6th Earl wrote to tell Miller: 'Croome ... is a good deal altered since you saw it, but I fear will never deserve the encomiums you have so plentifully given it.'[14] He seems unsure about it all, probably as there was still so much to do. Structural work may have begun on the wings around 1754 but was not complete until 1757 when the finials and weathervanes were placed on the corner towers, and the south portico was not finished until 1761, when Vassalli was paid for the plasterwork on the ceiling. The imposing Coade stone sphinxes guarding the south entrance were not to take up their positions until 1795 (see p. 11).

As for the completion of the interior, the bills suggest that the Drawing Room to the west of the Saloon and the room above, the Red Room or Red Damask Room (later known as the Lord's Dressing Room and then the Alcove Bedroom), were the first to be made habitable, probably by 1756–57. These would have provided basic accommodation

Croome Court, south elevation, showing
early fabric behind a basement window

Croome Court, west elevation

OVERLEAF
Croome c.1650, by David Birtwhistle, 2016

PAGES 102–103
Croome c.1750, by David Birtwhistle, 2016

PAGES 104–5
Croome c.1800, by David Birtwhistle, 2016

for the Earl. By the late 1750s, the rest of the rooms were being fitted out too, but not until 1761 did Vassalli start on the stucco and plaster-work in the Saloon, Drawing Room and Dining Room. Although the end wings were completed by 1757, the west wing remained a shell until the early 1760s and access routes would have been kept to a minimum. Even by 1760, Croome was certainly no place for a consumptive invalid like Countess Maria.

Various anomalies in the design, structural work and decoration bear witness to the problems encountered. For example, there were minor problems with the ashlar facing, and some of the wedge-shaped blocks of Bath stone were laid the wrong way to the quarry bed causing them to laminate off and weather badly. It was decided to render rather than remodel or reface the arcade of chimneys, which seems a regrettable compromise in view of their prominence. Then there is the horizontal misalignment of the Venetian windows with the rest of the fenestration on the *piano nobile*, or principal storey. Neither was much effort made to conceal the original basement window openings in the south elevation, which were just given squint reveals. Occasionally the old masonry slightly overlaps the new windows and is visible externally as well as internally. On the west and east side elevations, the corner towers seem to constrict the main structure, and the great canted, or angled, western bay appears to bulge outwards between them. Internally, it is also notable that, even adjacent to the main public circuit, evidence of

the old house, of early brickwork, hacked cornices, altered vaults, openings and doors, remains on view. Then there are the staircases. These were treated almost as afterthoughts in the design and layout of the house: quite possibly they were.

It is tempting to suggest that all this betrays Brown's and Coventry's inexperience, and it cannot have been easy for Brown to accommodate Lord Coventry's strong views and his bouts of thrift and indecision. By his very nature, Coventry was never satisfied and he continued to make alterations to the interior layout and decoration for the rest of his life. Neither should the problems associated with squeezing the stubborn old fabric of the building into its smart new suit of clothes be underestimated. This raises another question. Why did Lord Coventry with his notoriously critical eye tolerate such imperfections, and occasionally such blatant bodging? The answer may lie in his intended use of the house originally as a place for entertaining and the principal feature of the new landscape. As long as the public rooms were of the desired quality he was satisfied, for he still planned to disappear to his Cotswold retreat whenever possible. However, as these anomalies can be dated to the late 1750s and beyond, it seems he may have had other reasons too. It is quite possible that it pleased him to allow the history of the house to assert its presence. This was his home and he saw no reason to spend money unnecessarily so he chose to recycle materials wherever feasible, alter as little as he could get away with, and spend his money on things that mattered to him, like the public suite, the offices, or on something genuinely rare or beautiful for his collections.

On 28 November 1751, Sir Edward Turner wrote to Miller: 'Lord Coventry is furnishing his house with elegance. He complains of its amplitude'.[15] This remark has caused confusion about the date the structural works were completed. As the fitting and decoration of Croome Court did not begin until the mid-1750s and continued well into the 1760s and beyond, Turner may have meant that Lord Coventry's *plans* for the furnishing and decoration of his new house looked promising. Or more likely he thought that Coventry was *endowing* the old house with a new elegance and sophistication.

The Plan of Choice
The interior of Croome Court now had a central and symmetrical Entrance Hall and Saloon flanked by reception rooms. A lateral corridor ran east–west through the building alongside the central wall, which was repeated on the upper floors and linked all the important access routes and staircases. On the ground floor it was echoed by a second lateral route along the south *enfilade* (see p. 108).

The Entrance Hall was no longer an additional living space but simply served as a large vestibule and waiting area, providing access to all the principal rooms. Rectangular in form, it was not heated originally.[16] There was also no space for a lofty ceiling, and its awkward proportions were disguised by a screen of four fluted Ionic columns at its southern end, which subdivided the main space from the lateral passageway and made the room appear square in plan. This impressive colonnade with its paired columns drew the eye towards the great doorway into the Saloon, building anticipation of access to its soaring vault and the opulent delights within, as well as providing the visitor with glimpses of the enticing river and parkland beyond.

To the west of the new Entrance Hall was the Billiard Room. This was created partly from the infilled north front, which explains the irregular disposition of its windows. The corridor at its southern end was merely suggested by opposing east and west doors, and these were repeated at the northern end of the room to impart a sense of symmetry and balance, although the door to the north-east was false originally. East of the Entrance Hall there was now sufficient space for an impressive Dining Room, divided from the central corridor by a new south wall, which included a fireplace and flanking pair of doors. The east door was for service access but the west one was another false door that opened into a shallow cupboard.[17] A jib door in the north-east corner of the room led to a passageway through the former external wall and was angled to avoid the old external chimney breast, into the Lord's Dressing Room in the new east wing. This was Coventry's study where he entertained his male friends, and from the windows he could keep watch on unwary visitors and staff.

Along the south front, well-proportioned rooms existed already. Only minor adjustment of the partitions was needed to provide the necessary support for the new vault above the central double-height Saloon. The vault underlined the status of the Saloon within the *enfilade* of rooms, and the pair of fireplaces in the north wall was reused from the former layout. East of the Saloon was the Eating Room (later the Tapestry Room), where a fireplace was created at the centre of the north wall and the former access route in the north wall was blocked. Probably an original opening in the former external wall was used to provide access to the Earl's Library in the east wing. West of the Saloon was the Drawing Room, where the former flue on the north wall was reused and a jib door marked the route of the original arched passageway through to the north range. From the Drawing Room, the public progression along the *enfilade* continued into the Long Gallery in the west wing.

OVERLEAF
Croome Court, plans of the semi-basement (above, p. 108), ground floor (below, p. 108), first floor (above, p. 109) and second floor (below, p. 109), 2016, showing room layout following remodelling by Lancelot Brown and further alterations by Robert Adam during the mid-eighteenth century

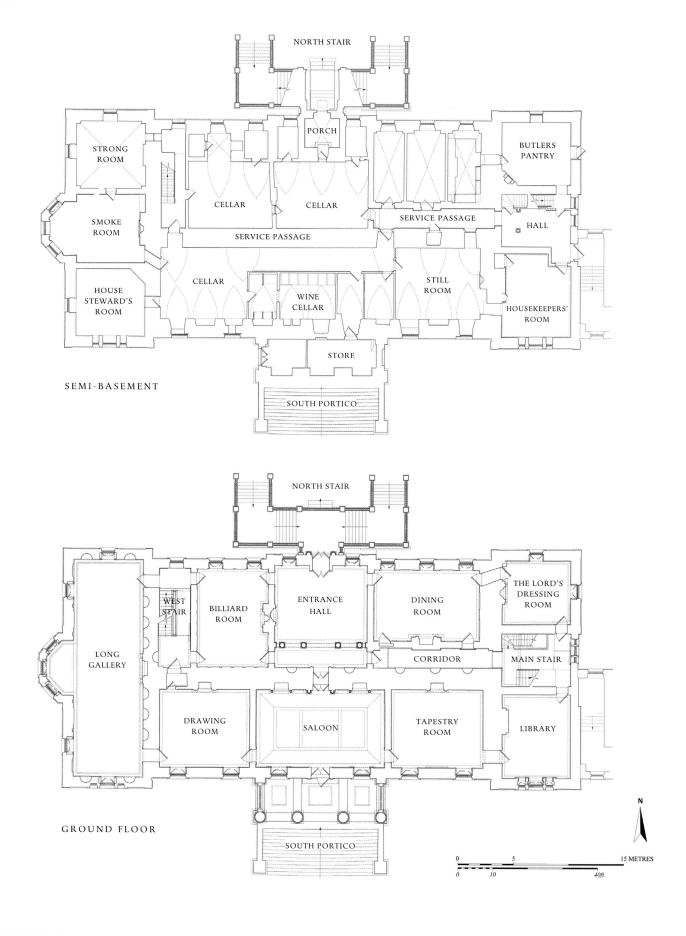

NORTH STAIR

PORCH

STRONG
ROOM

BUTLERS
PANTRY

CELLAR

CELLAR

SERVICE PASSAGE

HALL

SMOKE
ROOM

SERVICE PASSAGE

HOUSE
STEWARD'S
ROOM

CELLAR

WINE
CELLAR

STILL
ROOM

HOUSEKEEPERS'
ROOM

STORE

SEMI-BASEMENT

SOUTH PORTICO

NORTH STAIR

WEST
STAIR

BILLIARD
ROOM

ENTRANCE
HALL

DINING
ROOM

THE LORD'S
DRESSING
ROOM

LONG
GALLERY

CORRIDOR

MAIN STAIR

DRAWING
ROOM

SALOON

TAPESTRY
ROOM

LIBRARY

GROUND FLOOR

SOUTH PORTICO

N

0   5   15 METRES

0   10   40ft.

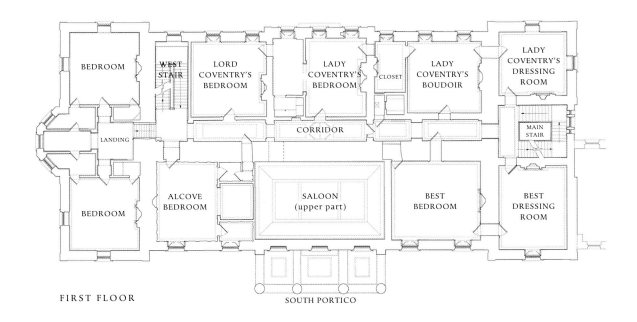

BEDROOM

WEST
STAIR

LORD
COVENTRY'S
BEDROOM

LADY
COVENTRY'S
BEDROOM

CLOSET

LADY
COVENTRY'S
BOUDOIR

LADY
COVENTRY'S
DRESSING
ROOM

LANDING

CORRIDOR

MAIN
STAIR

BEDROOM

ALCOVE
BEDROOM

SALOON
(upper part)

BEST
BEDROOM

BEST
DRESSING
ROOM

FIRST FLOOR

SOUTH PORTICO

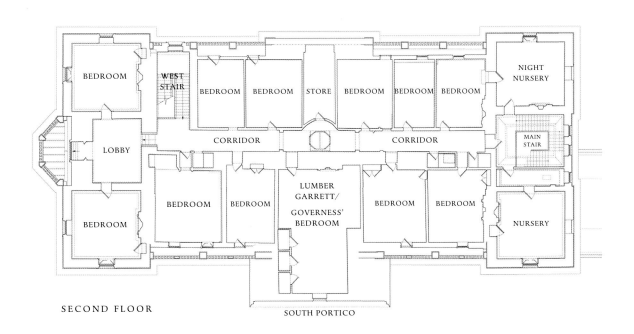

BEDROOM

WEST
STAIR

BEDROOM

BEDROOM

STORE

BEDROOM

BEDROOM

BEDROOM

NIGHT
NURSERY

LOBBY

CORRIDOR

CORRIDOR

MAIN
STAIR

BEDROOM

BEDROOM

BEDROOM

LUMBER
GARRETT/

GOVERNESS'
BEDROOM

BEDROOM

BEDROOM

NURSERY

SECOND FLOOR

SOUTH PORTICO

Croome Court, West Stair. Some of the string detail is now missing and the balustrade includes modern balusters.

The new wings, so important to the form and profile of the Palladian building, provided spacious and well-proportioned rooms that contributed much to the scale and grandeur of the interior. The Long Gallery in the west wing was a particular success, the space left undivided and the ceiling raised in height to enhance its appearance. The central full-height bay window took advantage of the superb parkland views and flooded the centre of the space with bright light, which balanced its length and cast strong shadows, later used by Adam to brilliant effect. The Long Gallery was accessed by doors at either end of its eastern wall that are likely to have reused original openings in the former external wall. From the southernmost door, the full extent of the new layout could be appreciated. However, the northernmost door led into a confined lobby set beneath the half-landing of the West Stair and, immediately adjacent to the Long Gallery entrance, a new service stair was introduced to access the basement. This was convenient, but the sheer anti-climax and contrast created by this abrupt juxtaposition was at best confusing, exposing any unsuspecting guest to potential calamity.

On the first floor, the infilled north front made space for a new private suite of rooms intended eventually for the use of the Earl and Countess, and were to include Lord Coventry's Bedroom and Lady Coventry's Bedroom, a closet, Boudoir and Dressing Room. The sequence of small rooms and closets recorded on the south side of the house in the 1719 inventory was largely removed to create the void above the Saloon. To the east of this was the Blew Bedroom, later the Best (or state) Bedroom, which referred to its seventeenth-century precedent, and was most probably Maria's room originally. To the west of it was the former Red Room or Red Damask Room, probably the Earl's bedroom previously, which became his functional dressing room and closet. The rooms in the east towers were used as dressing rooms, while those in the west towers enjoyed the best views in the house and were kept for key family members, often as bachelor bedrooms or for special guests, with the imposing canted bay serving merely to light the lobby in between them.

The second-floor attic storey of the old house continued to provide sleeping accommodation for staff and storage and minimal alteration was required, with day and night nurseries in the east wing and bachelor and guest rooms in the west wing. The old lumber garrett on the south side was enlarged when the south portico was added to create a pleasant Governess' Bedroom, and the rooms along the north front were similarly increased in size by the infilling of the space between the north wings.

An extensive overhaul of the accommodation in the semi-basement was required to make it fit for purpose. The well-equipped and efficient management of the household formed an essential part of the Earl's vision and he and Brown would have discussed the options at length. The decision to house the principal rooms, the kitchen, servants' hall and house steward's accommodation in the remodelled service wing would have been straightforward. This meant that much of the remaining area in the basement, with its parallel barrel vaults and the space gained that flanked the former porch, could be carved up into a series of smaller rooms, each fulfilling a more specific function. Only the main cellar in the north range, probably used in part as the beer cellar, was little altered and was not subdivided until the mid-twentieth century as indicated by a 1940 floor plan.

The area to the north-east of the basement, possibly once occupied by the original kitchen and Back Stair, was subdivided into three narrow rooms of equal size, each given new groin vaults. This area may have been previously altered in Gilbert's day and this question remains open to speculation. These formed part of the butler's suite of rooms and included a brushing room (where clothes were cleaned that could not be washed), probably a lamp and/or knife room, and a strong room for the silver. The latter was accessed from the new butler's pantry in the east wing through a passageway created through the archway of a fireplace in the former east end wall of the seventeenth-century house. On the south side of the east wing was the housekeeper's room, which also had a private passageway into the adjacent large room in the main house, possibly the new still room. Along the south front, two more narrow rooms were created. One may have been used as the still room stores. The other is entered via a massive seventeenth-century door and, at its southern end, an old chamfered window opening was made into a doorway that led into the space beneath the south portico. This may have been how the casks were brought into the adjacent wine cellar, as suggested by grooves in the brick floor.[18]

Beneath the west wing, there was additional accommodation for the butler or the steward, and the land agent's office and smoke room, well lit by the west bay window and accessed via another modified seventeenth-century door. This office doubled as a smoking room for male family members, conveniently close to the wine cellar, and from it a large iron door, now in the Estate Office at High Green, once led through to a spacious vaulted strong room beneath the north-west tower, where important documents, weapons and other valuables were kept.

It was clear from the start that the Main Stair could not play a prominent public role within the layout simply as the old fabric did not allow for this. On plan, the location of the new Main and West Stairs at either end of the building appears to present a practical and elegant solution. Adjacent to both was constructed a separate flight of stone service stairs that led to the basement, their treads reinforced by inserts of Forest stone, tough Pennant sandstone, to withstand the constant wear and tear. Although the Main and West Stairs all worked well functionally within the layout, their visual contribution to the whole was compromised quite ruthlessly.

The Main Stair had be located in the east wing, the private end of the house, as there was nowhere else for it to go. The east wing itself had been squeezed in between the original building and the service wing, necessitating the demolition of the western end of the early eighteenth-century wing. So the staircase was slotted into the space between the corner towers and approached off the Entrance Hall down the dark eastern end of the central corridor, effectively a service corridor between

Croome Court, east elevation

Croome Court, Main Stair

the offices and the eating rooms. As it was also the route to the Best Bedroom this was far from ideal.

Despite these issues, the Main Stair is a fine and gracious example of its type, open-well in form and of cantilevered construction with an elegant iron balustrade and ramped mahogany handrail. It was lit by a large semi-circular or Diocletian window on the ground floor and a tripartite Venetian window with a tall, arched central light and Ionic pilasters on the first floor. These should have added a distinctive note, but due to the restricted space and the intrusion of the adjacent service wing, the fenestration had to be misaligned. Externally, the windows appear squashed between the north-east tower and service wing; internally, the elegant staircase is deprived of its Palladian symmetry. The outlook over the offices and stable court did not help either.

The plasterwork detail is restrained, perhaps as the Earl saw little point in drawing attention to the inherent failings within the design. Instead, 12 plaster busts of unknown identity and a suitable selection of paintings enlivened the ascent and distracted from the view. In November 1763, Adam billed for a 'Section of Staircase at Croome & outside elevation'. The drawing is lost but it is a fair assumption that this was part of an early attempt to address the problems inherent within its design. In the 1780s, Adam was obliged to make a further attempt to resolve these defects, a task that would have required no small degree of tact.

The West Stair was located between the Long Gallery and the Billiard Room and provided access to the family suite, the Earl's functional

Dressing Room (or Alcove Bedroom) and the bedrooms in the west towers. Even today, with its joinery partly damaged and replaced, this timber open-well staircase has a particular dignity and charm. With its broad shallow treads, columnar newel posts, moulded handrail and delicate carving, it is generally assumed to be part of the remodelling, although stylistically it appears to date from the earlier part of the eighteenth century. As it links the Billiard Room and the Alcove Bedoom, both of which are fitted with early eighteenth-century style bolection-moulded panelling, it may have been a deliberate attempt to associate it with them stylistically (see p. 124).

This staircase is also let down by its fenestration. The half-landings fail to relate to the window openings, and the low ceiling of the half-landing located immediately outside the prestigious Long Gallery is cramped and crudely finished, the interior compromised for the sake of maintaining the symmetry of the Palladian exterior. The detail and mouldings of the staircase are also strange. The dado is only complete in part, the cornices differ and appear to have been hacked about, and later alterations to the joinery confuse the picture still further.

All this prompts the question whether the West Stair could even belong to the 4th Earl's phase of alteration? The staircase would have been only 40 years old and may have appealed to Lord Coventry as part of this early eighteenth-century scheme of refurbishment. This might provide an alternative explanation for the anomalies in its construction and finish, and the timber-framed partition wall between the West Stair and Billiard Room could well date from this time. Hobcraft is recorded as having undertaken work on this staircase in 1757, but the bill only mentions fitting balusters, and in 1764 he was paid for filling in a niche.[19] So maybe he was just fitting replacement balusters? That similar balusters are found around the light well on the second-floor corridor and were installed on the staircase in the south range of the service wing adjacent to Lord Coventry's apartment raises further questions. Were these salvaged from an earlier staircase or were they just made to match those on the West Stair? Keeping this early eighteenth-century staircase would have had undoubted practical benefits for it would have maintained access to the upper floors throughout the remodelling process.

The Red Wing
Brown's adaptation of the old basement into a functional sequence of rooms was ingenious, and his remodelling of the existing offices east of the house was equally inspired, resolving a project that had thwarted the 4th Earl, and may have sapped Deerhurst's confidence in the late 1740s.[20]

Croome Court, north elevation of the Red Wing (or service wing) and the adjacent stable block

Brown's service wing is known today as the Red Wing, due to the contrast between its finely jointed, red-brick facing and the Bath stone of the adjoining mansion. The brickwork identified its separate function and linked it visually with the stables, barn and other offices to the east. The service wing was completed in two stages. Work on the south range lasted from around 1751 to 1753, when whatever existed by this time was raised in height to include two main storeys to provide ample accommodation for the house steward and a generous attic storey for further servants' bedrooms. The floors were kept at a lower level than those in the main building, which helped maintain the distinction between the two buildings internally and allowed for a greater degree of privacy. Probably this phase also included the remodelling and partial completion of the projecting eastern end to create the huge servants' hall and provide additional staff bedrooms on the floors above.[21] The structural evidence suggests that the wall at its north-eastern end was left unfinished as an internal wall and the roof structure above was similarly adapted in anticipation of the construction of the adjoining kitchen wing to the north.[22] This implies that there was some urgency to complete the south range to service the ongoing works and it is possible that the servants' hall with its large fireplace was used as a temporary kitchen at this time. A long passageway was created that ran right through this southern range from the basement entrance to the service yard at its eastern end. That the western section of this passageway lies on the south side of the building but changes to the northern side in its eastern half is again indicative of the wing's phased construction.

Recent dendrochronology has dated the roof timbers of this south range to c.1753, although the timbers could have been stored on site. During construction of the east wing around 1754–57, this end of the range was partly demolished and the apex of the roof had to be truncated to fit beneath the projecting cornice of the new south-east tower.

Around the same time, work began on extending the service wing to the north to create the new double-height kitchen. This included two big fireplaces, one for spit roasting with an integrated smoke jack, and a second one fitted with charcoal stoves that were vented through the brick walls to gaps within the eaves to protect the staff from the lethal fumes. Smaller rooms on the western side and at the southern end of the kitchen included the cook's pantry and pastry room, which also served as a sitting room, the scullery and a larder, which was yet more staff accommodation. Part of the attic storey in this north range had lime ash floors, made from the residue from lime kilns and laid on a thatch of reeds. This created a strong, flexible and economic surface that provided good insulation and which was also vermin-proof so useful for the storage of perishable items. The household bills for April 1759 refer

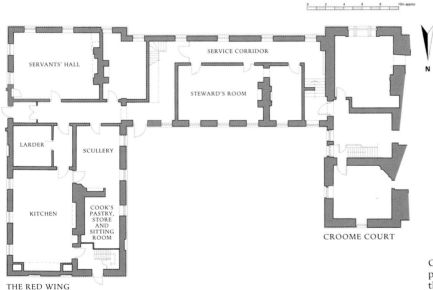

Croome Court, ground-floor plan of the Red Wing, showing the eighteenth-century layout

An impression of the late eighteenth-century kitchen in the Red Wing at Croome Court, by David Birtwhistle, 2015

to a 'very large octagon iron oven', as well as purchases of saucepans and crockery, which suggests that this is the date when the north range was being fitted out and it was certainly in operation by around 1760.[23]

Brown ensured the offices were effectively screened by planting, especially on the south elevation. However, the 6th Earl may have had second thoughts about its unprepossessing appearance, as in 1763 Adam produced a scheme to reduce the height of the southern range still further and to provide the entire northern elevation of the offices with a more impressive classical façade. This was never executed, possibly as it involved reducing the south wing in height and losing the valuable accommodation it provided. Later in the century, the service wing was linked to the laundry in the stable block to the east by a brick wing and a substantial screen wall and gateway were built to the north of this to enclose a kitchen court. This is now known as Laundry Green, although the actual green, later a drying yard, lay to the south of the linking wing.

The propriety and reserve of the service wing belie its generous proportions and the exceptional quality of finish. Its lofty ceilings, tall archways, spacious well-lit rooms and the high standard of its fittings and fixtures were indicative of Lord Coventry's concern for the welfare of his staff, the efficient management of his household and his interest in new technology. This was a place to be proud of, and it may have pleased him equally well to be seen to have the wealth and the will to invest in such prestigious offices. His decision to move into the service wing later in life is a further indication of the respect he held for his staff and for their place of work.

A Fitting Interior

Brown was responsible for the fittings and decoration of much of the interior during this initial main phase of activity in the late 1750s.[24] Its exuberant Rococo character exhibited an indulgent lack of restraint that spoke of Lord Coventry's eagerness to take his place among the great patrons of his day, but not yet to stand out and influence their decisions. This was to come with the second major phase of decoration that lasted from around 1759 to 1771 and which related to the contribution of Robert Adam.

The earliest surviving Hobcraft bill dates from May 1756, but most of the fitting out appears to have occurred between 1757 and 1759. In 1757, Hobcraft charged for taking the dimensions of the house and making a plan of the floors but, regrettably, this does not survive. The work on the West Stair must also have been completed in this year as this is when Hobcraft billed for turning balusters. The following year he made the mahogany handrail, dado and risers for the Main Stair, which may have been in use that year, even though the plasterwork detail and decoration by Vassalli remained incomplete until 1761 and Rose Jnr did not finish the ceiling until 1763. Several of the bills for fabric, wallpaper, curtains, window blinds and bedcovers are also dated 1757, and in 1758 payments began to Lovell for fine carving in wood and marble. From 1758 to 1760, there were further payments for carving to Linnell and to Wildsmith, and in 1759 and 1760 to Blockley for grates for the new chimney pieces and other metalwork. It was Blockley who later supplied the bell system for the house, which was fitted between 1766 and 1775. An invention of the 1740s, and based on a network of copper wires and pulleys, this novelty provided the occupants with greater privacy and more flexibility in the running of the household, and would have been of considerable interest and benefit to Lord Coventry.

The fitting out of the principal rooms charts the evolving taste of the 6th Earl. The relative restraint of the Entrance Hall was compatible with its intended function not as the main spectacle but as a place of access and anticipation, indeed little more than a grand lobby. Originally its austerity of form was enlivened only by Vassalli's graceful sequence of swags and festoons, by the plaster figures in the niches and by the fine joinery and carvings of Hobcraft and Lovell, which included swelling friezes decorated with oak leaves and acorns above the doorcases and a handsome cornice on consoles crowning the great double doorway into the Saloon (see p. 82).[25] Not until 1763 was the plaster ceiling completed by Rose Jnr, emblazoned with the Coventry eagle and with Adam's impressive lantern hanging from its claw. The result was enough to excite the curiosity while preparing the palate for the lavish treats to follow.[26]

The Dining Room was Vassalli's tour de force.[27] Here a profusion of plasterwork celebrated the pleasures of the table. Executed in 1761, fruit, flowers and ribbons spill down the panelled walls, framed by Hobcraft's and Lovell's ornate carving of 1758, which delineates every

Croome Court, the Dining Room. The bold paint colours on Vassalli's plasterwork date from the late twentieth century when the Court was in the ownership of the International Society for Krishna Consciousness. This photograph of 2010 shows a temporary exhibition.

Croome Court, the former Eating or Breakfast Room, later the Tapestry Room, showing salvaged panelling exposed in 2016 that was used to line the walls during the mid-eighteenth-century remodelling

Croome Court, the Saloon as photographed for the 1915 article in *Country Life*

surface. There was once a Linnell chimney piece carved with flowers and foliage, installed in 1758, but this was replaced in 1824, probably due to known damage from a leak from the closet on the floor above. Such an overt and extravagant Rococo theme, so apposite to the room's function, shows how well a congenial and considerate host like the Earl appreciated the need to set the scene and stimulate his guests' appetite for fine food and lively conversation. Behind the false door to the right of the fireplace, the shallow cupboard contained shelves pierced with 'holes for ye pots', maybe chamber pots to be used once the ladies had withdrawn.

The three large rooms along the south front formed the central section of the *enfilade* and occupied the former location of the Little Parlour, the Great Dining Room and the Great Parlour in the earlier house. Restoration work a few years ago exposed much of the work undertaken by Brown's team to convert the Little Parlour into the new Eating or Breakfast Room (now the Tapestry Room). This has confirmed the view that the large seventeenth-century fireplace in the east wall, an adjacent service access or window, and the entrance from the central corridor in the north wall were blocked. The walls and altered openings were covered with some fairly random sections of salvaged panelling, some of which resembles the panelling used to screen the void above the Saloon vault. Before the tapestries were hung on the walls, the reused panelling was probably covered with silk damask. Wildsmith billed for a chimney piece in the room in 1760, which may have been replaced by Adam's orange Veronese and white Carrara marble piece believed to date from 1762.

The double-height vaulted Saloon must have been an important challenge for Brown and its design anticipated later work, notably the ceiling of the Picture Gallery at Corsham Court in Wiltshire, built for Paul Methuen in the early 1760s.[28] The Saloon was fitted out with great extravagance as befitted its special status. Hobcraft's and Lovell's fine joinery and carved detail included eared window architraves with volutes, and doorcases also with eared architraves and swelling friezes carved with palm branches. The north entrance doors were flanked by fluted Corinthian columns, above which was a full entablature surmounted by a broken pediment containing a bust of Apollo. The vault itself was also richly decorated. The octagonal and oval panels with their foliated borders may have been intended to hold paintings, although no evidence exists of this. Instead the eye is drawn down to the detail of the deep coving, enriched by Vassalli with a scrolled frieze with baskets and, above it, a broad rosette and modillion cornice. Vassalli's bill is intriguing. He states that it is for the 'Ceiling in the saloon according to my designe, that done before according to Mr. Stuard [*sic*] design. For drawing the designs at first for the ceiling & cove in the Saloon not put in execution'.[29] This

implies that James 'Athenian' Stuart was approached to provide designs for this special room. As he, Lovell and Vassalli were all working at Hagley around this time this seems quite plausible; indeed Miller may have been instrumental in introducing him to Lord Coventry.

Lovell billed for the pair of chimney pieces in 1758. However, just two years later, Wildsmith submitted an invoice for eight days' work for a mason 'repairing & piecing & polishing over the slabs & chimneypieces in the Saloon'.[30] The same year, Sefferin Alken invoiced for 'Two Chimney pieces carved alike in stone, to both 4 Term trusses, the sides raised scroles & flowers on the Eye' for this room.[31] So the chimney pieces must have been subsequently repaired and altered, or even replaced entirely not long afterwards. Their design is unusual, combining Ionic columns with petalled paterae, jasper inlay and a Vitruvian scroll or wave frieze that changes direction in the middle. Furthermore, as John Wilton-Ely has observed, the Ionic volutes are set flat rather than at the correct angle. Vassalli's reference to 'Mr Stuard' and the uninformed use of neo-classical detail on these chimney pieces would seem to suggest that Lord Coventry was now attempting to inject some avant-garde, neoclassical elements into his decorative scheme.[32]

Elsewhere in the Saloon, Rococo excess exuded from every surface. Three carved white and gilt bow cornices were set above the south door and windows. Between them was placed a matching pair of gilt and white pier tables and, above them, oval wall mirrors, richly carved with shells, acanthus scrolls, festoons and swags, all supplied by the leading cabinetmakers and upholsterers, Vile and Cobb.[33] The finishing touch to this sumptuous spectacle was contributed by Linnell's eight opulent gilt and enamelled picture frames. Intricately carved with acanthus scrolls and shells, and surmounted by coronets, these contained Lord Coventry's royal and family portraits, including those of King George II, King William III and, his own ancestor, the Lord Keeper.[34] This was now a room fit for kings, which was just as well as, in July 1788, Coventry had the great satisfaction of entertaining George III in the Saloon to a feast of salmon, lampreys, carp and the finest port wines.

On the west side of the Saloon was the Drawing Room, known as the Blue Drawing Room prior to its refurbishment in 1793. Completed in 1758, it was again decorated in a Rococo style and to a similarly high standard of finish by Vassalli, Hobcraft and Lovell, and was where the 6th Earl hung some of his finest paintings, including the full-length portraits of George III and his consort, Queen Charlotte, by Thomas Gainsborough, which the King had presented to the Earl on his visit in 1788. The swelling friezes above the doors in this room are notable for their laurel-leaf ornament, which recurs on the delicate oval plasterwork decoration of the ceiling.[35] The chimney piece appears to have been subject to another attempt by the Earl to update the predominantly Rococo theme. No bill exists for the original chimney piece, only one submitted by Lovell to dismantle it, make alterations and set it up again in 1758. Although the floral drops and the frieze, with its festoons of fruit

Croome Court, the Drawing Room chimney piece

and flowers, make reference to the ceiling decoration, the consoles are ill-fitting and may well have belonged elsewhere. The fine central tablet, with its draped urn, was a later addition by Lovell. The banded and reeded detail around the fireplace opening was repeated on the window embrasures and door architraves within the room and may also have been added by Lovell.[36] So perhaps the chimney piece existed in the 5th Earl's time and was simply updated by Lovell for use in this room using salvaged and new pieces of carving?

The final room completed during this early main phase on the ground floor was the Billiard Room, west of the Entrance Hall. It contrasted most effectively with the extravagance and splendour of the Rococo decoration elsewhere on this floor, and this was quite deliberate. Even here, on the *piano nobile*, the 6th Earl wanted to impart a sense of history into his fashionable scheme, evoking a steady stylistic evolution rather than a radical rebuild, underlining his lineage and demonstrating a genuine respect for the past.

The 4th Earl had created a new bowling green in the grounds at Croome and, according to the 1719 inventory, he also owned a billiard table. So bowls and billiards were part of the house's recent history and may have played a prominent role in the 6th Earl's childhood memories. This room is linked stylistically by the timber West Stair to the Alcove Bedroom, the Earl's second dressing room, on the first floor, and it has been noted already that both rooms were fitted out with the very same early eighteenth-century bolection-moulded panelling. Possibly this was the panelling that George Chine, the joiner, had worked on in 1716 and which the 1719 inventory records as being stored on site. That Hobcraft's bill of 1759 refers only to making doors and architraves in this room would support this assumption.[37] Quite where this wainscoting was intended for originally is uncertain, but some of it may already have lined the walls of the floor above, as here some panels survive with minimal alteration. In the Billiard Room, Hobcraft had some difficulty trying to fit the panels within the room's awkward dimensions and on close examination it can be seen that they vary in size. So either they were altered to fit or else new ones had to be made to match. It is a tribute to his skill that the room became a masterly exercise in apparent symmetry.

Croome Court, view north from the Billiard Room, showing the bolection-moulded panelling

The new fireplace in the east wall has an ornate Rococo chimney piece that fails to complement its setting and this is unlikely to be its original location. It is possible that one of the pair of *c*.1700 bolection-moulded fossil chimney pieces that survives in the house was moved here originally, especially as the other survives in the dressing room upstairs. It is certainly a characteristic of the Croome chimney pieces that they were swapped around and altered with remarkable frequency.

The fitting out and decoration of the bedrooms on the first floor during the late 1750s was markedly less lavish but still of equal quality. Hobcraft and Lovell fitted out the suite along the north front between 1758 and 1759, where the joinery is mainly of a similar style and finish, with moulded skirtings, dado rails, moulded architraves to the windows and doors, and deep cornices, but an unusual scheme of varnished hardwood architraves and skirtings was adopted combined with painted softwood doors and chimney pieces.[38] The chimney piece in Lord Coventry's Bedroom was carved by Lovell with laurel leaves and berries, similar to the swelling friezes in the Drawing Room, which occur on the same bill.[39] That in Lady Coventry's Bedroom is plainer with a scroll frieze, although these mouldings and those of the door cornices appear remarkably crisp and may be late twentieth-century copies.[40]

The contemporary bills show that most of the main bedrooms were wallpapered in a red or blue sprig pattern or embossed yellow and blue silk, and were painted in dead white or dead stone colour with some mahogany graining.[41] A bill for bedcovers was also submitted in 1759 by Vile & Cobb, which included three of silk damask – one green, one red and one blue – each destined for one of the principal bedrooms.[42]

By the end of the 1750s, most of the main part of the house was nearing completion, but not yet the wings. A temporary library had been set up in the east wing and Lord Coventry's Dressing Room, his official dressing room or study, was probably in use by this time, but work on the west wing had still not begun. Although content with the sumptuous Rococo theme for some of the rooms, Coventry was now feeling sufficiently confident to introduce a more fashionable neoclassical element into the overall theme. He was after something bolder and more distinctive, and the search had begun for someone with originality and flair to give expression to his evolving taste.

The Alignment of Sights

Towards the close of Brown's initial phase of work, the Croome landscape was changing significantly. The old structures around the house had gone, and all around lay swathes of grassland framed by shrubberies, shelter belts and clumps of new and mature trees. Better still, the land was drying out. It was now sound for grazing sheep and cattle, draining through giant culverts into the artificial river that wound its way in sinuous curves through the park, inviting exploration of the shining lake with its little islands.

The domestic offices, stable court and walled garden had been remodelled and screened by judicious planting and, nearby, an alluring walk meandered up to the Rotunda clasped like a jewel within its cedar grove up on the marl ridge, awaiting its finishing touches by Vassalli in 1761.[43] The new church was under way too, its site sculpted to perfection by Brown's team to take advantage of the most dramatic views of the house and parkland against the broad western horizon. Already it would be apparent just how brilliantly Brown had contrived the overall effect, how seamlessly the parkland advanced into the surrounding countryside and how the views appeared, as if by chance, to unfold one upon another.

The house now took centre stage and had begun to orchestrate the whole. While working at Stowe, Brown would have observed how the house had presented only two of its elevations to the landscape. Croome Court presented three, and when Brown moved on to build Claremont, in Surrey, an entirely new house for Lord Clive of India from 1769 to 1773, he set it on a rise and open to the landscape on all four sides, in many ways an even more challenging proposition.[44] That the 6th Earl decided not to rebuild his house on higher ground had heightened Brown's awareness of the potential of such a low position: the house could be viewed in its entirety from many angles, including from above where its relationship to the overall design could be read like a map. If the eastern ridge denied the house a fourth aspect, it was used by Brown to full advantage to exploit the spectacular views to the west and inject a sense of theatre to the main approach from the London road. And he learnt to toy with the eager visitor's imagination. Quite suddenly, as you turned into the driveway, the vast Severn plain was exposed to view. Only on reaching the brink of the ridge did its full extent become apparent and there the drive swept south in a serpentine curve, in the classic Hogarthian manner, to reveal the house itself, embedded within the heart of its designed landscape. Innumerable clever variations on this oblique approach appeared in Brown's later designs.

The subsequent extension of the Croome landscape to include an outer circuit with park features in the middle distance enabled Brown to fully integrate the park with the surrounding landscape. The earlier 'three-mile walk' was supplemented by a 'ten-mile ride' so that views between structures, from windows, between columns, from bridges and across steely sheets of water added further complexity to the overall scheme. It became impossible to distinguish where the designed landscape ended

Croome Court, Worcestershire,
by Richard Wilson, 1758

Croome Park, the Rotunda

Croome Park, by E.F.
and F.T. Burney, *c*.1784

and the borrowed landscape began. Not just the Malvern Hills to the west,
but from the lake the giant barrow mound of Bredon rose beyond the
ridge to the south-east as if deliberately placed to enhance the pictorial
composition. That the form of the artificial river mimicked the sinuous
course of the nearby River Severn blurred the distinction still further. It
was as if the entire county had been shaped by Brown's hand.

The design of the church, and of the tower in particular, made a key
contribution to the overall composition. The deed of conveyance, drawn
up on 4 July 1758, had proposed a classical design with a tetrastyle portico, just visible in Wilson's early sketch for his famous landscape painting. The decision to have a Gothic church could have been influenced
by the Earl's friend, Richard Bateman, who had just built a wonderfully
elaborate little church at Shobdon, a Strawberry Hill confection inspired
by his close links with Horace Walpole. More probably it was due to
Miller's influence, directly or indirectly, as the revised Gothic design with
its three-stage tower and pinnacled parapet bears striking similarities to
that of Wroxton church, and their interiors are very alike too.[45] This was
the Earl's first opportunity to indulge his taste for the Gothic and it does
seem to have had a very personal, romantic and even patriotic resonance
for him. Material was salvaged from the former Gothic church, some of
which was incorporated in the detail of the new building to provide the
sense of continuity that clearly mattered. The church occupies one of
the best viewpoints in the park, which was described by William Dean
as follows:

Richard Wilson's sketch for his landscape
painting of Croome (see pp. 14–15), 1758

Croome church

the Stranger will naturally pause to contemplate, from its high grounds, the grand prospect ... in full display before him – offering a grand near view of the House, seated in the vale below – thence extending over the lawns, the woods, and the waters, of the park – shut in by the long waving line of the Malvern hills, melting into the wide horizon.[46]

The National Trust commissioned a detailed study of the views and sight lines at Croome and this has shown just how carefully and meticulously they were created. It is notable that 80 per cent of them emanate from the Court itself.[47] They are so precisely judged that it seems almost as if the fenestration was determined after the park's completion rather than the other way round. This was Brown, the artist, at his best, or, as he preferred to see himself, Brown the author and editor, for according to his friend, Hannah More, he compared his art to literary composition:

'Now there' said he, pointing his finger, 'I make a comma, and there', pointing to another spot, 'where a more decided turn is proper, I make a colon; at another part, where an interruption is desirable to break the view, a parenthesis; now a full stop, and then I begin another subject.'[48]

Dean wrote of the views from the Saloon:

Among the attractions of this room, not the least, is the delightful prospect which its windows command – over the fine verdant level of the park-diversified and adorned by its winding waters, its clustered trees, its spreading groves, its herds of noble deer; terminated on every side, by the grand sweep of the woods, which bound the whole.[49]

The views from the canted bay window of the Long Gallery are even better, for these take in the Temple Greenhouse, the Panorama Tower, the lake, the river and Chinese Bridge and the Malvern Hills. This was the only point within the public part of the building from which these westerly views could be appreciated to the full. There is even a fine cedar framed perfectly within the central sash of the bay window. Interestingly, as the Venetian window at the southern end of the gallery has blind outer lights, its splendid outlook was compromised for the sake of symmetry within: the only notable exception where internal aesthetics took priority over the views from the house.

Croome Court, view west from the Long Gallery

The Grave Young Lord and the Gardener

At Croome, Brown had staked out his future career and the project evolved to span his entire professional life. It demonstrated all his key skills as a landscape designer, as a hydraulic and structural engineer, and as an architect, and it proved to the world that poor drainage and challenging topography need not be a deterrent to vision and ambition.

The basic characteristics of the Brownian natural landscape were well suited to disguise this type of terrain. Clumps and belts of trees and shrubs and artificial water features had all been used before, by Henry Wise, Charles Bridgeman, Philip Southcote and Kent among others, but Brown's inspired way of incorporating them in his work was special. He had an extraordinary aptitude for reinterpreting a landscape, making it look its best, and he could think on a broad scale. He knew how to open up the woodlands, to frame and screen to create viewpoints and backdrops, to define boundaries, to position trees as specimens, sometimes moving trees of great girth. His skills as a water engineer enabled him to form lakes and artificial rivers that appeared seemingly endless, adding reflection and movement where it was most needed. He understood the effects of changing light, the colours of the seasons, and how nature would mature, mellow and unify his compositions. His landscapes were also relatively easy to manage and maintain, and they were functional too, to accommodate country pursuits, for breeding livestock, and for scenic rides, parties and picnics.

While the approach was always familiar, the design was crafted to its context. During his first phase at Croome, Brown was also working on several other important landscapes, like Packington (begun c.1750), Petworth (1752–63), Burghley (begun 1754) and Syon (begun c.1754), and it is likely that the layout at Croome influenced and was influenced by these significant contemporary projects, each of which maintained its own special character. As his work grew rapidly in popularity, Brown was criticised for the sheer ubiquity and blandness of his work. The architect, Sir William Chambers (1723–1796), launched a particularly vehement attack in his *Dissertation on Oriental Gardening* (1772), and later Brown became an ideal target for the leading figures of the Picturesque Movement, such as Richard Payne Knight (1750–1824) and Uvedale Price (bap. 1747–1829). There was something so enticingly English, so sensible, safe and undemonstrative about his approach, that such reaction was inevitable. But its appeal was enduring, and his various imitators and followers, not least among them William Emes (1729–1803) and Richard Woods (1715–1793), continued to gain from the benefit of his example many years after his death.

Brown became an accomplished architect, partly as his appreciation of contextual design was so well honed, partly as there was something so purposeful about his designs, an innate and cautious restraint and concern for function rather than gratuitous show that could not fail to please his clients. In his *The Theory and Practice of Landscape Gardening* (1803), Repton praised the comfort, convenience, taste and propriety of design evident in the several mansions and other buildings that Brown planned. Always aware of his lack of professional architectural training, it is to his credit that he acknowledged his limitations and continued to rely on support from the Holland family for any major commission. It is also true that, like his landscapes, his architectural designs reveal an innate understanding of English taste and preferences. Henry Holland, his partner, probably gauged the true measure of his skills when he wrote in 1788:

No man that I ever met with understood so well what was necessary for all ranks and degrees of society; no one disposed his office so well, set his buildings on such good levels, designed such good rooms, or so well provided for the approach, for the drainage, and for the comfort and convenience of every part he was concerned in. This he did without ever having had one single difference or dispute with any of his employers. He left them pleased, and they remained so as long as he lived.[50]

Croome Court had been an unforgiving testing ground for his talents. Miller had conceived the outline design for Croome but Brown had the thankless task of realising it, and juggling the structural issues with his patron's preferences would have been no easy task. Contemporary opinion was not always favourable. Dean considered the design of Croome Court to be 'too low for its extent, and plain in its style of architecture', while Arthur Young deemed it 'excellent' rather than 'magnificent'.[51] Certainly, the profile and overall proportions of the house were not as compact as might be desirable, but the new wings and central features balanced the elevations well. The south elevation, in particular, was impressive, with its grand and imposing portico, and if the Venetian windows appeared somewhat compressed, the generous spacing of the bays imparted a pleasing dignity and repose to the whole. The ridge stacks and spacing of the bays on the north front may hint at the house's seventeenth-century origins, but, arguably, this contributes to the building's character. The design of the side elevations, and of the east elevation especially, is less forgivable, and the manner in which the staircases were incorporated within the new layout was unfortunate, but these would be lessons that Brown would not forget. The point is that none of this mattered. Croome Court looked the part and, in terms of comfort and convenience, it was second to none. If the house was best seen from a distance, then that was because it was designed to do so.

Brown's ingenuity and skill were also evident in the design of the offices. Here he had a slightly freer hand but adapting the shell of the existing old service wing into spacious, efficient and impressive accommodation that appeared to be purpose-built was no less an achievement. The new service wing made a dignified transition between the house and the adjacent remodelled stable court, the fine new agent's house and associated outbuildings and was accomplished with considerable flair.

The work on Croome Court taught Brown much about managing an architectural project on such a scale and the benefit of a strong team, of men like Eltonhead, Newman and Hobcraft, and it gave him the confidence to tackle similar large and complex building commissions, such as Newnham Paddox, another remodelling project for the 5th and 6th Earls of Denbigh (1754–68, demolished in 1952); Redgrave Hall, Surrey, for Rowland Holt, which he began in 1763 and was another

A print as part of a theme entitled 'Nabob Houses and the Indian Style', showing Claremont House, Surrey, designed by Capability Brown for Robert Clive, 1770–72

Berrington Hall, Herefordshire, view of the grounds and the West Front

instance where he encased a brick Jacobean house in stone; Broadlands, Hampshire, remodelled for Henry Temple (begun in 1764); Fisherwick Hall, Staffordshire (1768–76, demolished in 1816), rebuilt for the 5th Earl of Donegal; and Claremont, Surrey (1769–74), for Lord Clive, possibly his most celebrated architectural achievement, where he was joined by his new partner, Henry Holland. All of these developed the theme he had mastered at Croome, with their giant porticos, and most had pedimented openings and balustraded parapets. However, their design was generally more compact than Croome Court and only Fisherwick incorporated the corner towers.

After he went into partnership with Holland in 1771, Brown's designs show an increasing restraint in accordance with current taste and the setting continued to take priority. One of his final projects was at Berrington, in Herefordshire. Designed by Holland in 1778–81 for Thomas Harley, the estate was set deep within the heartland of the burgeoning Picturesque Movement and home to some of Brown's cruellest critics. Holland's simple and elegant neoclassical mansion is raised upon a plateau above Brown's landscape and echoes of Croome are still evident in its composition, with the offices attached to one side, tree screens nearby, and, stretching out before it, a wide and open landscape framed by distant hills.

Miller's lingering influence remained particularly evident in Brown's Gothic designs. In a letter to Miller of 1756, Lord Dacre referred to Brown's recent work at Burghley and Brown's remark that he would 'give the world he [Miller] should see his designs: having the highest opinion of his skill in this way.'[52] This influence is apparent in his small park buildings, at Burleigh, Shropshire, and at Tong Castle, Burton Constable,

East Yorkshire, for example, and it may be no coincidence that Brown's ornate little Gothic bathhouse at Corsham Court, Wiltshire, of c.1760 (later remodelled by John Nash, 1752–1835), was located not far from Lacock Abbey, also in Wiltshire, where Miller had recently been working.

Croome may have been important to Brown as his first major achievement, but it was also important because of its patron. As Young remarked: 'Brown spent much of his time at Croom [sic]; it was his favourite residence; he never found himself so much at home as when there, nor at any time so happy.'[53]

Brown established friendships with many of his aristocratic clients and regularly enjoyed their hospitality, among them Lord Bute of Luton Hoo, the Duke of Northumberland of Syon and Alnwick, and Lord and Lady Chatham of Burton Pynsent, but his friendship with Lord Coventry seems to fall into a category of its own. Young underlined Coventry's proactive role in the creation of Croome when he remarked that Croome Court 'under Brown's management (who was upon this, as on all other occasions, very much assisted by his Lordship) has been rendered an excellent stone edifice'.[54] Together, they had developed the detailed aspects of the house and its landscape, both learning on the job, steadily gaining each other's respect and trust, and establishing a working relationship that soon flourished into a close personal bond.

As Miller seemed reluctant to produce a design for the lodge at Springhill, Brown was commissioned to build a house there for John Bulkeley Coventry, who paid Brown £1,300 from 1756 to 1758 for a neatly proportioned and reticent classical design, set within a fine park and pleasure grounds, which was completed in the early 1760s.[55] Many years later, the 6th Earl wrote to Repton from Springhill: 'I certainly held him [Brown] very high as an artist and esteemed him as a most sincere friend. ... I write from a house which he built for me which, without any pretension to architecture is, perhaps, a model for every internal and domestic convenience.'[56] It was probably also on the Earl's recommendation that Brown drew up a scheme to landscape the grounds at North Cray Place, in Kent, for his cousin, Thomas Coventry, around 1782, where he widened the River Cray to form a lake.

Although an exacting client, Brown may have appreciated his patron's close involvement. Before he arrived at Croome, he had learnt how to work for a demanding but rewarding patron under Lord Cobham and he would have gauged quickly how to handle Lord Coventry's petulant moods and learnt to appreciate his wit and vision.

Brown, in turn, helped Lord Coventry to gain confidence in his ideas and broaden his perspectives in every sense. They recognised in each other a kindred spirit and felt comfortable in each other's company. The

Croome Park, memorial to Lancelot Brown

dearth of correspondence that survives between Brown and Coventry is frustrating, but among Brown's papers is a letter from Coventry dated November 1772 concerning a leak in the river at Croome, which ends with an invitation to 'a Christmas Gambol' – presumably an informal family gathering and an invitation extended to Brown as a close friend.[57] As Brown had many of the most beautiful estates in England, from Bleinhem to Chatsworth, under his direction, there would always be plenty to discuss. After Brown's appointment as Surveyor to His Majesty's Gardens and Waters at Hampton Court in 1764, and his purchase of a small estate in Fenstanton in Huntingdonshire, there would have been even more reason to compare notes. Above all, Lord Coventry found in Brown someone who shared his passion for Croome, who had witnessed and contributed to its development right from the outset, who appreciated his fascination for plants and for beautiful and well-made things, and who understood utterly his obsessive drive and commitment.

Young believed that Brown had hoped to end his career at Croome, just as he had begun it there, and that he had even expressed a wish to be buried there. When he died on 6 February 1783, while returning to his daughter's house in Hertford Street after dining with Lord Coventry in Piccadilly, his eldest son, Lancelot, wrote to Coventry to see if the epitaph that William Mason had prepared for his memorial in Fenstanton Church met with his approval:

> *The great Friendship your Lordship honoured my Father with, when living, convinces me that <u>every</u> tribute paid to his memory will be acceptable to your Lordship ... Few people have as yet seen them* [the lines of the Epitaph] *and I do not wish them to be made very public 'till the Monument is completed.*[58]

So Brown's family acknowledged the significance of their friendship. Lord Coventry's own memorial to Brown beside the lake at Croome, erected in 1797, was brief and to the point, paying tribute to his 'inimitable and creative genius'.

But Coventry did not rely on Brown's genius alone. Back in 1760, when Brown's first major phase of work was complete, the 6th Earl was only just getting into his stride. As an inspiring and proactive patron, he was on a constant quest for a greater degree of refinement and originality in his commissions. Brown had performed the transformation and it was now time for Robert Adam to cast his spell.

THE REFINEMENT OF GENIUS

The study of what is elegant and beautiful, sensibility, discernment,
and a correctness of eye, are become more general; and arts formerly
little known begin to be naturalized amongst us. Cherished by the
patronage of a people, opulent, discerning, and capable of
estimating merit, the genius of native artists has been
called forth into new and laudable exertions.

From Robert and James Adam, *The Works in Architecture* (1778),
preface to the fifth part of Volume I

Such ill-disguised flattery would not be wasted on Lord Coventry. The
Adam partnership worked for him for over 30 years, both at Croome
and at his London townhouse in Piccadilly, and he proved to be its most
loyal client. Much of this work was undertaken between 1760 and 1783,
and Robert Adam's final designs for Lord Coventry are dated as late as
1791. Many of these designs were never executed, but that was not necessarily Adam's intention. He had learnt quickly that his patron did not
always appear susceptible to his persuasive manner, but his designs kept
Coventry coming back for more. It was a small price to pay to maintain
his loyalty and prompt his varied and prestigious commissions.

The remarkable career of Robert
Adam has been studied in depth and
continues to reward further analysis. He
returned from his Grand Tour in early
1758 and rented a house in St James's
Place, London, before setting up in business with the support of his family at
75 Lower Grosvenor Street. His brother
James returned from his own travels
in 1763 and joined him in partnership,
running the business side of the practice. James is credited as being more the
theorist than the designer. As author

OPPOSITE
Croome Court, south elevation

Robert Adam, attributed to
George Willison, c.1773

137

of the prefaces to the *Works*, he might have been a more familiar figure today had it not been for the exceptional qualities of his brother.

Their father, William Adam (1689–1748), the eminent Scottish architect and owner of the family estate at Blair Adam, had brought his family into contact with many of the leading Scottish intellectuals of the day. He also enjoyed a well-established network of patronage that was destined to benefit his sons' new London business. Robert's personal charm, commercial acumen and brilliant design skills quickly confirmed his new practice as the most fashionable and successful of its day. The Adam style had widespread appeal, and was well attuned to changing contemporary taste. It challenged the pomposity of Palladianism, seeking a more light-hearted spirit, full of movement, grace, contrast and colour, with a unique and inventive interpretation of antique form and detail that was infinitely adaptable to a client's individual whim. So familiar is it today that it is difficult to appreciate just how strikingly different, refreshing and exciting it must have appeared in the 1760s.

After abandoning his studies at Edinburgh University, Robert had joined the family practice, working for his elder brother, John (1721–1792). By 1754, he had earned sufficient money to embark on his travels in the company of Charles Hope (1710–1791), the brother of Lord Hopetoun (1681–1742), an important family patron. In Florence he encountered the sculptor Joseph Wilton (1722–1803), with whom he worked on various later commissions, and Wilton introduced him to the architectural draughtsman, Charles-Louis Clérisseau (1721–1820), from whom he took instruction in drawing and watercolour. Clérisseau taught him the art of observation, which helped counter his innate inventiveness, and under his guidance he developed an expressive sketching technique. It was also Clérisseau who sparked Adam's interest in French design and ornament.

Adam travelled to Rome with Clérisseau, where he parted company with Hope, intent upon studying and recording the architectural feast that confronted him. Rome seethed with talent by this time. Adam was introduced to his future rival, William Chambers, and, in June 1755, he met the great Venetian printmaker, Giovanni Battista Piranesi (1720–1778). Piranesi's *Le Antichità Romane* (1756–57) won him election to the Society of Antiquaries in 1756, and his creative approach accorded well with Adam's own enthusiasms.

Adam gathered much architectural source material to launch and sustain his career, visiting places such as Ravenna and Herculaneum. He absorbed all he could about antique, Etruscan and Renaissance art, and was inspired in particular by the ingenuity of Roman domestic interiors. By 1757, his limited funds curtailed his travels further south to Greece. Instead, he travelled with Clérisseau and a team of draughtsmen to

Spalatro on the Dalmatian coast to survey Roman Emperor Diocletian's
vast fortress-like palace on the main seafront. The work was completed
within five weeks and provided material for an architectural treatise that
was eventually published in 1764. Dedicated to George III and flaunting a
list of over five hundred subscribers, it failed to acknowledge Clérisseau's
substantial contribution.

Back in England by early 1758, Adam was eager to introduce his ideas
to a wealthy and receptive audience. Quite how he caught Lord Coventry's
eye is unknown, but as they lived not far from each other in Mayfair, it
would not have taken long for rumours of Adam's talent and interest
in antiquity to reach him. Coventry must have sensed his potential and
recognised in him a designer who could articulate and extend his maturing tastes and inject an edge of originality into the Croome project. Adam
would have welcomed Coventry's patronage as a useful advertisement
for his new practice and as well suited to the projection of his ideas. An
unidentified drawing of a bathhouse, somewhere in southern Italy, almost
certainly by Adam, survives within the Croome archive.[1] No record exists
of its purchase or origin, and it is interesting to speculate whether it was
a gift from Adam to Lord Coventry, a souvenir of his travels and of sun-
drenched lands unknown to the 6th Earl, intended to fuel his interest
and impress him with Adam's knowledge and expertise.

Lancelot 'Capability' Brown's reaction to the introduction of this young architect is unknown. Adam may have been inexperienced but he was scholarly, well trained and brimming with confidence. It could have threatened Brown's friendship with the Earl and presented an unwarranted intrusion on their shared vision. More likely is that Brown was somewhat relieved. The Earl's plans were escalating and Brown was inundated with choice commissions by this time. He had neither the time nor the personality to bear grudges. Neither did he have the professional architectural training that Adam had.

In any case, collaborations were commonplace on long-term projects on the scale of Croome. Brown and Adam went on to collaborate on numerous projects, for example at Syon, Alnwick, Luton Hoo, Bowood, Harewood, Corsham, Ugbrooke, Mamhead, Compton Verney and elsewhere, and on several of these they were both concerned with structural work.[2] Probably it was at Croome that they became fully aware of each other's abilities. Although Adam was interested in landscape design and Brown in architecture, it seems unlikely that this would have troubled either of them. They knew their own worth and would soon learn that they shared a compatible approach to design, and, as astute businessmen, they may have recognised at an early stage that, rather than threatening each other's livelihoods, they were both likely to benefit from a productive working relationship.

Dorothy Stroud has pointed out that Adam usually won the commissions when they both submitted designs. Among a number of similar unidentified drawings at Sir John Soane's Museum, London, is a design for a greenhouse for Croome dated 14 June 1759. Clearly not by Adam's skilled hand, perhaps this was by Brown and it was rejected by Lord Coventry and passed on to Adam so that he might improve upon it? That Lord Coventry continued to rely upon Brown's advice even during the period when Adam was also hard at work has already been noted.

Brown and Adam must have met at Croome and elsewhere. They frequented similar circles, and later too, when Brown moved to Hampton Court, his neighbour, the actor David Garrick, was one of Adam's closest friends. Perhaps they even dined at Lord Coventry's dinner table together: a truly fascinating idea. There must have been some discussion on the siting of buildings at the very least. Both ascended to the peak of their professions from a different starting point: Adam, the aesthete and intellectual, and Brown, the practical man. Both approaches had their own advantages that each would recognise. Whether Adam acted condescendingly to Brown or valued his judgement and whether Brown smiled knowingly at Adam's pretensions we shall never know.

Design for a Greenhouse for
Croome by an unidentified
architect, 1759

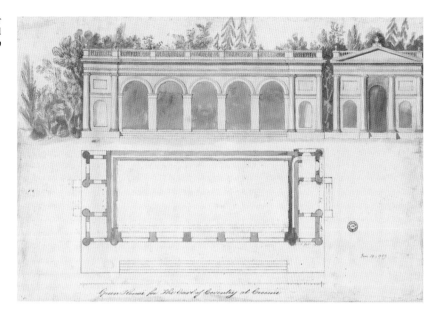

Adam was appointed Joint Architect of his Majesty's Works with
William Chambers (who was knighted in 1770) in 1761. This may have been
slightly irritating for Brown who was still awaiting his royal appointment
but, after 1764, their royal connections as well as their collaborations and
clients provided an irrefutable bond. What is certain is that both were
keen observers, blessed with a brilliant and innate understanding of their
chosen specialities that overlapped so closely and conveniently; there
is no doubt each would have recognised and respected a fellow genius.

The Interiors

Adam's involvement at Croome is well documented, in particular his
work on the decoration, fittings and furnishings of the house itself.[3]
His first design for Croome is generally believed to have been for a
greenhouse or orangery, now known as the Temple Greenhouse, dated
August 1760, possibly Adam's improved version of the unidentified
design at Sir John Soane's Museum.[4] Originally, it included end niches
holding statues of Flora and Ceres, and these and the laden basket in
the pediment, eventually carved by Sefferin Alken, were a foretaste of
the achievements to follow. Very soon afterwards, in September 1760,
Adam made his first design for the Long Gallery ceiling, although this
was subsequently rejected.

It was at this point that the 6th Earl's first wife, Countess Maria, died.
There followed a space of six months before Adam submitted his next
design for the ceiling, and then the commissions slowly gathered pace

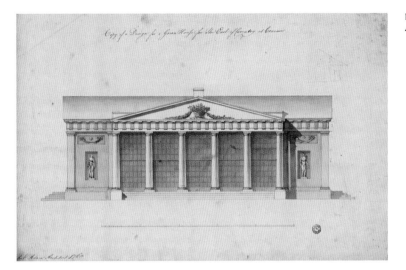

Design for the Temple Greenhouse, Adam office, 1760

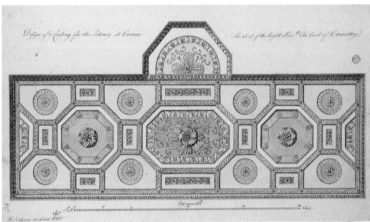

Unexecuted design for the Long Gallery ceiling, Adam office, 1760

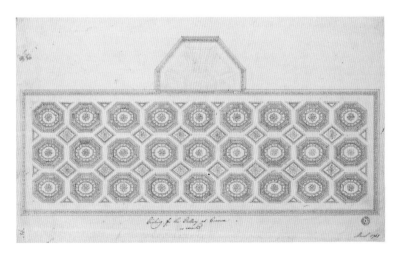

Second design for the Long Gallery ceiling, Adam office, as executed 1761

reaching a peak in the mid- and late 1760s. It was almost as if Maria's death injected a renewed sense of vigour and purpose into the second major phase of work at Croome. Once again, the Earl sought an outlet for his grief in remorseless activity and he was to emerge a few years later as an altogether bolder and more innovative patron.

Adam billed for his designs for the Long Gallery mouldings and his section for finishing the Gallery 'in the Manner of a Library' in November 1761. But Lord Coventry appeared uncertain about the function and layout of the new rooms on the *piano nobile* and not until the summer of 1763 did Adam produce an alternative section for the Long Gallery that met with his patron's approval. Meanwhile, he was kept busy with a number of other varied commissions that enabled him to demonstrate his remarkable versatility and skill.

Among the latter was a design for a classical bridge of May 1761. Other bridge designs followed, but the date of this early design is important. Could it have been a replacement for William Halfpenny's Chinese Bridge at Croome, perhaps proposed by Adam as he believed it an unwelcome intrusion on the views to and from his new Temple Greenhouse? It

Design for the east window of Croome church, Adam office, 1762

is the most likely site. The chances of Lord Coventry replacing the bridge, his very first park feature, were exceedingly slim, but Adam never ceased producing tempting alternatives.

Over the next 18 months, Adam made designs for various chimney pieces and for the arms for the north pediment of Croome Court, as well as for an alcove bedchamber for the house in Grosvenor Square. Most important of all were his designs for the interior of the new church at Croome. During 1761, Brown was still putting the finishing touches to the structural work and Lord Coventry may have been burdened by feelings of guilt that it was not complete in time for Maria's funeral. He dedicated the new church to St Mary Magdalene as a tribute to her memory, and it seems likely that the head stops on the interior hood mould of the west doorway were portraits of the Earl and his late wife.

It was an inspired decision to commission Adam to design the church interior, and, as it was his first Gothic interior, it was a risk. That the columns either side of the nave are too large for the entablature may indicate that he was brought in only after interior work had commenced. Adam billed for the drawings of the cornices and ceiling mouldings in July 1761, for chairs the following November, and for his spectacular designs for the pulpit and reading desk and for the unexecuted painted glass for the east window in April 1762.[5] Further designs for other

Section of the Church at Croome for the Right Honble the Earl of Coventry

mouldings, pews, altar rails, for the entrance doors and for ironwork and three different seating plans followed in May. Last of all came the design for the beautiful font with its intricate carving, for which Adam billed in January 1763.

Had the interior been completed as he had proposed, it would have been a small masterpiece. Regrettably, it became an early lesson for Adam in his patron's indecision and thrift. As Eileen Harris has observed, his intended fan vaulting, dado panelling and painted glass, which included armorial hatchments in the aisle windows, would have created a magical medieval effect of delicate interlacing and jewel colours. But all this was a step too far for the Earl's sensibilities.[6] Subsequent rearrangement of the interior and alterations to the fittings has further diminished the intended impact of Adam's original concept. Despite all this, the church was, and remains, a great success. Set high on the eastern brink of the park as a principal eye-catcher and viewpoint, the soft western light illuminates every outline of the finely crafted detail and of the elaborate monuments within the chancel.

Design for the interior of Croome church, Adam office, 1762

With the church interior in hand, Adam could return his attention to the Long Gallery. Measuring almost 20 metres in length, it was the largest room in the house with extensive views to the west. The commission represented another important opportunity for the Adam office. It was also the first but not the only time Adam decorated a principal room of a new structure by Brown, the Picture Gallery at Corsham Court being a notable case in point.

The first ceiling design of 1760 had been formed of three large octagonal compartments, which complemented the room's proportions and corresponded well with the central canted bay window. The approved design of March 1761, with its coffered design of elongated octagons and lozenges, may have appealed more to the Earl because of its neoclassical credentials, as it was modelled on Andrea Palladio's vaulted ceiling at the Temple of Peace in Rome that had been illustrated in *Quattro Libri* and Giacomo Leoni's translation. Rosettes of three different designs are set within the octagons to add interest but the repetitive effect of the coffering was intended primarily to enhance the room's apparent length. Adam used it to similar effect for the Drawing Room at Syon and the Library at Kedleston. The downside was its awkward junction with the canted bay window and this problem was exacerbated by a heavy structural beam. On the original drawing in Sir John Soane's Museum, the hesitant pencil marks in this area betray the frustration this caused Adam in attempting to overcome the problem and which he never fully resolved.

The original intention had been to use the room as a library, as indicated by Adam's initial section of November 1761. That the Library was to feature so prominently within the layout was not just because Lord

Section for finishing the Long Gallery 'in the Manner of a Library', Adam office, 1761

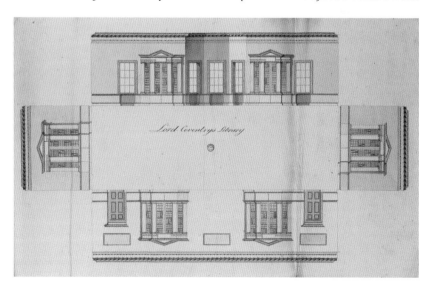

Coventry was a scholarly man who collected books. It seems very probable that this was his late brother's idea, as Thomas Henry had expressed his admiration for the new library of his friend and neighbour, Edward Turner, in a letter to their mutual friend, Thomas Walter Younge, in 1739:

> *Sir Edward Turner returns to his seat at Amersden [Ambroseden] where he has laid out a great deal of Money in making an elegant Library. The Wainscot is mahogoney [sic], and all the other Furniture answerable to the grandeur of it. In short nothing is wanted but a curious collection of Books; this perhaps you will say is a great deal; but when a Man has a taste to make a proper choice, and Money enough to answer the demands, that design may soon be put in Execution.[7]*

Adam's section had shown the room furnished with six aedicule bookcases, that is, framed by columns with a pediment above. These were of the Ionic order, an order that he favoured for libraries, and were of a tripartite design that made reference to the canted bay. There was to be a pair set along the east and west walls and one at each end of the room obscuring the windows. For some reason, the space where the fireplace was to be located was left blank in the drawing. Evidently, the design appealed to Adam, as he proposed a similar idea for the Long Galleries at Osterley and Syon that same year, although only the design for Syon was executed from c.1762 to 1763.

Lord Coventry may have not wanted the end windows totally obscured, and he was also having doubts about whether the room was suitable as a place for quiet study. He was already using the room in the south-east tower as a makeshift library and, by late 1762, he had decided that his new Library should remain at the east end of the building near to his Dressing Room. By redecorating and furnishing the room much as Adam had proposed for the Long Gallery, its status would still be acknowledged within the hierarchy of rooms, as would its personal significance at the very core of his public and private life. That winter, Adam billed for a section showing how his bookcases could be adapted to fit the more confined space of the Library with its awkward offset fireplace. There was also the question of the informal eating room next to it. This was the only room left along the *enfilade* that was relatively undistinguished and the obvious place for the Tapestry Room Coventry desired. So Adam was commissioned to provide designs for the ceilings and mouldings for both of these rooms, and from June 1763 until Coventry's marriage in September 1764 he was presenting new designs for Croome almost every month.

The question now was what to do with the Long Gallery. Adam's great coffered ceiling warranted a bolder and more comprehensive

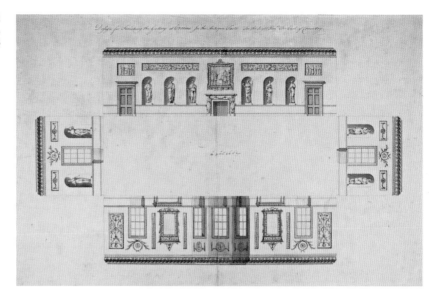

neoclassical theme based on a mutual interest in the antique. That June, Adam billed for an impressive new section of the Gallery 'finished in the Antique Taste'. This showed the space laid out as a sculpture gallery, with Holkham-style niches, believed by Harris to derive from a *horreum*, a type of Roman public warehouse. This was similar to his contemporary design for the dining room at Syon, and it would reappear at Harewood House, West Yorkshire, and Lansdowne House, London W11. Having never gathered a collection of antique sculpture in Italy, Lord Coventry would have to content himself with plaster replicas to achieve the desired effect, which were eventually supplied by John Cheere (1709–1787). That the side lights of the Venetian window at the south end of the room were not to be expressed internally was a considerable compromise on Coventry's part, but, by way of compensation, Adam made a huge feature of its partner window in the Library.

The Long Gallery was completed between 1763 and 1766 with every detail down to the door furniture designed by Adam as a complete work of art: one of the earliest rooms, and maybe the very first room that he decorated and furnished in its entirety.[8] Joseph Rose Jnr began on the stuccowork in 1763, while John Hobcraft worked on the joinery from 1764, with Alken executing the more intricate details from 1765.[9] The magnificent caryatid chimney piece with its statues of the Nymphs of Flora was completed by Wilton in 1766, for which he charged £300.[10] Adam had already designed similar statement chimney pieces for the Great Dining Room (now the Salon) at Hatchlands, Surrey, in 1759 and for the Drawing

Room at Kedleston, Derbyshire, in 1760, and he repeated the design again
in 1777 in the Gallery at Harewood. The grate and fender were the earliest
examples of their type by Adam. They were embellished here with the
anthemion motif, a floral ornament based on a flat radiating cluster of
either honeysuckle or palm leaves, used by Adam elsewhere in this room
and at Croome Court.

Adam's furnishings complemented the theme perfectly. They included
an outstanding pair of console tables and pier glasses that flanked the bay
window. These tables had innovative tapered legs carved to appear as
pilasters with female masks on the capitals. This design had been rejected
by the Duke of Northumberland for Syon, but the 6th Earl loved it and
had little doubt about its potential in the new Long Gallery.[11] The pier
glasses, probably those purchased in Paris in the summer of 1763, were
set within aedicule frames with anthemion borders carved by Alken to
Adam's design. These matched the frame for the grisaille painting of a
Roman sacrifice that hung above the chimney piece, and in January 1766
Adam designed two large and four small grisaille panels for the west wall,
an idea he had employed previously in the Dining Room at Shardeloes,
Buckinghamshire, of 1759–63. The larger ones were placed at the ends of
the wall and the four narrow ones flanked the pier glasses.

Important highlights within the muted 'dead stone' colour scheme
were the ten mahogany sofas or stools and the eight armchairs with
double anthemion back splats that Adam designed for the room in

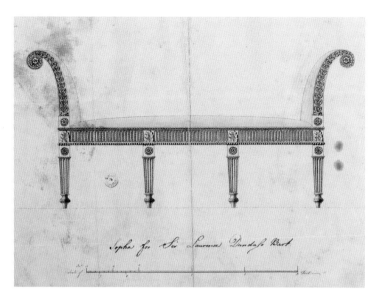

Design for a 'Sopha' or scroll chair for the Long Gallery, originally designed for Sir Lawrence Dundas, Adam office, 1764

1764, which were all finely carved by Alken and covered in blue morocco leather. These were Adam's very first experimental neoclassical designs for seat furniture and a landmark in the evolution of the Adam style. The scroll-end stools were made by the leading new firm of France & Bradburn, while the armchairs were the work of the master cabinetmaker, John Cobb. Former employees of Vile & Cobb, William France and John Bradburn had taken over the company's Royal Warrant in July 1764, following Vile's retirement in April 1764. This would indicate that Adam and his patron were eager to follow this shift in royal patronage.

The entire scheme was a cleverly contrived illusion aimed at enhancing the Long Gallery's proportions and emphasising its splendid westerly outlook. The chimney piece faced the bay window to add breadth and accentuate the central focus. The pier glasses also contributed to the apparent breadth and even the floorboards grew broader at the centre to enhance this effect still further. However, their contribution was partly diminished by the handsome carpet supplied by Thomas Moore in 1767, one of several made for the Earl by the Moorfields manufactory.[12] The cool austerity of the monochromatic scheme complemented the Roman architectural character of the coffered ceiling, and this, together with details such as the palmette frieze inspired by the Temple of Concord, the chimney piece and replica statues, all helped to provide the desired note of authenticity. Light flooding in through the bay window enhanced the sculptural qualities of the decoration, while the window itself provided a grandstand from which to take in the spectacular views. It was an early taste of Adam's theatricality that became a common theme of many of his most celebrated contemporary interiors.

The Library was redecorated between 1763 and 1765: a relatively short period of time as the basic scheme had evolved already during discussions on the treatment of the Long Gallery. The marble chimney piece by John Wildsmith, with its turtle doves and foliage in high relief, was already *in situ*. Although Adam billed for both the Library and Tapestry Room ceiling designs, only an office copy of one of the designs survives. This is inscribed erroneously as being for the Library, as its dimensions are those of the Tapestry Room, and this is where the design was executed. The detail of the Library ceiling, with its alternating border of anthemia and double calyces, a sepal-like ornament, was a variation of the frieze in the

Croome Court, the Long Gallery photographed for the 1915 article in *Country Life*

Long Gallery. It has a central laurel wreath and medallions at each corner containing heads in high relief set within laurel wreaths and placed on *thyrsi* (staffs or spears usually associated with Bacchus).[13] David King has also noted a similarity between this ceiling and an unexecuted and more elaborate ceiling design for Shardeloes.[14] The ceiling was probably subject to later repair and alteration, for the cornice, with its rosette and medallion motif, similar to that in the Tapestry Room, Dining Room and Best Bedroom, is cut off abruptly at the chimney breast.

The Ionic order used on the bookcases was echoed on the Venetian window, while the addition of anthemion cresting to the bookcases is believed to be a fashionable reference to the Choragic Monument of Lysicrates, illustrated in James Stuart and Nicholas Revett's *Antiquities of Athens*.[15] The first volume had appeared in 1762, but an engraving of the Choragic Monument had been circulated in 1755 as a specimen to attract subscribers, among them the 6th Earl's late wife, Maria. It may be assumed this was an inspired gift to her husband that could have prompted the additional decoration. In any case, this type of highly topical reference was something that both the Earl and Adam enjoyed.

The jib door in the north-east corner of the Library was concealed ingeniously by a *trompe l'oeil* painting, which Hobcraft's bill of 1764

Croome Court, the Library
photographed for the 1915
article in *Country Life*

describes as being comprised of '108 Blank Books, the wood & fixing; 108 ditto bound; 74 of ditto tooled & filleted'.[16] The rest of the room was decorated in the Earl's favourite colours, with the walls painted a sombre 'dead stone' colour and the windows emphasised by festoon curtains of crimson silk damask. These matched the crimson velvet of the Earl's suit in the iconic portrait by Allan Ramsay that hung above the fireplace (see p. 36).[17] The bill for these curtains refers to an arched panel covered with the same damask that fitted into the top of the Venetian window, presumably to reduce glare for reading purposes. In 1772, additional bookshelves were also fitted into the window recess to accommodate the Earl's increasing book collection. Poised between the public and private areas of the house, the Library fulfilled its dual purpose as secluded retreat and public showpiece in considerable style.

The Tapestry Room would prove a more complex task. There was a long tradition of such rooms in English country houses, a tradition that the Earl felt should be perpetuated at Croome, particularly as Lord Lyttelton now had an enviable new tapestry room at Hagley. The Hagley tapestries, woven to a French Rococo design by Joshua Morris at the Soho factory in 1725, were much admired and had been hung within an elaborate setting that included a ceiling painted with zephyrs by James

'Athenian' Stuart. The Earl was determined to surpass this spectacle with something more unusual and different. Adam's chimney piece of orange Veronese and white Carrara marble set the tone. Despite the apparent confusion in the Adam office over the ceiling design, its geometric layout, with its wheel moulding and garlanded trophies, worked well with the room's dimensions. Rose Jnr started work on the ceiling and the rosette and modillion cornice in 1763 and, between 1763 and 1764, Hobcraft and Alken executed the joinery and carving.[18] The chimney piece itself was taken down by Wildsmith at this time, polished and enhanced by the addition of a lapis lazuli plaque provided by Wilton.

With the Seven Years' War reaching a conclusion early in 1763, and with the function and decorative schemes established for the Library and Long Gallery, and work well in hand on the new Tapestry Room, the Earl left for Paris in the summer of 1763, eager to purchase some suitable tapestries as well as mirror glasses for the Gallery and determined to make a statement second to none.[19] He headed straight for the Royal Gobelins Manufactory. Recent improvements undertaken there by the director, Jacques-Germain Soufflot (1713–1780), and the master-weaver, Jacques Neilson (c.1718–1788), to attract more private customers had included technical changes to the weaving process and looms to produce tapestries more quickly and at a lower cost without loss of quality. This in itself would have been of interest to the Earl. But what impressed him most was a striking new design that had been created in conjunction with the leading artist, François Boucher (1703–1770). Medallions containing scenes by Boucher were placed on backgrounds woven to simulate crimson silk damask richly decorated with flowers, birds and vases, which appeared to be suspended from frame-like borders. The design was eminently adaptable and could be tailored to a room's dimensions like wallpaper, perhaps an idea that originated during the Earl's discussions at the factory. This clever combination of contemporary art with an innovative design and manufacturing process was an irresistible combination for the Earl, and he placed an order without further delay. He also ordered matching tapestry covers for a set of seat furniture. Better still, he knew he was the first Englishman to purchase the new design.

Adam was summoned to Croome that October and was shown the proposed Gobelins design, now lost apart from the detail of the design above the chimney piece. Following the success of his scheme for the Long Gallery, Adam attempted to persuade his patron to adopt a more restrained neoclassical theme for the room and submitted a design for 'Altering the French Design for the Tapestry Room', as well as a design for 'Finishing the sides of the Tapestry Room'. His alternative scheme

was more elegant, disciplined and two-dimensional in appearance, but Lord Coventry, still buoyed up by the success of his Parisian expedition, was not to be persuaded.

He had plenty of time to dwell on his successful shopping trip. He returned to the Gobelins Manufactory to check on progress and discuss details on his 1764 trip to Paris but was obliged to wait a tiresome eight years before everything was delivered. In the summer of 1771, the leading cabinetmakers, Ince & Mayhew, sent a skilled team to hang the tapestries and fix the tapestry backs to the giltwood seat furniture, now believed to have been made by Ince & Mayhew in 1769–70 to a Gobelins design. This included a pair of settees that flanked the chimney piece, and six oval-backed chairs, which were the earliest-known English seats of their kind. Their form echoed the oval medallions in the tapestries and became a standard neoclassical type that was widely imitated. Ince & Mayhew also supplied the crimson silk festoon curtains and box cornices for the windows, as well as the fine gilt pier glass that was set between them. The frame was designed, perhaps by Adam, like a Kentian picture frame, with a shell at its top, a ram's head at its base and husk detail to match the seat furniture, and this was flanked by a pair of gilded wood pedestals. Not until 1794 did the finishing touch arrive, an ornate pier table, also supplied by Ince & Mayhew, which supported an impressive marble top inlaid with semi-precious stones and minerals that had been made by Wildsmith back in 1759. This included a square of lapis, which matched the plaque that Wilton had added to the chimney piece seen reflected in the mirror above the table. The simple geometry of this plaque anchored

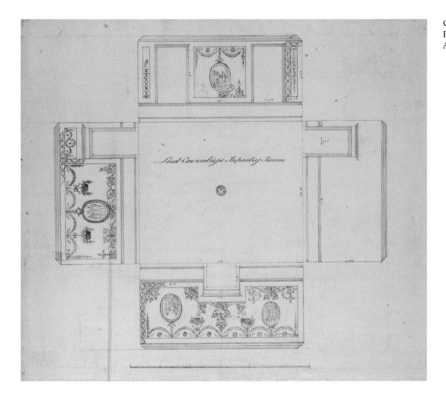

Croome Court, design for 'Altering the
French Design for the Tapestry Room',
Adam office, 1763–64

the sheer exuberance of the scheme so that the contribution of each
part was easier to assimilate.

In 1824, William Dean described Lord Coventry's Boucher-Neilson
Tapestry Room as 'the most beautiful room hung with the finest tapestry now in England'.[20] Following the sale of the tapestries in the late
nineteenth century, the entire room itself was subsequently dismantled
and reassembled in the Metropolitan Museum of Art, New York, in the
mid-twentieth century, where it was reunited with the tapestries (see
p. 186). What exists today at Croome is actually a replica of the original
design of the room by Brown & Muntzer of London of 1949. This, in itself,
is a telling episode in the history of the decorative arts.[21]

Lord Coventry's Tapestry Room fulfilled all his intentions as one
of the most exceptional and influential rooms of its day. It inspired
similar rooms at Weston Park, Newby Hall, Moor Park, Osterley Park and
Welbeck Abbey, and it became an important example of his ability to
influence the evolution of the Adam partnership's characteristic style.
The room was also a potent demonstration of his informed appreciation of contemporary French taste, of his receptiveness to new ideas
and of his close involvement in the design process at Croome. Above

Design for a bed, Adam office, c.1763

all, it underlined his impact as a leading tastemaker of his day.

The first floor was also being refurbished from around 1763. This had been fitted out by John Hobcraft and James Lovell from 1758 to 1759, but more as a matter of expediency in view of Maria's failing health.[22] Quite possibly the private suite was still incomplete and, in any case, required some upgrading to conform to the standard of the rooms on the *piano nobile*, and in preparation for Lord Coventry's second marriage.

Lady Coventry's Bedroom was fitted out with a western alcove with flanking closets. This alcove is believed to have been the destination for the magnificent domed bed that Robert Adam designed for Lord Coventry, the drawing for which is undated. This was completed in 1763 by the new partnership of William France and John Bradburn, who went on to produce the seat furniture in the Long Gallery at Croome. The magnificent mahogany structure, with its spiral-fluted posts with Corinthian capitals, and coved and fluted cornice, was crowned with a richly embellished dome supporting a vase finial. It was upholstered with curtains and covers of green silk damask, acquired in 1765 from the French supplier, Triquet & Vansommer.[23] It was the very first of several important domed beds designed by Adam, of which only the state bed at Osterley of 1775–76 survives, complete with its original textiles.

Lord Coventry had no wish to alter his own adjoining bedroom but he commissioned Adam in 1764 to undertake a similar refurbishment of his Dressing Room, now known as the Alcove Bedroom, on the south side of the house. Always a room of high status, it had been fitted out with bolection-moulded panelling and a fossil chimney piece in the 4th Earl's time. In 1759 Hobcraft had billed for altering it to conform to the new room layout and this earlier bill makes a specific distinction between the old and new joinery.[24] These earlier bills also imply that an alcove and closet existed in the room already. Adam's design included a central alcove with flanking closets on the east wall and a new chimney piece. Lord Coventry decided to keep the original chimney piece and as much of the old joinery as possible, probably as they were part of the historic decorative theme that linked the room with the Billiard Room.

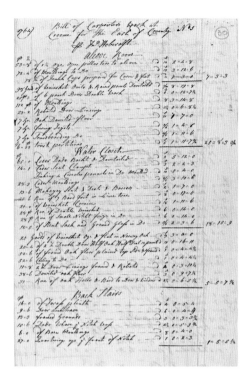

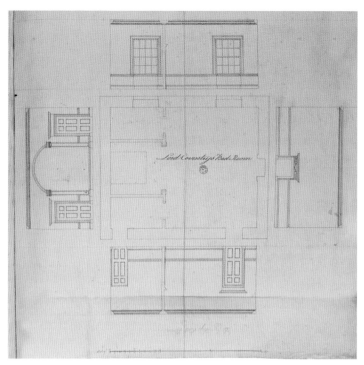

Consequently, only part of Adam's design was executed, which included the new eastern partition with its archway, Ionic pilasters, fielded panelling and matching closet doors.

One innovation the 6th Earl was keen to have in his new closet was some proper plumbing. A pumping engine was installed east of the service wing that took advantage of an existing well and the remains of a former outbuilding. A bill dated 13 April 1764 sent from Kedleston by Adam's plumber, William Chapman, describes the proposed installation in some detail.[25] Apparently the engine had a hand-cranked iron flywheel, over five foot in diameter, set within a sturdy oak frame, that served two cisterns, one in the cellar and 'the other in a Dark Closett in ye Passage'. The bill also states that its purpose was to supply a 'Statuary marble Bason for ye Water Clossett', almost certainly the one in the Alcove Bedroom, a notably early example of a water supply system to sinks and basins in a country house.

The other first-floor room to be redecorated at this time was the Blew Bedroom on the south side of the house, which was to become the state bedroom also known as the Best Bedroom and the Chinese Bedroom following its redecoration. Although first fitted out in the late 1750s, when a chimney piece by Lovell was installed, the Earl was keen

Hobcraft's bill of 1764 for work in the Alcove Bedroom and water closet, Croome Court

Design for the Alcove Bedroom, Croome Court, Adam office, 1764. The drawing is inscribed 'Lord Coventry's Bedroom'.

to give it a fresh identity and commissioned Adam to refit it in a manner appropriate to its intended status. Adam designed a chimney piece for the room in 1763, enriched with swags, husks, rosettes and dentil mouldings, that is, mouldings formed from rows of square-shaped blocks like teeth. These details recur on the joinery so it may be assumed that this was all replaced too. The room was also given a new cornice by Rose Jnr that matched the rosette and modillion cornices on the *piano nobile*. To complete the transformation, the walls were covered with elaborate Chinese landscape wallpaper, supplied by Compton & Spinney.

Also prior to the Earl's second marriage, to Barbara St John, further improvements were made to the stable court and offices, including a new model dairy. Although the Earl had rejected Adam's proposal to give the offices a more distinguished classical appearance back in January 1763, the dairy may have been a treat for Barbara. Located in the western range of the stable court, Adam billed for his initial drawings that November. Further designs followed the next year, including detailed interior elevations that show a decorative tiled frieze and a pair of tall niches on the north wall to hold elegant vases. All of this was executed much as proposed.

This dairy was among the last projects undertaken during Adam's early phase of work at Croome. In October 1764, Lord Coventry bought a new London townhouse in Piccadilly.[26] The timing of the purchase, within a few weeks of his second marriage, suggests that this was for his wife's benefit, at least in part, for it would have been difficult to erase Maria's overwhelming influence from the house in Grosvenor Square. As Frances Sands has noted, Coventry was not unique among Adam's patrons to do so as a similar situation occurred at 20 St James's Square.[27] Coventry would also have been keen to acquire somewhere more spacious to advertise his prowess as a patron and collector within the capital.

Facing Green Park at the eastern end of Piccadilly, the site was part of the estate of William Pulteney, 1st Earl of Bath. Number 29 (now 106), had been built only a few years before, in 1759–62, for Sir Henry Hunloke, 4th Baronet, of Wingerworth Hall, Derbyshire. Hunloke had purchased a 99-year lease on a plot previously occupied by a former inn, known as The Greyhound. The architect of his new house is unknown, although Matthew Brettingham has been proposed as a possible candidate. Lord Coventry acquired the remaining 94 years of the lease of the property and immediately commissioned the Adam partnership to undertake a major refurbishment.

During the following six years, most of the work commissioned by the 6th Earl from Adam was associated with Piccadilly. Adam began by carrying out a detailed survey in 1764, and then made seven sketch

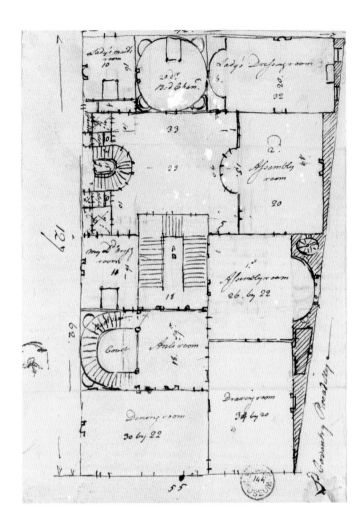

Lord Coventry's new London townhouse: 29 (now 106) Piccadilly

Sketch of proposed new layout for 29 Piccadilly, Robert Adam, 1764

proposals for the revision of the layout with the aim of creating a new circuit of rooms of varied shape and size, some of which attempted to set the rooms around a central staircase. These proved too ambitious and would have involved gutting the brand new house, and prudence seems to have prevailed. Instead, a less extensive series of alterations was carried out, together with an elaborate scheme of decoration. Over 50 drawings at Sir John Soane's Museum bear witness to the grand scale of the project and include designs for the ceilings, walls, chimney pieces, carpets and furniture, many of them for the Great Room and Ante-Room that were to face the street on the first floor, and for Lady Coventry's Bedroom and octagonal Dressing Room set to the rear of these on the same floor.[28] This scheme has survived in part and the complex geometric layout of the Great Room ceiling is particularly impressive with its ornate

Design in the Antique style for the decoration of the octagonal dressing room at 29 Piccadilly, Adam office, 1765

plasterwork by Rose Jnr and paintings by Antonio Zucchi (1726–1795). However, the exquisite decorative scheme for Lady Coventry's octagonal Dressing Room is especially memorable, with its coved ceiling and elaborate wall decoration with grotesque panels all perfectly scaled to the room's dimensions.

Adam remained involved at Piccadilly after work was completed, as is evident from correspondence in the Croome archive that relates to his lengthy negotiations with a neighbour whose alterations threatened to block light from the main staircase. The scale and intensity of the work had demanded increased contact between Adam and the Earl during the mid-1760s, and this may have enabled them to establish a more secure and effective working relationship that benefited the ongoing works at Croome.

With his new townhouse complete, Lord Coventry could now assume his role as a leading tastemaker in the capital as well as one of the most inspirational patrons of his day. As the tide of cultural influence began to ebb away slowly from the great country houses back to the capital, this became increasingly important, particularly now that Croome was becoming of such immense personal significance to him. It was no coincidence that, over the next few decades, Coventry began to mark out his territory at Croome with increasing rigour and decided to create a hidden retreat at the very heart of the building.

The Adam Eye-catchers

Adam's park buildings at Croome were his first chance to design new buildings for Lord Coventry and, although many of his ideas were never executed, they show an unfailing determination to impress his patron and make the most of any opportunity.

Richard Wilson's painting of 1758, probably the first visual representation of a landscape by Brown, had underlined to the 6th Earl the importance of pictorial composition in the redesign of his park (see pp. 14–15). The Rotunda, with its Vassalli plasterwork, belonged stylistically to the early Rococo phase of the project and marked an historic viewpoint, whereas the new church and Temple Greenhouse belonged to the second main phase when the complex network of viewpoints and vistas that were defined by Brown's planting were endorsed in brick and stone. These and subsequent park structures gave explicit form and fresh perspectives to Brown's seemingly naturalistic and incidental planting, designed to be either glimpsed from the house or to emerge suddenly during circuitous explorations.

The Temple Greenhouse had demonstrated Adam's skill at siting a building, its elegant lines balanced brilliantly by the church tower on the hill. The structures round the lake, Brown's grotto, completed in the 1760s, and Adam's tiny Island Temple, for which no drawing has been identified and which was not built until 1777–78, served merely as pausing points and picnic places. Lord Coventry was now eager to create more landmarks and to establish eye-catchers at key points within the park, especially on its boundaries to define his territory and place it in its wider context.

A ruin was essential, particularly for a man of antiquarian leanings like the Earl. Adam's designs do not survive but the bills imply that he presented his first design in 1765, which was rejected, and it was not until October 1766 that he billed for 'a new drawing of the ruin with alterations'.[29] Work commenced immediately.

Dunstall Castle, by E.F. and F.T. Burney, c.1784

Built from Bredon Hill stone, the ruin, known as Dunstall Castle, forms an L-shaped screen, more a semblance of a ruin, with towers at each end and at the angle, a tall round archway in one wall and the remains of a traceried Gothic window in the other. Intended to be viewed from a distance, the shallow site on Dunstall Common meant that it had to be tall, and its simple form enabled it to fulfil its purpose to maximum effect at minimal cost. Adam was making a point here, but he was also on familiar ground. He drew inspiration for these and his many castle designs from his Scottish heritage, from John Vanbrugh and from his travels abroad, and they were well suited to his irrepressible creativity as they were capable of infinite variation. David King has noted the similarity of this early design for Dunstall Castle to an unexecuted design by Adam at Mellerstain in Berwickshire and to several designs for Tulloch Castle in Ross-shire.[30]

Also in October 1766, Adam billed Lord Coventry for a design for a garden seat, although this was not completed until the early 1770s. This was to be perched high above the southern tip of the artificial river on the north-east ridge, drawing the eye along the ridge to the new ruin. Adam designed garden seats for at least nine of his clients, notably at Kenwood and Richmond in Outer London, and Mamhead, Devon, but this was probably the only one that was built. His initial proposal had included unusual spiral-fluted columns, three apses and a decorative frieze, but, as executed, the design was simplified. The rear apse was omitted and the seat was set within an arched entrance on Tuscan columns with the pediment supported on larger outer columns of his favourite

Spalatro design for added definition. Like the Island Temple and the new ruin, the design was to be viewed from one side only and was very much a stage set.

During the 1760s, the Earl was already looking further afield to the pastureland to the north and west. Work had begun on Pirton Park to Brown's plan of c.1763 following the Inclosure Act of 1762 and the Award of 20 September 1763, and in 1764 the exchanges began for small parcels of land to the west of the lake where the Menagerie was to be built. The Croome bills indicate that Adam submitted at least three designs in the autumn of 1766 for a 'building between the woods', only two of which appear to have survived and none of which were executed. These are generally assumed to have been for an eye-catcher up on Knight's Hill, on the heathland known as Cubsmoor, where the land fell away to the west towards the Severn vale. This was an essential slice of the middle distance to complete his view, but it was to be another decade before the Earl succeeded in acquiring this land.

Adam's designs paid little heed to matters of cost and detail here. One of them, now at Sir John Soane's Museum, shows an ornate square domed structure. Steps on each elevation are guarded by sphinxes and lead to large pedimented apses set behind screens with broad end pilasters and flanking niches that hold urns. The complexity of the design does seem strange in view of its proposed isolated location. Presumably Adam decided to take advantage of the prominent and spectacular site to demonstrate his talents, content in the knowledge he could use the drawing elsewhere if it was rejected. The sphinxes were to reappear later at Croome flanking the steps to the south portico.

Another drawing is more like the structure eventually built by James Wyatt.[31] Again it is square in plan and on each side are recesses behind a three-bay screen with flanking niches containing urns set beneath reliefs. On this occasion Adam included a flat roof that formed a platform from which to take advantage of the superb views, accessed by a spiral staircase crowned by a small central dome. This ingenious feature was filed in the Earl's memory for future use.

Design of a building between the woods, assumed to be the site of the existing Panorama Tower on Cubsmoor on the western perimeter of Croome, Adam office, 1766

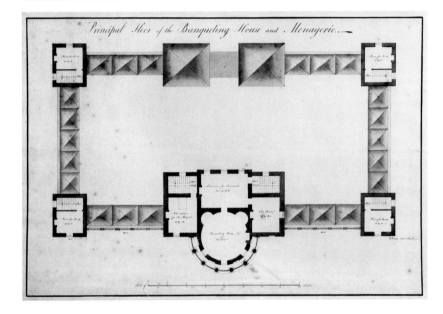

Design for a Banqueting House and Menagerie at Croome: elevation and plan, Adam office, 1766

That same year Adam endeavoured to dazzle his patron further with a resplendent design for a Menagerie and Banqueting House for which he charged a substantial 21 guineas. He proposed a generous rectangular courtyard, the long sides measuring almost 55 metres in length, with pavilions at each corner that appear to have elliptical domes, and a further pair along one side. The walls were rusticated and arcaded and lined with aviaries, and there were superior aviaries in the pavilions too. The Banqueting House, Tea Room and Keeper's Lodgings were housed in a large two-storey structure at the centre of the main elevation, with the Banqueting House set in an impressive semi-circular first-floor room lit by a magnificent seven-bay, full-height bow window.

The design far exceeded Lord Coventry's requirements. In truth, it threatened to eclipse Croome Court itself. Perhaps that was the intention: a demonstration by Adam to his patron of a lost opportunity. So

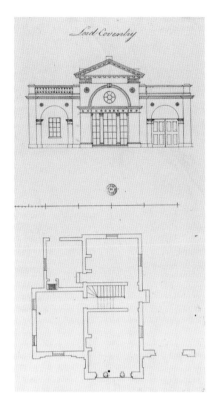

Design for altering the Keeper's Lodge at the Menagerie, Croome, Adam office, 1781

the project was shelved, and Barbara's birds were housed in a simple, if extensive, brick enclosure with rudimentary aviaries. Not until 1781 did Adam submit a much more modest proposal to remodel the Keeper's Lodge. This gave the existing brick building a distinctive and symmetrical classical façade, and visitors were invited to take shelter in a small but well-proportioned tea room, otherwise used by the keeper as a sitting room, from where they could view the attractions through an elegant tripartite window.

It may be significant these ambitious designs for park buildings by Adam were all proposed in 1766, and many of them billed for in October as, only a few weeks later, Lord Coventry wrote an anxious note to Brown:

> I shall not leave this place till tomorrow fortnight, which I do not mention from any hopes I entertain of seeing you here within that time, but I should be wanting to myself if I threw away any chance of such an event by neglecting to acquaint you with my motions. I don't know that Croome ever stood more in need of your assistance, or that the master ever wished it more ardently.[32]

He may have been confident to make decisions with regard to the house, and even to alter work executed under Brown's supervision, but he remained dependent upon his advice when it came to the landscape. Brown's common-sense approach may have served as a valuable counterpart to Adam's tempting excesses.

The Creative Edge

Although Lord Coventry's relationship with Adam never attained the easy familiarity that he shared with Brown and remained on a strictly professional basis, it was enduring. They were both men of great personal charm and intellect and they shared similar tastes. Over time they established a mutual respect and trust from which each gained a good deal. The parameters of their relationship had been carefully drawn out ever since Lord Coventry had accused Adam of overcharging early in 1764. Adam's reply of 3 April is quoted here at length as it is so revealing and skilfully composed, conveying the extent of his damaged pride without risk of offending his valued but demanding patron:

> My Lord
> I received the Honour of your Lordships Letter with the Draught for £250. I have returned the Bill discharged to your Lordship. I am extremely Sorry your Lordship should have thought of deducting any part of the money, as almost every person I have done Designs for, upon considering

that it is my only Branch of Business, & that I have never stated a Sixpence for Surveying (when every Carpenter & Bricklayer who call themselves Architect claim with not half the justice I might) have generally sent me a present over & above the Bill itself & not long since of delivering one of Seventy Five pounds, I received a Hundred with this compliment. That he knew how many thousands I had spent in acquiring knowledge, & if he was to offer seven times that sum he did not know where he could have got Designs that would have pleased him so well. I am very far from either asking or expecting any thing of that kind from your Lordship, But cannot help wishing from the Respect & Esteem I have for your Lordship, that you had considered me incapable of stating more than I thought was just, when I compute the Time employed by my Clerks, the high wages I pay them & the particular attention I have always given & will continue to bestow on every thing [sic] that is your Lordships.

Your Lsp will at once be convinced that it consumed the same Time & requires the same money from me for Drawings, executed or not Executed, as your Lordship knows I have charged nothing for the Execution though I have done everything that gives a title to that claim ... I must beg that your Lordship will be so obliging not to mention my taking less than the Total of my Bill, ... as I do assure you that it is not the difference of the payment that is capable of giving me the Smallest Concern, and will exert myself in the other Buildings for Croome ...[33]

Lord Coventry paid Adam in full straight away. Quite possibly when Adam received the lucrative commission for Piccadilly later that year this helped to resolve their differences, especially as the scale of the London project would place their relationship on a firmer footing. Certainly Coventry never risked a similar objection.

In Adam he had found a designer who had taken the Croome project onto a more daring and challenging level in terms of its originality and style. He admired his pictorial skills, and the sense of movement and theatre conveyed in his designs. He may have envied Adam's first-hand knowledge of antiquity, the vast reference source of material he had established on his Grand Tour, and he must have delighted in his erudite allusions that reflected on himself. Above all, Adam had helped to clarify his vision.

Adam, in turn, knew Lord Coventry to be a patron worth cultivating. He was wealthy and well informed, he had wide experience and good connections, he was sympathetic to his aims, and he was acquiring a reputation for his innovative taste. He had helped to nurture his interest in contemporary French neoclassicism too, perhaps more than any other of his Francophile clients. He also furnished him with a broad and interesting range of commissions. Adam's work at Croome was not of the scale or spectacle of his greatest work, it was not a Syon or a Kenwood, but it offered many opportunities to extend his skills and develop his career. Although he enjoyed similarly close relationships with some of his other patrons, among them the Duke of Northumberland and Robert Childe of Osterley, Lord Coventry proved the most loyal. Adam worked at Croome for three decades and in many respects it became a fundamental component of his professional life.

Just how much Adam valued Lord Coventry's patronage is evident from a letter he sent to him on 17 October 1771 that accompanied one of his designs for a bridge (see inside back cover).[34] This design is also of interest in itself in that it shows an actual elevation implanted within an improbably rugged landscape that is almost Chinese in inspiration. If this was another attempt to replace the Chinese Bridge perhaps the reference was intentional. The detail of the bridge is relatively restrained: a few roundels and paterae, and some plaques carved with fantastical amphibious beasts to lighten the mood. The letter begins:

> *I received the Honor of your Lordship's Letter from Croome, & have made out a Drawing of the Bridge a good deal altered from the one your Lordship saw, and I flatter myself you will approve.*
>
> *It is drawn to the Size of the Copper plates of the Work my brother & I are to publish. I shall give your Lordship our Ideas about this Work when I have the Honour of seeing you in Town. In the meantime, I beg that you will not fold the Drawing but keep it Rolled up, as I shall get the engraving done from it with your permission, as I have taken a good deal of pains upon it & done it all myself . If you like the design I shall get a Copy done for the Workmen & the Parts at large made up for the Execution.*[35]

Not only does Adam seems keen for his patron to be aware that the drawing was all his own work and that he had taken trouble over it, but also that he intended to publish it in the *Works* to advertise the quality of his clients: a classic example of Adam's charm and shrewd commercial tactics coming into play. Regrettably, Lord Coventry would still not be persuaded, so Adam never published his drawing and his plans for a bridge across Croome River remained unbuilt. But by this time Adam understood his patron pretty well and was sufficiently confident of his loyalty to enjoy the challenge.

THE FINAL FLOURISH

The early 1770s had marked a crucial stage in the evolution of the 6th Earl of Coventry's plans for Croome. The second main phase of Lancelot Brown's work on the landscape had drawn to a close, Robert Adam had finished his initial major sequence of work and, in 1771, the Tapestry Room was completed at last, perhaps the most celebrated statement of the Earl's innovative and influential taste. Now that the house in Piccadilly was asserting his cultural status within the capital, it might have been time for Coventry to relax and reflect on his achievement.

Nothing could have been further from his mind. The boundaries of the park had not quite reached their full extent, drainage problems persisted and the business of developing his collections had barely begun. But with the clarification of his vision, he could now afford to obsess about the detail and the content as well as the context.

Vitruvius Britannicus

The Earl subscribed to Volumes IV and V of *Vitruvius Britannicus* and the inclusion of Croome Court in the pages of Volume V of 1771 must have afforded him deep satisfaction. Certainly the elevation included in the volume looked the part, not least because it had been simplified by the omission of the chimneys and the weathervanes from the tower roofs, giving the building a more desirable Palladian profile.

OPPOSITE
Croome Court, north and west elevations, with the adjoining Red Wing

Elevation of Croome Court from Colen Campbell's *Vitruvius Britannicus* (1771), Volume V

The ground- and first-floor plans in *Vitruvius* are of particular interest as they are the earliest known of the remodelled building. They also reveal several striking differences from the house as it survives today. On the ground floor, it appears that the doorway from the northern end of the Entrance Hall into the Billiard Room was still blocked with a false door at this time, and as no fireplace is shown in the Entrance Hall this would confirm the accepted opinion that the existing one was not installed until the mid-nineteenth century. However, the passageway from the Dining Room into the north-east tower and that from the foot of the West Stair into the Drawing Room are also missing, as is the adjacent niche. Similarly, on the first floor, the passageway from the central corridor into the Alcove Bedroom is not shown, nor is that between the Best (or Chinese) Bedroom and the south-east tower. In Lady Coventry's Bedroom it is noticeable that there are doors at the western end of the alcove leading into the closets, but no door is shown from the south closet onto the corridor as now exists. Interestingly, too, the original layout of her Boudoir, washroom and water closet can also be clearly seen. Although the omissions from the elevation were simple matters of presentation (and date if the sphinxes are also taken into account), these anomalies in the layout are less easy to explain. Some may be due to subsequent alteration but the omission of the various passageways through the central and end walls is more likely to represent a simplification of the plan or possibly even an oversight.

Making an Entrance

Designs for Croome continued to trickle through from the Adam office during the 1770s and 1780s. They included ideas for lodges, bridges, an elegant scheme to remodel Severn Bank House in Severn Stoke, and the revised proposal for the Menagerie tea room. Among the few that were executed was Adam's proposal for a grand entrance portal at the main entrance from the London road.

Brown had devised a dramatic sequence of vistas leading down the sweeping driveway to the house. Adam responded by delivering a most fitting proscenium arch through which one could experience this spectacle.[1] The gateway, known as the London Arch, was designed in February 1779 and assumed the form of a triumphal arch in the Roman manner, with flanking pairs of Ionic columns. There was also a bucranium frieze, with not forbidding ox skulls but the friendly faces of the Earl's own cattle, complete with tousled forelocks. The gateway design made erudite reference to the Temple of the Sun at Palmyra, although David King has noted a much more convincing resemblance to the Arch of the Sergii, the Roman arch at Pula, which Adam would have seen on his visit

The London Arch, Croome Park, by E.F. and F.T. Burney, c.1784. Above the arch can be seen the statue of Day.

to Spalatro.[2] The blocking course held statues of Day and Night. Day is now missing, but was seen on entering the park as a gesture of welcome to the Earl's enlightened realm.

Coade Stone

Much of the additional work on the embellishment of the park was made easier by the publication of the Coade catalogue, *Etchings of Coade's Artificial Stone Manufactory*, in 1777–79. Coade stone, or *Lithodipyra*, was an artificial stone invented by Eleanor Coade (1733–1821) around 1770, who ran the business under various names for 50 years. Many key features were acquired from this source. These included the Druid statue, which was located near the Temple Greenhouse; the plaques of the Aldobrandini Wedding for the Island Temple; the statue of Sabrina, nymph of the Severn from John Milton's *Comus* (1634), designed by John

Bacon (1740–1799), which was placed beside the grotto; and the terms that lined the walk to the Rotunda through the Home Shrubbery. The pair of Coade sphinxes, supplied in 1795 for the south portico, may have been additions recommended by Adam or prompted by one of his proposals for a 'building between the woods' of 1766 (see p. 161). Among the Earl's final acquisitions from Coade was the casket in memory of his friend and collaborator, Lancelot Brown, which was placed beside the lake in 1797 (see p. 135).

The Apartment

Although Adam had continued to produce designs for the park during the 1770s, it was not until 1781 that the Earl demanded his services back at the Court and this time he was in need of a secret retreat.

In March 1781, Adam billed for a 'Plan for an Apartment', and in June for a 'Sketch of part of front end of House', a 'Section of the 4 sides of the upper part of the Staircase', and for two detailed drawings for the cornice of the Main Stair. Robert Newman, the master-mason, also billed that year for creating an access route via a jib door from a half-landing on the Main Stair into the new apartment located on the first floor of the service wing. However, shortly after the apartment was finished in 1783, Newman billed for 'Alterations of the Staircase between the Towers, taking off the roof and cutting out the walls for letting in the timbers of the new roof'.[3] It was little more than 20 years since Brown and Henry Holland had completed work on the east wing roof and it appears that neither its design nor its construction had proved entirely satisfactory.

It can be no coincidence that the decision to create a private apartment occurred during a period of personal turmoil for the Earl caused by the behaviour of his eldest children and the death of his friend, Brown. His dark moods returned and his need for privacy and solitude became more critical. Springhill was no longer an option, which was now the home of his brother and intended for his favourite second son, John. In any case, his total commitment to Croome rendered any other alternative impractical. That he was content to inhabit the service wing is indicative of the informality and relaxed relationship he enjoyed with his staff. The new apartment was also located conveniently close to his Library and private office, and as far from the public areas of the main house as possible (see pp. 172–73).

Regrettably Adam's drawings are missing, but James Wyatt drew up a plan of the apartment in 1799, when he was commissioned to make alterations to it, and this gives a clear indication of the layout. His plan shows a large sitting room with a recess, a light closet, a bedchamber, dressing room and a water closet. The main rooms all faced north, following the traditional layout of this part of the service wing, and Lord Coventry seems content to have maintained this arrangement, although the partitioning was devised to permit some views south. More significant was his decision to panel the walls of the main rooms with salvaged Jacobean wainscoting, perhaps from the old house or even the church. He also installed one of the pair of bolection-moulded fossil chimney pieces in the Bedchamber. That the other chimney piece was still located in the Alcove Bedroom – the traditional bedroom of the Earls of Coventry – again suggests that they may have had a special significance for him. A new access and staircase were installed at the eastern end of the apartment, a private route to and from the stable court, and the balustrade of this staircase matched that of the West Stair in the main house that led to the Alcove Bedroom. It would certainly make sense that Coventry wanted his apartment to reflect, not the man of taste and fashion, not the public figure, but the very private man who cherished his lineage and sought comfort and solace in memories of the old Croome of his youth.

In 1792 Adam died and Lord Coventry was a pall-bearer at his funeral in Westminster Abbey. He would have recognised the honour, and he would have been keenly aware of the immense personal loss. He had come to rely on Adam, who had brought a sense of continuity to the Croome project following Brown's death. He now had a void to fill and, once again, the loss spurred him on to another period of intense activity. It was as if his life depended on it, and maybe it did. That year the author of an anonymous letter to The *Gentleman's Magazine* gushed: 'Never did I see a more beautiful spot; nor any kept in such perfect order ... In short, Mr Urban, if there be a spot upon this habitable globe to make a death-bed terrible, it is Lord Coventry's, at Croome, in Worcestershire'.[4]

In 1796, the fourth major phase of drainage began and lasted until 1802, supervised by John Snape of Birmingham, whose beautifully detailed plan of the park now forms an invaluable record (see pp. 6–7). Arthur Young, with his informed and critical eye, could barely contain his admiration for Croome's exceptional collection of plants and the immaculate and well-kept parkland. He proclaimed Croome second to Kew as a botanical garden, adding that 'not a thistle or a weed can be seen, not a single tree or shrub is out of its proper place'.[5] But there was a hint here, too, of the obsessive spirit that controlled it all.

In 1799, the Earl took on a remarkable new head gardener, or botanic gardener as he preferred to style himself: William Dean. Dean brought fresh energy to the project and a botanical knowledge that helped sustain the Earl's passion for plants during the last years of his life. On the south side of the great walled kitchen garden, Dean supervised the construction

David Birtwhistle Me fecit MMXV

Cross section showing an impression of the 6th Earl's apartment on the first floor with the house steward's accommodation on the ground floor of the Red Wing at Croome Court, by David Birtwhistle, 2015

of a new vinery and also a hollow hot wall heated by five fires from 1805 to 1806: proof, if it was needed, that even in his 80s the Earl's enthusiasm for new technologies remained undimmed. Dean stayed at Croome until his death in 1831, long after the Earl himself was gone, managing and maintaining the plant collections for the 7th Earl, George William, with admirable vigour and efficiency. In 1824 he published his *An Historical and Descriptive Account of Croome D'Abitot*, which included his invaluable *Hortus Croomensis* and four delightful engravings of Croome by C. Turner, after J. Pitman, of the Court, the church, the Temple Greenhouse and the Rotunda.

The Contribution of James Wyatt

Fearing that the project might stall, Lord Coventry wasted little time in seeking a replacement for Adam and settled upon James Wyatt.[6]

The son of a Staffordshire timber merchant and builder, Wyatt had travelled in Italy in the 1760s with the patronage of the Bagots of Blithfield, where he studied architectural drawing with Antonio Visentini (1688–1782) in Venice. During this period, he had met Richard Dalton, librarian to George III, and, on his return, possibly as a result of this encounter and his own undeniable talent, Wyatt had won the competition for the rebuilding of the Pantheon, Oxford Street, London, of 1770–72. The building was a resounding success. Although its debt to the Saloon at Kedleston incited the annoyance of the Adam brothers, who accused Wyatt of plagiarism in the introduction to the *Works* in 1773, it became the chosen setting for many a memorable masquerade until 1792, when it was destroyed by fire.

Not that this presented a problem for Wyatt. As a result of its success, and the influence of his powerful friends and patrons, among them the Dukes of Devonshire and Northumberland, his career flourished. In 1776 Wyatt succeeded Henry Keene (1726–1776) as Surveyor to Westminster Abbey and, in 1782, he was appointed architect to the Board of Ordnance. Then, in 1796, he followed Chambers as Surveyor-General, a position that he held until his own unfortunate death in a coach accident in 1813. His prestigious country house commissions included Heaton Hall, Manchester, of 1772 for Sir Thomas Egerton, interior work at Heveningham Hall, Suffolk, of 1781–84 for Sir Gerald Vanneck, and Dodington House, Gloucestershire, of 1798–1813 for Christopher Codrington, as well as several large houses in Ireland and work for Oxford University, all of which had helped to maintain his high profile.

It was not as a classicist or even as a pioneer of the Greek Revival that Wyatt is best remembered, for his favoured style was undoubtedly Gothic. According to his friend, Humphry Repton, he believed it to be

James Wyatt, by Joseph Singleton, 1795

best suited to the British climate, but it was also a style he endeavoured not merely to imitate but to understand. His first big Gothic house was Lee Priory, in Kent, of 1785–90 (now demolished). Described by Horace Walpole as the 'quintessence of Gothic taste', this had demonstrated an exceptional appreciation of Gothic detail and picturesque massing.[7] However, it was Wyatt's concern for archaeological authenticity in his cathedral restoration work and his familiarity with contemporary published research that was most significant to the history of English Gothic Revival architecture.

By the time he was taken on by Lord Coventry in 1793, he was already the most accomplished contemporary architect in the Gothic style of his day and certainly no young and undiscovered talent. In terms of his proven versatility, expertise and panache, he was the ideal candidate for what Coventry had in mind. That he had worked on projects by Adam previously, such as Shardeloes and Syon, would also have appealed to Coventry's instincts. However, their working relationship never approached the creative bond that Brown and Adam had enjoyed. Wyatt lacked their personal charm and his reputedly un-businesslike approach would not have endeared him to Coventry. The fact that Wyatt attracted controversy for his cathedral restoration work may have added to his suitability for the task rather than concerned Coventry, although his reputation was yet untarnished by the unfortunate outcome of his work for William Beckford at Fonthill Abbey, Wiltshire, of 1796–1812 (demolished).

Wyatt's task was to provide the finishing touches to the park and pleasure grounds, supervise ongoing minor alterations and redecoration work on the house, and from 1796 he was also employed at Springhill House and at Piccadilly.[8] His first payment dated 21 March 1794 was for 'Journies and Drawings' on account and he remained involved at Croome and elsewhere from around 1793 to 1805. During this time, Wyatt completed various tasks, including the installation of the statuary, the design of iron bridges on the lake, the alterations to the Dry Arch beneath the carriageway by the lake, and the design of new gates and lodges on the Worcester and London approaches. Wyatt also altered Adam's design of 1791 for the Pier Gates near the lake, which were surmounted by great oval Coade vases and renamed the Punchbowl Gates.

However, his principal undertaking was to complete the final eye-catchers.[9] The 6th Earl knew that time was running out and these seemed to take on a special significance for him. Pirton Tower, the second ruin in the park, was designed in 1794. Work began in 1797 up on the ridge of Rabbit Bank in Pirton Park and was carried out by a new mason, William Stephens.[10] Then, in 1801, Wyatt made his design for the Panorama Tower on Cubsmoor. He presented the Earl with fine watercolour drawings of

both towers, of which the Panorama was a proposal but the Pirton ruin was presumably a record of the completed work. Generally assumed to have been based on one of Adam's designs of 1766 for a 'building between the woods', work did not start on the Panorama Tower until 1805, and it was not completed until after the Earl's death as it is not shown on Thomas Hobcraft's plan of the estate of 1810.[11]

It is interesting that the Gothic ruins at Croome stand to the north and south of the house, and the classical Rotunda and Panorama Tower to the east and west. Also the ruins were both designed as two-dimensional screens to be viewed from the house, while the classical eye-catchers were intended to be viewed in the round: a contrast of sham and substance. This may have been determined largely by the topography but the Earl's motives were rarely that straightforward. That the Rotunda and the Panorama Tower were the first and last eye-catchers to be built within the park adds further intrigue to the puzzle.

Broadway Tower is more interesting still in terms of both its architectural ambition and its personal implications for the Earl. Perhaps it was this project alone that lured Wyatt to Croome: the opportunity to design a great prospect tower up on the scarp above Broadway, one of the most spectacular sites in the region. It was the kind of challenge Wyatt was unlikely to resist and the tower was to be the Earl's swansong.

During this late period of his life, Lord Coventry's ties with the Broadway estate had increased now that his son, John, was living there. During the 1780s and 1790s, he spent considerable sums refurbishing

Springhill House and its grounds for his son's benefit. A letter of 29 March 1790 refers to laying the floor and installing a chimney piece and grate in 'the new room'. Coventry also purchased the adjacent farm of Severn Wells around 1788, and in 1799 he acquired Campden Hill and Ash Little Farm (now Campden Ashes). A major scheme of tree planting was put in place, including the great beeches along the roadsides, and as the extension of the estate enabled direct carriage access north to the main London road, Wyatt was commissioned to build new lodges and gates.[12]

Springhill also held fond memories of Brown, but even before he had met Brown, this outpost of the Croome estate had a special hold on Lord Coventry. He had climbed up there to consider his plans with Sanderson Miller 50 years previously. Then he had been after a Gothic retreat in the Cotswolds, and the idea still enthralled him. It is easy to see why. From the lip of the scarp, a vast portion of the Croome estate can be seen stretched out across the southern half of Worcestershire and along the Gloucestershire borders. The sharp-sighted can even see the Court itself some 24 kilometres away. Its potential was difficult to ignore. Visible to all on the plains beneath, this site was where Coventry knew his influence and reputation would continue to exert itself long after he was gone. If ever he intended to stake out his territory and plant a statement of his patronage on his county and his country, then this was it. There could be no better place for a great prospect tower.

But its purpose was not just to command its site. It was to capture the Earl's youthful ideals by embracing all the romantic historicism of Miller's home at Radway. It was to secure a prominent place at the forefront of a long tradition of prospect towers. And it was to be endowed with a certain archaeological authenticity that paid respect to its forebears and proclaimed the Earl's position at the cutting edge of contemporary culture.

Wyatt had responded with the first of his beautiful watercolour drawings in 1794. This included a plan and elevation of the proposed design, and showed a picturesque neo-Norman tower, standing over 20 metres high, with a battered base, balconies, a cluster of turrets and a roof terrace from which to admire the view. Wyatt described it on his drawing as a 'Saxon Hexagon Tower'. Precedents for designs of this type were numerous. Among the most relevant were Gibbs's Gothic Temple at Stowe of the 1740s, the construction of which had been

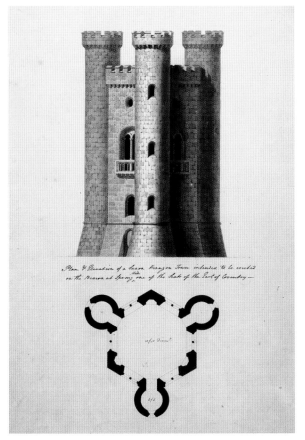

Proposed design for a 'Saxon Hexagon Tower', now known as Broadway Tower, on the escarpment south-east of Broadway in Worcestershire, James Wyatt, 1794

Croome Park, panorama view looking south-west from Church Hill

supervised by Brown; the tower at Aske Hall, North Yorkshire, built in 1740 by Daniel Garrett (d.1753) based on designs by William Kent; and Henry Flitcroft's King Alfred's Tower or Stourton Tower on the Stourhead estate, designed in 1765 and completed in 1772. Adam was also a master of the genre, and John Vanbrugh before him. Perhaps Adam had even discussed the idea with Lord Coventry.

More interesting still is that, in 1783, William King had published his *Observations on Ancient Castles*, in which he had actually proposed a medieval precedent for prospect towers of this type with main central structures on battered bases, and with subsidiary towers, placed within panoramic settings.[13] John Frew has pointed out the close similarity between Broadway Tower and the twelfth-century Orford Keep in Suffolk, which had been described and engraved in King's book. It is very likely that Wyatt was aware of King's research, particularly as it would have given a greater authenticity to his own design.

Although 'Saxon' was a usefully vague term in this period to describe all medieval architecture of pre-Gothic date, Wyatt's approach to the detail of the design also had more scholarly pretensions. In 1771, James Bentham had published his *History and Antiquities of the Conventual and Cathedral Church of Ely, Cambridgeshire*, which had provided an authoritative analysis of the stylistic evolution of Saxon, Norman and Gothic

architecture.[14] As Frew has observed, the detail of Wyatt's design actually alludes to Bentham's book: the round-headed openings, and the intersecting arches of the balustrades with their squat columns and cushion capitals were the most obvious attempts at historical accuracy, and made direct reference to Bentham's theory on the origin of the Gothic arch.

It was unfortunate that, despite Wyatt's well-intentioned attempts at authenticity, his church restoration work, in particular, caused consternation within the Society of Antiquaries in the late 1790s. It might have been some consolation to him that, just a few decades later, in September 1876, while staying at Broadway Tower, William Morris (1834–1896) drafted his famous letter to *The Athenaeum* that led to the founding of the Society for the Protection of Ancient Buildings. Lord Coventry would have appreciated the irony.

Although he never lived to see the tower completed, it fulfilled Lord Coventry's every intention. Perched high on the hilltop and commanding views across the Croome estate, the county and the region that he had loved and served, it paid tribute to the ideals of his youth and anticipated the stylistic revolution that was to follow. Even at the end of his life, it seemed that his aesthetic instincts remained as astute as ever. The tower became a regional and a cultural landmark. It marked a beginning and an end, and it saluted the achievements of a lifetime.

THE COLLECTIONS

Introduction

The collections at Croome were important components of the whole. Like many prominent collectors of his day, Lord Coventry's motives for collecting were numerous. He did it partly to embellish his homes, to edify and impress his guests, and as an investment, but also it was to satisfy his curiosity, to possess something novel and different, and, above all else, to project his identity. This lay at the heart of Coventry's mission.[1]

The 6th Earl was fortunate in that he was blessed with all the necessary attributes of a successful collector, including wealth, taste, knowledge, an obsessive personality, an enquiring mind and an unswerving commitment to his goals. As a patron, he enjoyed the creativity and control associated with commissioning works of art, but as a collector he relished the thrill of the chase, an opportunity to abandon thrift and caution for the immense satisfaction of securing rare and beautiful objects, and also plants: especially plants.

Not surprisingly, the quality and originality of his principal collections were difficult to ignore. An ardent Francophile, Lord Coventry was prominent among a select few of Adam's clients who helped to nurture his enthusiasm for French design. Many of Coventry's finest and most fashionable acquisitions of French decorative art were bought in Paris, either directly from the manufacturer or from the *marchands-merciers* who congregated in and around the rue St Honoré. These included Simon-Philippe Poirier, and dealers like Thomas Joachim Hébert and Mme Dulac, and he also bought items from the leading London dealer, Pierre Langlois. His purchases bear witness to his adventurous and influential taste and played a significant role in the dissemination of the new French style.

Lord Coventry's lavish spending on his principal collections began in the mid-1750s and reached a peak from 1763 to the mid-1780s, with the exception of the purchase of plants, which he tracked down with an unwavering enthusiasm throughout his adult life. These principal collections fall into six distinct categories: furniture, tapestries, porcelain, paintings and sculpture, books, and plants. Most of these have been and remain the subject of extensive scholarly research. The intention here is simply to highlight some of the most memorable items with reference to these valuable studies.

Many items from the collections have been sold and dispersed. A substantial number of paintings were sold after the Earl's death; the tapestries were sold in the late nineteenth century, and numerous other items formed part of the major sales of the late 1940s. Wherever possible, special emphasis is given here to items intended for Croome and to those that have remained part of the substantial collection held by the Croome Estate Trust. This includes many of the most significant pieces and provides a glimpse of the sheer ambition of the whole.

The Furniture

The quality of Lord Coventry's furniture collection and especially the many highly original and influential pieces has attracted widespread interest. Some items were specially commissioned but a significant number were acquired in Paris where Coventry's avant-garde taste soon earned him the respect of the Parisian *marchand-mercier*, Simon-Philippe Poirier, who supplied furniture and works of art to the French royalty and aristocracy. Based at 85, rue St Honoré, Coventry found him to be an excellent source of unusual designs à *la grecque*. Anthony Coleridge has analysed Coventry's buying habits in considerable detail. It appears that on his very first visit to Poirier in 1763, he made several extravagant

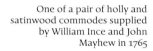

One of a pair of holly and satinwood commodes supplied by William Ince and John Mayhew in 1765

purchases including 'un secrétaire en armoire garni de bronze d'oré' and 'une commode à la grec garnie de bronze doré'.[2] Coventry returned there in 1764, and he continued to purchase items from Poirier through various agents in the late 1760s. So confident did he become of Poirier's goodwill that, in June 1769, Poirier was obliged to send a statement of unpaid bills dating from 1766 and 1768, which totalled a substantial £1,778 12s 9d.

Such an amount was far from exceptional. From 1758 until the turn of the century, Lord Coventry made purchases from most of the leading English makers and suppliers of fine furniture, including Ince & Mayhew, France & Bradburn, Chippendale & Rannie, Vile & Cobb, Gordon & Tait, Marsh & Tatham, George Seddon & Sons, and Robert and George Gillow, many of whom were patronised by the Crown. He also commissioned work from various individual specialist craftsmen, among them Sefferin Alken, William Linnell and James Lovell. Ince & Mayhew supplied important items for around 30 years from 1764 to 1794 and, according to Coleridge, their accounts for this period totalled £1,359 15s 8d, a sum that included some major orders, such as that for the suite of furniture in the Tapestry Room. However, Coventry spent twice as much with William Vile and John Cobb. From 1757 to 1773, he bought over 1,300 items costing well over £3,000, probably around half the furniture that he purchased during this intense period of acquisition.[3]

Although the sheer quality of the Earl's furniture collection owed much to his own exacting standards and sophisticated taste, Robert Adam's role was also significant and his response to the Earl's specific and unusual requests often resulted in some of his most outstanding designs. He found the Earl willing to accept some of his more avant-garde designs that had been rejected by his other clients, and this helped to reinforce their relationship and encourage Adam's inventiveness.

Once approved, Adam's designs would be passed on to the chosen cabinetmaker, often with instructions to employ Alken to undertake any specialist carving, and this combined expertise produced such memorable results as the remarkable neoclassical seat furniture in the Long Gallery. With competition rife in the cabinetmaking trade, it also helped that both Adam and Lord Coventry were keen to secure the best quality and service by patronising so many different firms. Coventry proved himself more than a match for Adam in his astute business dealings.[4]

This was particularly the case with Thomas Chippendale (bap. 1718– 1779). Chippendale supplied the Earl between 1764 and 1770, but only seven items have so far been identified, including a casket on a stand in 'fine Gaudelupe wood' billed for in 1764, a black rosewood shaving table and two fire screens billed for in 1765, and two dining tables with compass ends and a looking glass billed for in 1770. This may be attributed in part to Chippendale's inflexible approach to pricing. A notable example of this was when Sir Rowland Winn (1739–1785) of Nostell Priory was charged £36 by Chippendale for six mahogany chairs 'in the Antique taste' in January 1768. Three years earlier, the Earl had succeeded in paying Vile & Cobb only £30 for eight chairs of a similar type and quality for the Long Gallery. This would have added considerably to his pleasure in their purchase.

The Satinwood and Holly Commodes

A striking pair of neoclassical bedroom commodes were without doubt among the most outstanding purchases within Lord Coventry's collection (see p. 181). They were supplied in August 1765 by the leading cabinet-makers, Ince & Mayhew, for £40 and are described in the bill as '2 very fine Sattin wood and Holly Commodes, Neatly Grav'd and Inlaid with Flowers of Rosewood, the one with Drawers, the other with shelves to slide, Lind with paper and Green Bays falls to ditto Brass Naild'.[5]

Veneered with vertical stripes of the two contrasting woods, their bold geometry was startlingly novel and provided a surprisingly effective background for the wonderful inlaid decoration. This included sacred urns set within garlands of flowering myrtle on the front panels and laurel wreaths on each side, the whole elegantly defined by Etruscan black mouldings. Ornament of this type is now believed to derive from the centre of the Corinthian frieze of the Temple of Solomon from Villalpandus, which had been illustrated in Roland Fréart's *Parallèle de l'architecture antique et de la moderne* (1650), an architectural pattern book that had been recently published in English. No evidence of this book has been found in the Earl's library, nor did Adam appear to own a copy, but the timing suggests that Adam's influence is quite possible. The extraordinary combination of material and detail was so utterly à *la grecque* and so highly original it would have fuelled the Earl's appetite for similar spectacular pieces.

The Water Stand

One such piece, also supplied by Ince & Mayhew in 1767, was the remarkable water stand made for the Tapestry Room. This extraordinary item, with its rams' heads and intricate carving, was designed to hold a superb Sèvres jug and basin that the Earl had acquired earlier that year (see p. 189). The stand was made from padauk or padouk wood, known then as Redwood, and its design was based on an *athénienne* or classical tripod.

According to Coleridge, tripods of this type were first seen in a painting of 1762, *La Vertueuse Athénienne* by Joseph-Marie Vien (1716–1809), exhibited at the Paris Salon in 1763. Vien was a protégé of the Comte

A padauk wood water stand supplied by William Ince and John Mayhew designed to hold a Sèvres jug and basin, 1767

de Caylus, an important promoter of *le goût grec* and a man to whom Lord Coventry had been favourably compared by his brother-in-law, Gilly Williams, in 1766. The painting had been engraved by P. Filipart in 1765, so possibly Coventry had seen the painting or acquired a copy of this engraving for Adam to copy. On 6 May 1767, Adam invoiced for 'A Tripod altered from a French design for a Water Stand', and Eileen Harris has identified a preliminary sketch at Sir John Soane's Museum for this design, which she refers to as 'conclusive evidence of Adam's knowledge and use of French Neo-classical designs communicated to him by Lord Coventry and other patrons'.[6]

However brilliant the concept, it is evident from Adam's design that he was unaware of the form and appearance of the jug and basin at the time. The design had to be adapted by Ince & Mayhew, who also billed for further alteration and repairs to the stand on 22 April 1769. As executed, the stand was supported on four slender elegantly braced legs with cloven-hoofed feet. The legs were carved with rams' heads at the junction with the deep basin holder and had a square undertier to provide a safe base for the Sèvres jug. Although the tripod idea was abandoned, the ram's head and feet are similar to those in the Vien painting and the intricate carved decoration is unmistakably French in concept.[7] The ram's head motif also relates to that on the frame of the pier glass in the Tapestry Room supplied two years later, which may support the view that Adam contributed to the design of this mirror too.

Drawing for a tripod stand,
Robert Adam, 1767

The Handkerchief Card Table
There were several card tables in the Earl's collection, and the form and detail of the one within the Croome Estate Trust's collection is particularly appealing. It is one of a pair of card tables supplied by John Cobb, who charged the Earl six guineas for them on 30 July 1772. The bill describes it simply as 'an Inlaide Hankerchief table on a Carvd pillar and claws'.[8]

The ingenious design was adapted from a French *table en mouchoir*, although similar examples have been recorded in London in the 1730s. It was made from mahogany, its top veneered in pollard oak, which folds up like a square envelope to reveal an inlaid circular design formed from each triangular panel and uniting to create a central sunburst medallion. The top is supported on a fluted vase-shaped pillar set on an elegant tripod base, and the whole is so well proportioned that it looks equally

A handkerchief card table, made from mahogany veneered with pollard oak, supplied by John Cobb in 1772

good when the envelope top is either open or closed. Such a clever and graceful design was ideal for a game of piquet or quadrille, and its combination of beauty, function and French origins could not fail to please Lord Coventry.

The Tapestries

The Tapestry Room at Croome has been described by Christopher Rowell as 'a significant landmark in the 6th Earl's collecting and in the Parisian formation of his taste'.[9] Its sumptuous splendour combined the very best of contemporary English and French design and craftsmanship.

Lord Coventry seems to have been determined to make a statement with his Tapestry Room right from the start. He had arrived at the Royal Gobelins Manufactory in August 1763 with impressive haste and had placed an order for its latest design even before Louis XV. Known as the *Tentures de Boucher*, this design had been developed under the direction of Jacques-Germain Soufflot, in collaboration with the decorative artist, Maurice Jacques (1712–1784), and with the supervision of master-weaver, Jacques Neilson. The involvement of the popular artist, François Boucher, was a master stroke. His allegorical scenes were adapted as tapestry cartoons to form central features of each section in the design. These scenes were placed within medallions that appeared to be suspended from illusory gilt-wood frames, and set against a crimson and dark pink ground that simulated silk damask, lavishly embellished with swags, vases, abundant foliage and perched and fluttering birds. The design was as opulent as it was commercially astute, for it could be adapted in terms of its size, colour and composition to suit a customer's requirements. The idea of covering the entire wall surface with tapestry was also

a completely new concept for the Gobelins Manufactory and Coventry may well have influenced this decision.

Lord Coventry ordered a design known as *Les Amours des Dieux*, which depicted the four elements: Earth (Vetumnus and Pomona), Air (Aurora and Cephalus), Water (Neptune and Amymone) and Fire (Venus and Vulcan). Soufflot is now credited with the excellent idea of creating matching seat furniture, in conjunction with the designer Louis Tessier (1719/20–1781), in order to generate additional income as well as impact. Coventry ordered two settees and six gilt-wood armchairs, which were made by Ince & Mayhew. The armchairs were notable for their oval backs, which complemented the medallion designs and set an important precedent for neoclassical furniture of this type.

Boucher-Neilson tapestries were ordered subsequently by six other prominent English patrons, and the tapestry rooms created at Weston Park and Osterley resembled the original room at Croome most closely. The Croome Tapestry Room survives today in the Metropolitan Museum of Art in New York as a prime example of the Earl's influential role as tastemaker, of his receptiveness to new ideas, his close involvement in the design process and as one of the most important patrons and collectors of his day.[10]

Croome Court Tapestry Room: north wall as recreated at the Metropolitan Museum of Art, New York

The Sèvres Porcelain

Among the many treasures to be tracked down in Paris, Sèvres porcelain was high on the list. Much of the correspondence and also the bills that relate to these purchases survive in the Croome archive. These have been researched in detail by Rosalind Savill, and in her fascinating account of the Earl's porcelain purchases during the 1760s she has described the documents that relate to the purchases from 1767 as 'one of the most exciting sequences of bills relating to design, purchase and display to be recorded in the history of English patronage of Sèvres.'[11]

The Earl began acquiring porcelain in the 1750s, most probably through a friend or agent, but not until his visit to Paris in 1763 did his purchases begin in earnest. Most of his Sèvres collection was bought from Jean-Jacques Bachelier (1724–1806), who was a talented artist at this time as well as a dealer and worked for Louis XV and Madame de Pompadour, although he is remembered chiefly as the *directeur artistique* at Vincennes and Sèvres. Occasionally the Earl would acquire Sèvres from other dealers too, such as Poirier or Jacques-Antoine Rouveau, and by the late 1760s he was also purchasing items from Thomas Morgan in London. He continued to add to his collection well into the 1780s, buying items from Meissen and Worcester, but it was his patronage of Sèvres porcelain and the well-documented relationship he established with Bachelier, a man only two years younger than himself, that is of special interest and significance.

Ship-shaped Sèvres potpourri vase, c.1759–60, formerly owned by the Earls of Coventry

The Ship-Shaped Vase

Among the many important items of porcelain acquired by the 6th Earl was a ship-shaped vase. This is of particular interest not just because of its rarity and unusual design, but because of the intriguing mystery that surrounds its possible purchase that has been carefully unravelled by Savill. It was one of a set of three potpourri vases that date from 1759–60.[12] All had rose and green ground colours and were gilded and painted with scenes after David Teniers (1610–1690), but the ship-shaped vase was the most remarkable of the three. Only four ship-shaped vases of this type survive of the ten that are specified within the Sèvres sales record. All were sold between 1758 and 1762, so it is likely that this one was sold on to the Earl by a dealer. Frustratingly, no bill survives to confirm the purchase. However, the vase appears in an old photograph of the Tapestry Room, which must have been taken not long before it was sold by the 9th Earl of Coventry, George William, on 12 June 1874, and it is now in the collection of the J. Paul Getty Museum in California. Savill believes it was almost certainly the 6th Earl who acquired the vase as he was such an enthusiastic collector of Sèvres porcelain and it was just the highly

unusual type of item that appealed to him and that he would want to display among his other rare treasures in his Tapestry Room.

The Tea Service

Fortunately there need be no doubt at all about the 6th Earl's purchase of a small Sèvres tea service in 1764. The bill for this is dated 29 August 1764 and survives together with Bachelier's hand-written receipt.[13] Small it may have been, but the service cost around 30 guineas, an exceptional price that can only be attributed to its exquisite decoration. Comprised of a tray, a cup and saucer and a sugar bowl, it has an overglaze-blue ground and is decorated with pastoral scenes executed by the artist Charles-Nicolas Dodin (1734–1803), one of his earliest versions of Boucher's work. Savill has even proposed that this remarkable service may have been intended for a very special patron, possibly Madame de Pompadour, who died on 15 April 1764 just before the service was completed.[14] The service may have been destined for the Tapestry Room too, as its colour and decoration would complement the lapis lazuli incorporated within the scheme.

The Jug and Basin

Three years later, on 25 March 1767, Bachelier wrote to Lord Coventry concerning a jug and basin, *un broc et une jatte*, as well as four wine-bottle coolers that he had ordered. Together these cost a total of 968 livres or

Sèvres jug and basin, soft-paste porcelain painted with harebells and festoons of flowers, by Charles-Louis Mérceaud, 1767

approximately £40 6s, the jug and basin representing half of this amount. The letter begins:

> Milord
> J'ai remis à Monsieur Folley le broc et la jatte que vous m'avez chargé de vous faire faire; j'ose me flatter que vous en serez content. Cette nouvelle décoration a fait une très grand fortune à la Cour. Le Roi en a demandé de pareilles: Mad[am]e Durfort en a ordonné un Service de table; tout le monde en veut avoir.[15]

The new design referred to in the letter consisted of a white ground, richly embellished in bold reds, blues and purples with a broad and beautiful scrolled frieze of stylised harebells on a gold ground and with abundant festoons of flowers. Not surprisingly, the design became popular during the late 1760s and Savill has observed that it also appears on a Sèvres jug and basin of 1770 at Clandon Park. However, Lord Coventry's jug and basin were of particular quality and the most expensive of their type to be sold at Sèvres in the 1760s.

The jug and basin are both notably large in size and the basin is oval in form. Once again, these were acquired for the new Tapestry Room, as their colour and naturalistic detail matched the design of the tapestries perfectly. The plan was to display them on the water stand designed

specifically for this purpose by Robert Adam (see p.184). As is evident
from his drawing, Adam designed the stand with no knowledge of the
appearance of the jug and basin and it had to be modified by Ince &
Mayhew. Savill believes it unlikely that the jug and basin ever served
a practical purpose as the location of the jug on the lower part of the
stand would be very inconvenient. More likely, it was just intended to
enhance further the extraordinary quality of the room and its contents.

Paintings and Sculpture

Lord Coventry's collection of paintings and sculpture was substantial, if not exceptional. He added steadily to it throughout his life,
purchasing items by many leading contemporary European artists
and commissioning work from renowned British artists such as Allan
Ramsay (1713–1784), Joshua Reynolds (1723–1792), Frances Cotes
(1726–1770) and Richard Wilson.[16] The paintings seem to fall into three
main categories: the heirlooms, which included the inherited family
portraits, the vast *The Great Horse, or Jack-a-Dandy* (early 1700s) by
John Wootton (c.1682–1764), and some of the Flemish and Dutch works;
the commissioned works, which included the family portraits and the
famous Croome landscape by Wilson of 1758; and finally, a substantial
collection of works by Flemish, Dutch, French and Italian masters, most

of which were purchased in the late 1760s and 1770s, mainly by agents such as Robert Strange and a Mr Moore, and were destined for the walls of the Piccadilly townhouse.

The paintings kept at Croome were those that had a personal meaning and significance, and included the heirlooms and the commissioned works, not least the family and royal portraits and the Wilson landscape, his first topographical work on his return from Italy. These were displayed in appointed places in the Saloon, the Drawing Room and the Library, and on the walls of the Main and West Stairs. There was no place for paintings in the other rooms on the *piano nobile*, as Vassalli's plasterwork covered the walls in the Dining Room, and the Long Gallery and the Tapestry Room were works of art in themselves.

Following the Earl's death, there was a major sale on 16 February 1810 at Christie's in Pall Mall of the paintings and drawings kept at Piccadilly. Documents relating to this sale, correspondence from his agents, and also bills relating to the gilder and carver, John Touzey, who worked on frames for 36 of the paintings, provide some clue to their identity.[17] The collection included works by Hans Holbein, Peter Paul Rubens, Salomon van Ruysdael, Aelbert Cuyp, Willem van de Velde, Frans Snyders and Philips Wouwerman, as well as possibly by Nicolas Poussin and David Teniers, and a wide range of Italian masters, such as Annibale Carracci, Caravaggio, Canaletto, Domenichino, Parmigianino, Sebastiano Ricci, Salvator Rosa, Andrea del Sarto, Sassoferrato, Tiamingo, Tintoretto, Paolo Veronese, Giovanni Battista Zelotti and Francesco Zuccarelli. The work by Domenichino was said to be of a Bacchanalian subject; the painting by Caravaggio is described as being of two men playing musical instruments and a young woman standing by them; the work by Tiamingo depicted the marriage of a noble Venetian man; the painting by Zelotti was of a Venus, and the one by Carracci was of 'St James and St Carlo kneeling down in a Landskip'. The large Zuccarelli landscape, *The Rape of Europa*, was framed by Thomas Wolf of Soho to form a pendant to Wilson's painting, and this remains in the collection of the Croome Estate Trust.

Bronzes

The Earl did not collect antique sculpture but acquired various sculptures for decorative purposes. Most of these were supplied by John Cheere, including the ten plaster sculptures for the Long Gallery and the lead Flora and Ceres for the Temple Greenhouse. The origin of the sculptures for the Entrance Hall niches and the 12 busts on the Main Stair is not known, but these were cleaned by Cheere in 1765 and again in 1779. Similarly the sculpture in the park was purchased from the Coade catalogue.

However, as his Francophile tastes developed, the Croome accounts indicate that the Earl's interest in bronze vases and figures increased.[18] Much of his collection was probably destined for Piccadilly as it was in 1764 that he acquired his first bronze from Poirier, as well as various vases and figures from another Parisian dealer, Thomas Harrache. This was followed by the purchase of a pair of 'bronze boys candlesticks' and other unspecified French bronzes in 1767 and 1768. Then, in 1769, he bought a pair of bronze vases from Josiah Wedgwood (1730–1795).

Following a pause of around ten years Lord Coventry's purchases continued and a series of French and Italian bronzes were acquired from different English dealers, such as Thomas Martin, Richard Hayward and William Dermer. These included a Venus, a Flora, a Hercules, a Silenus and a pair of centaurs, as well as additional vases. The reason behind this fresh surge of interest is unclear, but the final purchase in 1804 from the dealer, Robert Blore, is particularly interesting. This was of a bronze figure of Greed for £20. Clearly Coventry's wit was as sharp as ever.

The Books

The Library ranked prominently in the Earl's priorities for his new house, as implied by his original intention to locate it in the west wing. It became a much-loved sanctuary, decorated under Adam's supervision to a similar high standard as the rest of the public rooms.

Like his portrait by Ramsay that hung above the chimney piece, the Earl's book collection served a similarly pleasing affirmation of his interests and achievements, with its notable emphasis on architecture, horticulture and antiquities. According to Mark Purcell, its contents were indicative, in general, of someone collecting, not just accumulating books to fill shelves.[19] This summary is based primarily upon Purcell's preliminary analysis of the collection and a review of the Earl's book bills and household accounts.[20]

Some impressive and expensive books have been identified, as well as many predictable purchases. They were not necessarily rare books, and some of the more important botanical works could have been inherited from his father or found their way to Croome from the collection of Anne Somerset, the 2nd Earl's widow, who corresponded with the 6th Earl and who wished to re-establish her connections with Croome and be buried in the new church.[21]

Poetry, music and history feature prominently within the collection, with poets ranging from Catullus to Edmund Spenser, Thomas Gray and Richard Jago. Among the favourite composers are George Frideric Handel, Arcangelo Corelli and Johann Sebastian Bach, while the histories include Francis Sandford's *Coronation of James II* (1687), William Robertson's

Croome Court Library bookcases designed by Robert Adam and supplied by William Vile and John Cobb, c.1763

History of America (1773) and the Roman studies by Edward Gibbon and Nathaniel Hooke. Other items of note include 24 volumes of Voltaire, for which the Earl paid a substantial £23 in 1773, the enormous *A Natural History of Uncommon Birds* by George Edwards, bought in three volumes in 1763 for 12 guineas, maybe for Barbara, and a 1587 Greek Bible in a fine French binding that was purchased at the *Loménie de Brienne* sale of 1724.

However, the books on architecture, horticulture and antiquities are the most revealing. Among these are William Tindal's *History and Antiquities of the Abbey and Borough of Evesham* (1794), John Dart's *The History and Antiquities of the Cathedral Church of Canterbury and the Once-Adjoining Monastery* (1726) bought in 1763, and a guide to Roman Bath. There was James Gibbs's *A Book of Architecture* (1728), essential reading for the amateur architect, Matthew Brettingham's *The Plans, Elevations and Sections, of Holkham ...* (1656), William Hogarth's *The Analysis of Beauty* (1753), James Paine's *Plans, Elevations and Sections of Noblemen and Gentlemen's Houses* (1767 and 1783), and William Chambers's *A Treatise on the Decorative Part of Civil Architecture* (1759). The Earl also subscribed to *Vitruvius Britannicus*, acquiring Volume IV in April 1770 and Volume V in May 1772, and every volume of Robert and James Adam's *Works* was purchased with tactful alacrity. The Library contained Robert Adam's *Ruins of the Palace of the Emperor Diocletian at Spalatro in Dalmatia* (1764), Antony Desgodetz's *The Ancient Buildings of Rome* (1771), which Adam had planned to revise, Giacomo Leoni's 1715 translation of Andrea Palladio's *I Quattro Libri dell'Architettura*, and works by authors such as Richard Dalton, William Hamilton and Julien David Le Roy, including a set of Sir William Hamilton's four volumes on Greek, Etruscan and Roman vases (1766–76).

The horticultural works were the most remarkable of all. These included a selection of grand and costly books, some with enormous colour plates that would have been important even when new. Among them was a first edition of Linnaeus of 1753, a set of the Comte de Buffon's *Histoire Naturelle* (1785–87), Sir Hans Sloane's *A Voyage to the islands of Madera, Barbados, Nieves, S.Christophers and Jamaica ...* (1707–25), Denis Dodart's *Memoires pour servir à l'histoire des plantes* (1676), and the magnificent and expensive *Natural History of Carolina, Florida and the Bahama Islands* (1729–47) by Mark Catesby.

The Plants

Lord Coventry pursued his passion for plants with a rigour and commitment that probably lasted longer and exceeded all his other great interests – and there were many. One need only consider the Croome plant bills if any evidence were needed. Over 600 of these survive, dating from 1746 to 1816, which bear witness to the extraordinary extent and range of Coventry's collection. These have been analysed in detail by the Croome Plant Research Group (CPRG), and the following summary can hope only to hint at Coventry's horticultural obsessions.[22] With his competitive instincts and love of the rare and unusual, he not only strove for quality and variety in his collection but also sought out the latest introductions and even brought several new species into England himself, earning the respect of the horticultural world.

His plant purchases had begun in the 1740s when he started buying large numbers of trees for the park, including elms, Scotch pine, beeches, sycamore, larch, cedar and cypresses, but perhaps it was his construction of a hothouse in 1750 in which to grow pineapples that first excited his interest in horticulture.

Many of his plants and seeds were bought from London-based nurseries. These would have been acquired from collectors abroad who would ship them to agents in England for distribution to landowners and nursery-men. Some of the bills are several pages long and reveal evidence of the Earl's care with his spending. Occasionally he scribbled notes on

Bill for plants from George Ferne, dated 6 January 1758. Lord Coventry has written on it: 'Very Very Dear – Pay no more'.

Bill for plants from George Ferne, dated 6 January 1758. Lord Coventry has written on it: 'Very Very Dear – Pay no more'.

them, so he must have scrutinised them in detail, and one early bill for American seed includes a stern reminder: 'Very Very Dear – Pay no more'.[23] Like many of his bills, it might be several years before they were paid. The Earl acquired plants and seeds directly from Barbara's contacts and relatives too, and as gifts from friends, like Lord Strafford, who provided him with Aleppo pines as well as pineapples, and Lord Rochford, who sent him boxes of seeds and plants from Madrid.[24] There were also other contacts, such as the eccentric Philip Thicknesse, who promised to supply him plants from Spain, and John Bush, who went to Russia to work for Empress Catherine II and sent back tales of the wolves and bears he had encountered in his efforts to secure the Earl's plants.

During the 1770s Coventry took on a talented head gardener, John Graefer (1746–1802), who may have encouraged his interest in rock plants. Then, in 1799, William Dean arrived. Dean's *Hortus Croomensis* (1824) includes a detailed list of over 5,000 varieties of plants and trees growing on the Croome estate, both of British origin and from all over the world. Among them were 27 different oaks, 27 pines, 14 types of poplar, 12 magnolias, 14 olives, 7 elms, 11 ash, 19 types of Prunus, 191 species of heather and many, many more. Similarly, in his *Arboretum and Fruticetum* (1838), John Claudius Loudon referred to over 90 trees of exceptional quality at Croome. As Arthur Young pointed out: 'no expence [*sic*] has been spared to render the collection complete', and, in his opinion, Croome was 'inferior only to Kew in the number, variety, and magnitude of the productions which it affords'.[25]

The Home Shrubbery, one of the Earl's favourite places, included magnificent specimens of cedar of Lebanon, ginkgos and evergreen oaks, a tulip tree, an oriental plane, and various cypresses and pines, including a Siberian stone pine near the Rotunda, said in Dean's 1824 guidebook to be the largest in the kingdom. To the north, behind the Church Shrubbery, were extensive orchards filled with a wide variety of fruit trees, of which 114 standard apple trees were bought in 1759. Beyond and to the north was the Arboretum and Flower Garden. In the Arboretum grew 300 labelled hardy trees of mainly foreign origin, but the Flower Garden was the real surprise. Laid out in the 1760s, at a time when the Earl was beginning to experiment more freely, it contained two greenhouses for his new collections of exotic plants – one for those of Eastern and Western origin, and another for Ericas, Proteas and other South African plants. During the 1790s, he added significantly to his collection of Ericas and Dean records an astonishing total of 205 species. Around 1759, the Earl acquired a collection of 39 different roses, a considerable number at that time. In the Flower Garden there was an orangery, with oranges, lemons, citrons and shaddock trees, and a conservatory filled with plants from New Holland, China and Otaheite, a South Pacific island visited by Captain Cook in 1796. There was also a small water garden with water lilies and gold and silver fish, a rockery, a collection of herbaceous plants and an American border, all of which enabled him to provide habitats for as wide a variety of plants as possible.

The great walled kitchen garden was another source of exciting horticultural experiment, now brought back into production by Chris and Karen Cronin. It included areas for a huge variety of soft fruit and vegetables, additional herbaceous borders, and, from the late 1750s, a wide selection of peaches, plums and nectarines were purchased to grow against walls, chosen for successive fruiting. In the north-western corner was a vinery, and to the south of this a fig house, a melon and cucumber house and then the pineapple pits or hotbeds covered by glass. This impressive array of structures was later joined in 1805–6 by the new vinery and hot wall constructed on the south side of the garden.

Croome Park, ginkgo in the Home Shrubbery

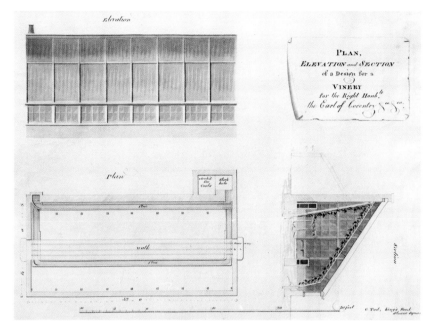

Plan, elevation and section of the Vinery, built together with the hot wall on the south side of the walled garden, George Tod, 1805,

The CPRG has noted several invoices for plants that predate their known introduction to Britain.[26] In February 1759, a prostrate Canadian juniper, *Juniperus communis var. depressus*, was bought for five shillings, a plant thought to have been introduced in 1783. Similarly, in February 1761, seeds of an American chestnut, *Castanea dentata*, and the Chinkapin oak, *Quercus prinoides*, were purchased, believed to have arrived in this country in 1783 and 1816, and there are other examples like this among the greenhouse plants and elsewhere. The Earl is also credited with bringing *Koelreuteria paniculata* and *Chimonanthus praecox* to Croome in 1763 and 1766. It was fitting that one of the first *Ranunculus asiaticus* to be introduced into Britain, the 'Earl of Coventry', was named after him, as was *Erica coventryana*, as a tribute to his exceptional contribution to the pursuit of botanical knowledge.[27] He was admitted as one of the first members of the Royal Horticultural Society in 28 March 1804, an honour that was hard-earned and well deserved.

EPILOGUE

Sacred to him the Genius of this place
Who reared these shades and formed these sweet retreats
With every incense breathing shrub adorned
And flower of faintest hue
His cultured tastes and native fancy bathed the scene around
Rise perfect and amuse who much he loved
Still joys to haunt it.
Crowned with length of days
He lived one wish alone unsated
Much his loyal heart had cherished
Fond hope to hail the day of Jubilee
And close his earthly course in Britain's hour of joy.

Inscription on the 6th Earl of Coventry's memorial in Croome Park

Croome Park, the 6th Earl of Coventry's memorial in the Home Shrubbery

The 6th Earl of Coventry died at his home in Piccadilly on 3 September 1809 aged 87. He never fulfilled his wish to witness his monarch's Golden Jubilee, but on 25 October 1809, the 49th anniversary of George III's reign, an elegant urn was erected to the Earl's memory beside his favourite walk in the Home Shrubbery. It was a discreet and peaceful spot and probably he chose it himself.

On 7 September, his body had been brought back to Croome and was placed in the Saloon, the coffin lit by candlelight and draped with crimson velvet. Two days afterwards his funeral took place. The long procession wound its way slowly round the park and up to the church, gathering in its wake the Earl's entire staff, around 200 tenants, officials, tradesmen and local worthies, his many friends, rivals and admirers from every sphere of his public and private life, and also the inevitable ranks of sightseers. The press reported that an 'astonishing number of people lined the road, and fell into the rear of the cavalcade', such was Lord Coventry's influence and reputation by this time.[1]

Only recently has it become clear that all his close family were present at his funeral and this would have pleased him. Following Barbara's death on 28 November 1800, Lord Coventry seems to have become increasingly withdrawn, afflicted with debilitating depression, arthritis and severe attacks of gout.[2] During this time he had been forced to confront the implications of his behaviour upon his legacy, particularly with regard to his sightless heir, George William, Lord Deerhurst.

Lord Deerhurst had rallied to confront his destiny with admirable fortitude. He had settled into a comfortable and respectable middle age with his second wife, Peggy Pitches, and had a fine townhouse at 14 Devonshire Place as well as a substantial estate in Streatham, which he was improving with an enthusiasm that echoed the tireless exploits of his father. He had also begun to re-establish his links with the county and was made lieutenant-colonel of the Worcestershire Militia on 10 May 1806, and in 1808 he had succeeded his father as Lord Lieutenant.

John, the Earl's favourite son, was living up at Springhill with his family and working on the improvements there with his father's blessing. Even his youngest son, Thomas William, had salvaged something of his shattered reputation. Disowned by his father, his unfortunate situation had been resolved by the generosity of his cousins, who offered him and his young wife, Catherine, a home at North Cray Place in Kent.[3]

Yet it was probably true that Lord Coventry was more familiar with the names and habits of his plants than those of his grandchildren. To be fair, he never neglected his duties and responsibilities towards his family. He continued to provide his estranged sons with regular financial support and this increased significantly as their families grew. This distant but dutiful attitude seemed to mellow in his final years. It also appears that his assumptions about the infinite virtues of John were challenged when John's wife, Anne, died in August 1809. Within days John married Anna Maria Eves (d.1837) of Clifford Place in Herefordshire, a widow with three children by her former husband, Ebenezer Pope. Lord Coventry died just a couple of weeks later: perhaps this unsettling change of circumstances proved too much to bear.

Lord Coventry's will is signed and dated 21 May 1802 and John was appointed his Executor. Croome, the core of his legacy, was left to Deerhurst in the correct manner, with generous allowances for Peggy and all his grandchildren. The Broadway property and the estates inherited from his father, the 5th Earl, were left to John, and there was provision for Barbara's nephews too, one year's wage to all his staff and £200 to the Worcester Infirmary. The remaining years of the leasehold on his townhouse in Piccadilly he left to John, with the sale of its fabulous contents to pay his funeral expenses, debts, mortgage and legacies and, if that amount was insufficient, John was to mortgage Springhill.

The house at 29 Piccadilly had served effectively only as an investment in his public image, but Lord Coventry gave Deerhurst the option to purchase the remaining leasehold and contents for £14,000 as long as he signified his desire to do so in writing to John within three months. This was rather clever. It seems as if he was holding out his hand to Deerhurst and offering him the chance to make a public and private apology, and to buy back his reputation. Deerhurst took up the offer, much as his father had predicted. In this way, Coventry ensured that he put right some of the damage he had inflicted, while also making sure that John and his family secured an ample portion of his fortune.

As his attitude towards his eldest and youngest sons began to soften, indecision set in. Just six months after he made his will, the first of many codicils appeared, one of them even dated Christmas Day and some of them not dated at all. These relate to gifts for his valet and other servants, but more significantly, on 22 February 1804, he left £2,000 to Deerhurst to spend on Streatham. Then, in 1806, he provided an annuity for Thomas William and a gift of money to Thomas Darby Coventry. The household accounts record the occasional gift from the 6th Earl to Deerhurst and his family, a harp for Peggy, and small items of furniture. There was also an annuity, a bequest and a gift of two unspecified pictures made to Jane Young. She was the wife of the Revd Arthur Young and the daughter-in-law of the Earl's friend of the same name. Jane had been mistreated by her husband, but she became devoted to her father-in-law, now a reformed character and fervent Evangelical. Her connection with the Earl remains a mystery, but it is possible she cared for him in his final years and perhaps she was also responsible in part for his decision to make amends to his estranged sons.

Through Lord Coventry's relentless efforts, Croome and its contents came to inspire the admiration and respect of the nation. His family acknowledged this achievement and endeavoured to maintain it as he would have wished. During the nineteenth century, the basic fabric of both house and landscape remained little altered, adapting only to Victorian standards of comfort and convenience. Only the sale of the magnificent Gobelins tapestries by the 9th Earl, another George William, served as a warning of imminent crisis. It was the 9th Earl who set up two Settled Land Trusts in 1887 and 1921 to protect the house, the park, the Coventry heirlooms and the surrounding estate. During the 1930s, his grandson, the 10th Earl, also George William, embarked on a major scheme of modernisation but was killed in action at Dunkirk in 1940 so never benefited from his investment. As the Second World War tore apart the social and economic fabric of the country, Croome braced itself for the future and played a special part of its own, providing a base for RAF

Defford, whose role in the development of radar technology made a significant contribution to the outcome of the war. By the late 1940s, the Croome Estate Trustees had little option but to put the house on the market. The family left and major sales dispersed many of its treasures far afield, but by no means all. A significant proportion of the collection remained, and the work of the Trustees ensured that Croome and its estate survived into the twenty-first century more intact than many other great houses and estates.

It continued to be a most accommodating and inspirational place. From 1950 to 1979 the Court became a Roman Catholic school, attached to nearby Besford School for disadvantaged boys, and from 1979 to 1984 it served as the worldwide centre for the International Society of Krishna Consciousness community. Following this period of benign management, the house was obliged to withstand the aspirations of various late twentieth-century developers. A sense of optimism returned in 1996 when Croome Park came into the care of the National Trust and a major scheme of restoration was put in place. Then, in 2007, the Croome Heritage Trust acquired the Court and leased it to the National Trust. The purchase of the Red Wing followed in 2011. This enabled the house to be reunited with its landscape park so that once again Croome could be appreciated as a single work of art and assert its true character as a place of creativity and experiment.[4]

⋆ ⋆ ⋆

Croome had brought the 6th Earl of Coventry security, solace and a sense of purpose. It became his stage and his sanctuary. It had been the focus of his aesthetic ambition, it had established his reputation as a man of exceptional and exquisite taste, and it had defined his stature as a patron of the arts. Croome was a collaborative creation, but it was under his auspices and close supervision that it became a place of experiment and opportunity, a place that nurtured the creative genius of Lancelot 'Capability' Brown and Robert Adam and that housed collections of widespread significance. His contribution had shaped and directed the project. He was responsible for both its strengths and its weaknesses, and for much of its special character and charm. Here the boundaries between patron and place begin to blur. For just as the 6th Earl had created Croome, so Croome had been the making of the Earl. It was fitting that his memorial recalled Alexander Pope's celebrated exhortation in its description of him as the 'Genius of this place'. The concept had been fundamental to the age in which he lived and to his own outlook. He had striven throughout his life to realise the latent potential in himself, in others and at Croome. He was, and still remains, its presiding spirit.

Notes

PROLOGUE PAGES 10–13

1   Letter from G.W. Coventry to Sanderson Miller, dated 22 May 1744. Dickins and Stanton (eds) 1910, p. 103.

AN ARISTOCRATIC AGE PAGES 14–27

1   See Cannon 1987.
2   See McKendrick, Brewer and Plumb (eds) 1982.
3   Mingay 1963.
4   In 1701 the Act of Settlement had sought to guarantee a Protestant succession and pronounced George I's mother, Sophia of Hanover, grand-daughter of James I, as heir to the English throne if William III and his heir Queen Anne died without issue. She was the closest living Protestant relative, although there were numerous Catholic relatives to choose from.
5   Mingay 1963. See also Turner 1999, pp. 13–20.
6   Hoskins 1955, pbk edn 2013, p. 167.
7   The ideas of the French natural historian, Georges Buffon (1707–1788), and Scottish geologist, James Hutton (1726–1797), were altering perceptions regarding the earth's history and mutability.
8   See Christopher Hussey's Introduction to Jourdain 1948, and Lees-Milne 1962, pp. 14–17.
9   Stourton and Sebag-Montefiore 2015, p. 9.
10   Turner 1999, p. 29.
11   See F. Herrman. The English as Collectors: A Documentary Sourcebook (1972) (London, 1999).
12   Stourton and Sebag-Montefiore 2015, p. 15.
13   G. Jackson-Stops (ed.). The Treasure Houses of Britain (New Haven and London, 1985), pp. 14–21.
14   Horace Walpole, The History of the Modern Taste in Gardening (1780; facsimile of 1982 edn, New York, 1995), p. 43.
15   The Stourhead so familiar today was the creation of Richard Colt Hoare in the 1790s.
16   See Hussey's Introduction in Stroud 1950.

AN ENVIABLE INHERITANCE PAGES 28–35

1   See Gordon 2000.
2   Edward Hyde, 1st Earl of Clarendon. The History of the Rebellion and Civil Wars in England, 4 vols (Oxford, 1702–4), I, p. 37.
3   The Lincolnshire property was alienated in the early eighteenth century while some of the smaller properties were disposed of in the early nineteenth century.
4   History of Parliament online (hereafter HoP), William Coventry, http://www.historyofparliamentonline.org/volume/1715-1754/member/coventry-william-?1676-1751 (accessed 8 January 2013).
5   Thomas Darby assumed the name Coventry and permission to use the Coventry coat of arms under the terms of his godfather's will. The Darby Coventrys moved to Versailles in 1821.

6   See A. Chilvers. The Berties of Grimsthorpe Castle (Bloomington, IN, 2010).
7   Letter from the 5th Earl of Coventry to the 7th Earl of Lincoln dated 1 April 1721. Newcastle correspondence, Catalogue of the General, Political and Family Correspondence of Henry Pelham-Clinton, 2nd Duke of Newcastle-under-Tyne (University of Nottingham, 1977), Ne C2914.
8   Survey of London, vol. XL (1980), pp. 117–66.
9   Dickins and Stanton (eds) 1910, p. 93.
10   See Rowell 2013, pp. 3–17.
11   Rowell has traced the missing portrait of George William Coventry to its reappearance at the Sotheby's auction of 29 May 1963. See Plate 19, Apollo (19 August 1963), p. xlvii. It was later re-advertised for sale by Charles Woollett & Son, 59/61 Wigmore St, London W1, but has not been located since.
12   Between 1720 and 1739 there were seven peers and sons of peers at University College, Oxford, second only to Christ Church, which had 21. See Cannon (1984), 1987, pp. 34–59.
13   WAAS 705:73 BA 14450/322 (1-19). History topics included 'War and the Role of the King', and 'The Causes of War' (apparently defence, the recovery of rightful property and punishment, or the French and the Scottish succession).
14   Ibid. (17).
15   Letter from Walpole to Horace Mann dated 23 November 1741, quoted in HoP, Thomas Henry Coventry, http://www.historyofparliamentonline.org/volume/1715-1754/member/coventry-thomas-henry-1721-1744 (accessed 8 January 2013).
16   Letter from T. Lennard Barrett to Sanderson Miller dated June 1744. See Dickens and Stanton (eds) 1910, p. 104–5.
17   HoP, Thomas Henry Coventry, http://www.historyofparliamentonline.org/volume/1715-1754/member/coventry-thomas-henry-1721-1744 (accessed 8 January 2013).
18   WRO 705:73 BA14450/331/4(1).
19   Letter from G.W. Coventry to Sanderson Miller dated 10 June 1744. Dickins and Stanton (eds), 1910, p. 103.
20   HoP, George William Coventry, http://www.historyofparliamentonline.org/volume/1715-54/member/coventry-george-william-(1722-1809) (accessed 8 January 2013). John Bulkeley took over the seat in 1751 until 1761. He had inherited the Bampton estates in Oxfordshire from his father and in 1764 he succeeded to the Nether Burgate estate on the death of his cousin, James Coventry Bulkeley, on condition that he adopted the Bulkeley surname under the terms of the will of his uncle, Sir Dewey Bulkeley.

EARL OF CREATION PAGES 36–49

1   See Ramsay's portrait of William Colyear, Viscount Milsington, of 1764 now in the collection at Penrhyn Castle (NT).
2   Lewis and Brown (eds) 1937–83. Walpole to Mann, 27 February 1752, 1960, vol. 20, p. 302. Hereafter referred to as Walpole Corresp.
3   See WAAS 705:73 BA14450/37, and Dolan 2009.

4   Quoted in Parker 1959, p. 91. Margaret Street was his father's family home.
5   Gaut 1932–42, pp. 118–41, p. 122.
6   See Gantz 1963, pp. 21–65.
7   Walpole Corresp, Walpole to Mann, 27 July 1752, 1960, vol. 20, p. 324.
8   Ibid., 1 November 1760, 1960, vol. 21, p. 451.
9   Mike Payne has established recently that Barbara did not die in 1804 as previously recorded, but on Friday 28 November 1800, aged 63.
10   WAAS 705:73 BA14450/299/9 (22).
11   Ibid., BA14450/23 (1) Jewellery and silver bills.
12   Walpole Corresp, Hertford to Walpole, 9 September 1763, 1974, vol. 38, p. 440, fn. 7.
13   WAAS 705:73 BA14450/288/7 (5).
14   Ibid., BA14450/287/9 (5).
15   Ibid., BA14450/153.
16   Ibid., BA14450/287/12 (1).
17   Ibid., BA14450/287/12 (6).
18   Ibid., BA14450/153.
19   Some accounts record the death of another child in January 1753.
20   See H. Rubenfold. Lady Worsley's Whim: An Eighteenth Century Tale of Sex, Scandal & Divorce (London, 2009).
21   WAAS 705:73 BA14450/100 Household bills, new items 1765–69.
22   Ibid., BA14450/287/7 (1).
23   See letter from H. Reade to Catherine Clinton, Countess of Lincoln, dated 26 June 1757, Newcastle correspondence, Ne C3127.
24   Dean 1824, p. 38.
25   Dickins and Stanton (eds) 1910, p. 214.
26   Quoted in Harris 2001, p. 41.
27   See R. Cooksey's account of the visit to Deerhurst: WAAS 705:73 BA14450.290/1.
28   See letter from Harriet Pelham-Holles to Henry Fiennes Clinton, 9th Earl of Lincoln, Newcastle correspondence, Ne C3631
29   Walpole Corresp, Letter from Lady Hervey, 19 December 1765, 1977, vol. 31, pp. 85–86.
30   Gordon 2000, pp. 88–89.
31   See R. Holden. Historical Record of the 3rd and 4th Battalions of the Worcestershire Regiment (London, 1887), p. 18.
32   Dean 1824, pp. 38–39.
33   See J. Lane. A Social History of Medicine, Health, Healing and Disease in England 1750–1950 (Abingdon, 2001).
34   See Noake 1868, p. 101.
35   See Willis 1984, pp. 382–91.
36   See the 6th Earl's account book with Child's Bank: WAAS 705:73 BA14450/359/4.
37   WAAS 705.73 BA14450 General accounts, notably /161/1-3, Household accounts 1758–80 /170 -9. I am grateful to Anne Owen for her work on the accounts.
38   See R. Floud, 'Capable entrepreneur? Lancelot Brown and his finances', in B. Elliott (ed.). Occasional Papers from the RHS Lindley Library, vol. 14 (October 2016), pp. 19–41.
39   Quoted in Reider 1996, p. 158.
40   Quoted in Coleridge 2000, pp. 8–19, p. 10.

THE HIDDEN HOUSE PAGES 50–69

1   AA: CVZ/Y/34.
2   BAM: QV1/1.

3 Gordon 2000, pp. 42–43.
4 See Colvin (1954) 1978, pp. 554–61 and pp. 870–74.
5 F.H.W. Sheppard. *Survey of London*, vol. XXXVI (London, 1970), pp. 25–34.
6 BAM: QV1/1.
7 Gordon 2010.
8 Cooper 2010.
9 BAM: QV1/1.
10 There is a possibility that the splendid Jacobean chimney piece at Pirton Court nearby was moved there from the house at Croome.
11 I am grateful to James Finlay, NT Advisor on Historic Interior Decoration, for this information.
12 For a full comparative analysis of contemporary developments in the design of the country house, see Cooper 1999.
13 West Woodhay was probably the work of Edward Carter, who had worked as Inigo Jones's deputy on the repair of St Paul's Cathedral.
14 AA: CVA/H3/4.
15 BAM: QV 2/1 & 2.
16 AA: CVZ/Y/34.
17 AA:CVA/H3/27.
18 Ibid.
19 See Gomme 2000, pp. 458–59. See also the 4th Earl's accounts: AA: CVA/H3/22 and CVA/H3/27.
20 AA: CVA/H3/22.
21 AA: CVA/H3/27.
22 Ibid.
23 This generous settlement was on condition the Countess was paid £500 annually in the event of Gilbert's death. When he died in 1719, she sued the 5th Earl for this annuity and won the case in 1724.
24 AA: CVE/Z/10.
25 No wing is shown on Doherty's plan of a similar date but this is rough and schematic and the accuracy of the architectural detail is questionable.
26 AA: CVA/H3/27.
27 AA: CVA/H3/27.
28 Ibid.
29 Ibid.
30 AA: CVE/Z/10.
31 AA: CVA/H3/22.

THE PRIMARY AUTHOR PAGES 70–81
1 See Hawkes 1964, and Meir 2006.
2 Lennard Barrett transposed his names when he inherited the title and was thereafter known as Barrett-Lennard.
3 See Dickens and Stanton (eds) 1910.
4 Miller records in his diaries that he used either a *camera obscura* or telescope to gauge the best viewpoints and picturesque effects. WCRO CR1382/1.
5 The idea was prompted by Lyttelton's familiarity with Cirencester Park and Stowe, and by his late wife's family home at Castle Hill in Devon and the small sham ruin nearby at Mount Edgcombe. See Meir 2006, p. 116, and also Cousins 2007, p. 47.
6 Hawkes 1969, pp. 99–107.

7 Letter from T.L. Barrett to Sanderson Miller dated January 1748, Dickens and Stanton (eds) 1910, pp. 135–36.
8 WCRO CR125B/147.
9 WAAS 705:73 BA14450 /287/3 (1).
10 WCRO CR125B/149.
11 Letter from Sir Edward Turner to Sanderson Miller dated 20 August 1748. See Dickens and Stanton (eds) 1910, p. 138.
12 WAAS 705:73 BA14450/288/1 (2).
13 Ibid., 222/1 (3).
14 WCRO CR125B/150.
15 WAAS 705:73 BA14450/288/1 (4).
16 See Milne 2014.
17 See WAAS 705:73 BA14450/288/1 (6).
18 WCRO CR125B/156.
19 WCRO CR125B/152.
20 Dean 1824, p. 46.
21 WCRO CR125B/152.
22 WCRO CR1382/1.
23 Hawkes believes Miller may also have been involved in the classical design of Gopsall Hall, Leicestershire, of c.1750 by the Hiorns of Warwick, where he advised on the grounds.
24 McCarthy 1976, pp. 214–25.
25 Cousins 2007, pp. 93–95.
26 Ibid. Prowse added corner towers to Kimberley Hall, Norfolk in 1754, a house of 1712 by Talman for Sir John Wodehouse, which resembles Hagley. Lancelot Brown designed the park at Kimberley in 1762.
27 WCRO CR125B/150. Deerhurst wrote to Miller on 13 December 1748, to ask him to design a Gothic front for a stable at Whitminster (probably never executed) for his friend, Richard Owen Cambridge.
28 WCRO CR2465 Box 4 Diaries CR1382/1.
29 WCRO CR125B/156.
30 Hester, Countess Temple, died in 1752. She was succeeded by her eldest son, Richard Grenville-Temple, 2nd Earl Temple, who was a close friend of Lord Coventry.
31 WCRO CR1382/1.
32 Ibid.
33 Ibid.
34 See Meir 2006, p. 199.
35 WCRO CR125B/153.

THE EMERGING GENIUS PAGES 82–135
1 See Robinson (1990), 1994 reprint, pp. 106–10. The temple is believed to have been designed by Cobham's nephew, Richard Grenville.
2 Quoted in H. Repton. *Sketches and Hints on Landscape Gardening* (London, 1795).
3 Brown 2011, p. 48.
4 Hyams 1971, p. 24.
5 Willis 1984, vol. 27, pp. 382–91. See also WAAS 705:73 BA14450/23 Brown's receipts 1763–1782 and the 6th Earl's account with Child's Bank BA14450/359/4.
6 Letter from Lord Coventry to Sanderson Miller dated 14 November 1752: WCRO CR125/153.
7 See Beresford 1996.
8 See Brown and Williamson 2016.
9 Brown visited Wilton in 1753: Brown 2011, p. 84.
10 The domes have always been attributed to Gibbs but the authorship of Houghton as executed remains unclear.

11 Roger Morris has been proposed as the probable architect. (See *Georgian Group Journal*, vol. XIV (2004), pp. 26–32 and 33–47).
12 Cousins 2007, p. 49.
13 See Gordon 2010. This schedule is based on a summary of the bills by Jill Tovey, Croome archivist.
14 WCRO CR125/153.
15 Dickens and Stanton (eds) 1910, p. 184.
16 The existing fireplace is a mid-nineteenth-century addition. Its Rococo chimney piece was relocated from elsewhere in the house so that the space might be used as an additional reception room.
17 This may mark the location of the former entrance to the seventeenth-century Back Stair.
18 See A. Little. *Hidden Treasures*, unpublished notes on the history of the basement, March 2016.
19 WAAS 705:73 BA14450/F62/30.
20 See Gordon 2012.
21 Tim Hickson has proposed that the small room next to the servants' hall could originally have provided accommodation for the Earl's French chef.
22 I am grateful to Nick Joyce of Nick Joyce Architects Ltd for information regarding the building's structural history.
23 WAAS 705:73 BA14450/100 Craftsmen and Manufacturers bills.
24 Sarah Kay's *Conservation Management and Maintenance Plan* of 2012 has collated and summarised most of the published and unpublished sources of information on the interior fittings and decoration and provides an invaluable reference source.
25 WAAS 705:73 BA14450/F62/15. Hobcraft itemises the outer doors as being made of oak and the inner doors of mahogany.
26 Ibid., F62/24. The lantern was sold in 1960 and the plasterwork eagle was removed in the 1980s.
27 Ibid., F62/18.
28 Brown's design for the Picture Gallery was intended originally for Burton Constable in East Yorkshire.
29 Ibid., F62/18.
30 Ibid., F62/16.
31 Ibid., F62/35.
32 The scroll frieze reappears elsewhere in the house at this time, for example on the Main Stair and in a first-floor bedroom.
33 The mirrors are similar to a design for 'Glass frames' dated 1760 in the third edition of Chippendale's *Directory*, so it is possible that he may have supplied the design. See C. Gilbert. *Furniture at Temple Newsham House and Lotherton Hall*, vol. II (London and Leeds, 1978), pp. 361–62.
34 The frames were sold to the Metropolitan Museum of Art, New York, by the Croome estate in 1960.
35 Its unusually shallow relief has raised questions concerning its origin.
36 WAAS 705:73 BA14450 /F62/19.
37 Ibid., F62/15.
38 See Hassall 2008.

39 WAAS 705:73 BA14450/F62/35.
40 Ibid., F62/6.
41 Ibid., F59, F62 and F69a.
42 Ibid., F60/6.
43 Ibid., F62/18.
44 Rutherford 2016, p. 99.
45 Hawkes has noted the close resemblance between Croome Church and Wroxton Church, and cites Magdalen College Chapel as the possible source of their design.
46 Dean 1824, p. 69.
47 Unpublished report by Whitton Associates on behalf of the National Trust, 2009.
48 R.B. Johnson. *Letters of Hannah More* (London, 1925), quoted in Stroud 1950, p. 198.
49 Dean 1824, p. 53.
50 Quoted in Repton 1803, pp. 168–69.
51 Dean 1824, p. 49, and Young 1801, p. 466.
52 See Stroud 1940, part I, pp. 14–18.
53 Young 1801, pp. 465–81, p. 478.
54 Ibid., pp. 466–67.
55 See Gordon 2000, p. 136. Also Bradney 2016–17.
56 Letter from the 6th Earl of Coventry to Humphry Repton from Springhill in 1793. Quoted in Repton 1803.
57 BL Add MS69795 Folio 42.
58 Letter from Lancelot Brown, eldest son of Lancelot 'Capability' Brown, to Lord Coventry, dated 27 November 1783. WAAS 705:73 BA14450/23/15.

THE REFINEMENT OF GENIUS
PAGES 136–165

1 John Wilton-Ely and Frances Sands, who have expert knowledge of Adam's drawings, are both of the opinion that Adam is the likely author of the drawing.
2 See Stroud (1950) 1957, pp. 98–99.
3 Sarah Kay's *Conservation Management and Maintenance Plan* of 2012 has collated and summarised most of the published and unpublished sources of information on the interior fittings and decoration and provides an invaluable reference source.
4 The Sir John Soane's Museum design is a copy. The original is at the Metropolitan Museum of Art, New York. The bothy was added *c*.1762.
5 Harris 2001, p. 45. Some of the fittings may have influenced later work at Alnwick Castle of *c*.1766–81, notably a design for the chairs of 1761.
6 Ibid., p. 43.
7 Letter dated 13 May 1739 from Thomas Henry Coventry in Oxford to T.W. Younge in Paris. WAAS 705:73 BA14450/299 (11).
8 Harris 2001, pp. 52–53.
9 WAAS 705:73 BA14450/F62/30, F62/32, F62/52.
10 Ibid., F62/51.
11 Harris 2001, p. 52.
12 An undated plan for a 'Matt in the Gallery' survives in the Croome archive. Also see W. Hefford. 'Thomas Moore of Moorfields', *Burlington Magazine*, vol. 119 (December 1977), pp. 840–48.
13 Harris 2001, p. 45.
14 King (1991) 2001, p. 232.
15 A much grander version of the design appeared at Nostell in 1766–80.

16 WAAS 705:73 BA14450/F62/30.
17 Ibid., F62/32.
18 Ibid., F62/30 and F62/35.
19 Letter from Gilly Williams to George Selwyn dated 4 August 1763. See J.H. Jesse. *Memoirs of George Selwyn and his Contemporaries*, 1902, vol. 1, p. 225.
20 Dean 1824, pp. 54–55.
21 The skirting at Croome may be the original one as suggested by the thick layers of paint that mask the mouldings.
22 WAAS 705:73 BA14450/F62/15 and F62/19.
23 Ibid., F60/32.
24 Ibid., F62/15.
25 Ibid., F62/29a.
26 See Gordon 2000, pp. 133–35, and Sands 2016, pp. 93–97.
27 Sands 2016, p. 94.
28 Ibid., pp. 93–97.
29 WAAS 705:73 BA14450/209/5 (2) and (3).
30 King (1991) 2001, pp. 328–29, fn. 20.
31 Ibid., p. 383.
32 BL Add MS69795 Folio 8.
33 WAAS 705:73 BA14450/209/6.
34 King (1991) 2001, pp. 206–7.
35 WAAS 705:73 BA14450/209/6 .

THE FINAL FLOURISH PAGES 166–179

1 His interest in theatrical effects had been reinforced by his work at the Theatre Royal, Drury Lane, in 1775 on behalf of his friend, David Garrick.
2 King (1991) 2001, p. 330.
3 WAAS 705:73 BA14450/F58/7.
4 *The Gentleman's Magazine* (July 1792), quoted in Dean 1824, pp. 47–48.
5 Young 1801, p. 467.
6 See Robinson 2012.
7 *Walpole Corresp*, Walpole to Hannah More, 31 July 1790, 1977, vol. 31, p. 342.
8 *ODNB*, vol. 60 (Oxford, 2004), pp. 572–77.
9 WAAS 705:73 BA14450/F58/6/1 and F58/7/1.
10 Ibid., F62/68e.
11 Ibid., F60A/49.
12 See Bradney 2016–17, Part 3, pp. 13–21.
13 Frew 1982, pp. 144–49.
14 J. Bentham. *History and Antiquities of the Conventual and Cathedral Church of Ely, Cambridgeshire* (Cambridge, 1771). Wyatt was commissioned to restore Ely Cathedral *c*.1794 and almost certainly consulted Bentham's book.

THE COLLECTIONS PAGES 180–197

1 Stourton and Sebag-Montefiore 2015, p. 27.
2 Coleridge 2000, pp. 8–19.
3 Ibid., p. 12. Also Lane 1997, pp. 25–29.
4 Coleridge 2000, p. 15.
5 WAAS 705:73 BA14450/207/3.
6 Harris 1963, p. 100.
7 See C. Rowell. *Furniture in National Trust Houses* (New Haven and London, 2015).
8 Coleridge 2007, pp. 1–4.
9 See Rowell 2015 (as in note 7 above), and Harris 2001, pp. 47–48.
10 Other principal sources are too numerous to list but include, in particular, W. Reider, James Parker et al. from the Metropolitan Museum

of Art, New York, and Geoffrey Beard, Eileen Harris, Susan Leech and Helen Wyld.
11 Savill 2015, pp. 134–60, p. 11.
12 Ibid., pp. 151–53.
13 Ibid., pp. 136–37.
14 Ibid., pp. 139–43.
15 WAAS 705:73 BA14450/209/1 (10).
16 Laing 2004.
17 See WAAS 705:73 BA14450/288/10 (1-2), and Lane 1997.
18 WAAS 705:73 BA14450/23.
19 M. Purcell, notes on Croome Court book collection, email to Sarah Kay dated July 2011.
20 See book bills WAAS 705:73 BA14450/147 and 354.
21 She died in February 1763, just months before the new church was consecrated.
22 M. Stone et al. 2016.
23 WAAS 705:73 BA14450/439/1 (8).
24 WAAS 705:73 BA14450/288/2 (3) and 288/6 (6).
25 Young 1801, pp. 465–81, p. 478.
26 Stone et al. 2016, pp. 18–19.
27 Ibid., pp. 54–55.

EPILOGUE PAGES 198–201

1 WAAS 705:73 BA14450/326 (1-5).
2 *Walpole Corresp*, Hertford to Walpole, 9 September 1763, 1974, vol. 38, p. 440, fn. 7.
3 Thomas William's wife died in 1806 and in 1813 he married Sarah Manton of St Martin Ludgate, London. He died three years later and was buried at North Cray, Kent.
4 For a more detailed account of Croome's nineteenth- and twentieth-century history see Gordon 2000; Kay 2012; and the work of the Defford Airfield Heritage Group (DAHG) now brought together at the RAF Defford Museum at Croome under the curatorship of Dennis Williams.

Select Bibliography

PUBLISHED SOURCES

Adam, R. and Adam, J. *The Works in Architecture of Robert and James Adam* (London, 1773–79) (pbk edn New York, 2006).

Beard, G. *Craftsmen and Interior Decoration in England 1660–1820* (London, 1981).

Beard, G. *The English House Interior* (London, 1991).

Bolton, A.T. *The Architecture of Robert and James Adam* (London, 1922), reissued 1984.

Brown, D. and Williamson, T. *Lancelot Brown and the Capability Men* (London, 2016).

Brown, J. *The Omnipotent Magician, Lancelot Capability Brown 1716–83* (London, 2011).

Cannon, J. *Aristocratic Century: the Peerage of Eighteenth-Century England* (1984) (Cambridge, 1987).

Carter Brown, J. et al. *The Treasure Houses of Britain: 500 years of Private Patronage and Art Collecting* (Washington, D.C., 1985).

Colvin, H. *A Biographical Dictionary of British Architects 1600–1840* (1954) (second edn London, 1978).

Cooper, N. *Houses of the Gentry 1480–1680* (New Haven and London, 1999).

Dean, W. *An Historical and Descriptive Account of Croome D'Abitot ...* (Worcester, 1824).

Dickins, L. and Stanton, M. (eds). *An Eighteenth Century Correspondence* (London, 1910).

Gantz, J. *The Pastel Portrait* (London, 1963).

Gomme, A. *Smith of Warwick: Francis Smith, Architect and Master-Builder* (Stamford, 2000).

Gordon, C. *The Coventrys of Croome* (Phillimore in association with the National Trust, 2000).

Halfpenny, W. and Halfpenny, J. *Rural Architecture in the Chinese Taste: New Designs for Chinese Temples. Improvements in Architecture and Carpentry* (London, 1750–52).

Harris, E. *The Furniture of Robert Adam* (London, 1963).

Harris, E. *The Genius of Robert Adam: His Interiors* (New Haven and London, 2001).

Hoskins, W.G. *The Making of the English Landscape* (1955) (pbk edn Toller Fratrum, Dorset 2013).

Hyams, E. *Capability Brown and Humphry Repton* (London, 1971).

Jourdain, M.J. *The Work of William Kent* (London, 1948).

Kelly, A. *Mrs Coade's Stone* (London, 1990).

King, D. *The Complete Works of Robert and James Adam and Unbuilt Adam* (Oxford, 1991), reprint 2001.

Lees-Milne, J. *The Age of Adam* (London, 1947).

Lees-Milne, J. *Earls of Creation: Five Great Patrons of Eighteenth-century Art* (London, 1962).

Lewis, W.S. and Brown, R.S. (eds). *Horace Walpole's Correspondence* (New Haven and London 1937–83).

McKendrick, N., Brewer, J. and Plumb, J.H. (eds). *The Birth of a Consumer Society: The Commercialization of Eighteenth-Century England* (London, 1982).

Meir, J. *Sanderson Miller and his Landscapes* (Chichester, 2006).

Mingay, G. *English Landed Gentry in the Eighteenth Century* (London, 1963).

Mowl, T. *Gentleman Gardeners: the Men Who Created the English Landscape Garden* (Stroud, 2000).

Noake, J. *Noake's Guide to Worcestershire* (London, 1868).

Phibbs, J. *Capability Brown: Designing the English Landscape* (Milan, 2016).

Reider, W. 'The Croome Court Tapestry Room, Worcestershire, 1771', in A. Peck et al., *Period Rooms in the Metropolitan Museum of Art* (New York, 1996) (second edn New Haven and London, 2006).

Repton, H. *Observations on the Theory and Practice of Landscape Gardening ...* (London, 1803).

Repton, H. *An Enquiry into the Changes of Taste in Landscape Gardening ...* (London, 1806).

Robinson, J.M. *Temples of Delight* (London, 1990), reprint 1994.

Robinson, J. M. *James Wyatt 1746–1813: Architect to George III* (New Haven and London, 2012).

Rutherford, S. *Capability Brown and his Landscape Gardens* (London, 2016).

Sands, F. *Robert Adam's London* (Oxford, 2016).

Stourton, J. and Sebag-Montefiore, C. *The British as Art Collectors* (London, 2015).

Stroud, D. *Capability Brown* (London, 1950), reprint 1957.

Summerson, J. *Architecture in Britain 1530–1830* (London, 1953) (pbk edn 1970).

Turner, R. *Capability Brown and the Eighteenth-Century English Landscape* (1985) (Chichester, 1999).

Woolf, J. and Gandon, J. *Vitruvius Britannicus*, vol. V (London, 1771).

Young, A. *Annals of Architecture and Other Useful Arts*, vol. XXXVII (Bury St Edmunds, 1801).

ARTICLES

Bradney, J. 'Springhill: The 6th Earl of Coventry', *Gloucestershire Gardens and Landscape Trust Newsletter*, Parts 1–3, Part 3 (Winter 2016-17), pp. 13–17.

Coleridge, A. 'English furniture supplied for Croome Court: Robert Adam and the 6th Earl of Coventry', *Apollo*, vol. CLI (February 2000), pp. 8–19.

Coleridge, A. 'John Cobb's "Hankerchief" table', *The Furniture History Society Newsletter*, vol. 167 (August 2007), pp. 1–4.

Cousins, M. 'Hagley Park, Worcestershire', *Garden History*, vol. 35, supplement 1 (special edition published with the support of the Hereford and Worcester Gardens Trust by The Lavenham Press, 2007).

'Croome Court, Worcestershire: The Seat of the Earl of Coventry', *Country Life*, vol. 13 (1903), pp. 536–42.

'Croome Court, Worcestershire: The Seat of the Earl of Coventry', *Country Life*, vol. 37 (1915). pp. 482–89.

Frew, J. 'Some observations on James Wyatt's gothic style 1790–97', *Journal of the Society of Architectural Historians*, vol. 41 (August 1982), pp. 144–49.

Gaut, R.C. 'Croome Park', *Transactions of the Worcestershire Naturalists Club*, vol. IX (1932–42), pp. 118–41.

Grice, F. 'The park ornaments of Croome D'Abitot', *Transactions of the Worcestershire Archaeological Society*, vol. 5, 3rd series (1976), pp. 41–49.

Harris, E. 'Robert Adam and the Gobelins', *Apollo*, vol. 7 (April 1962), pp. 100–6.

Hawkes, W.H. 'Miller's work at Wroxton', *Cake and Cockhorse*, vol. 4, no. 6 (Winter 1969), pp. 99–107.

Lane, J. 'The furniture at Croome Court: the patronage of George William, 6th Earl of Coventry', *Apollo*, vol. 145 (January 1997), pp. 25–29.

Leech, S. 'A story of loss and survival: Croome Court's lost Tapestry Room and its replica', *NT Bulletin* (Spring 2015), pp. 13–14.

McCarthy, M. 'The building of Hagley Hall', *Burlington Magazine*, vol. 118, no. 877 (April 1976), pp. 214–25.

Parker, J.C. 'Croome Court: the architecture and furniture', *Metropolitan Museum of Art Bulletin* (November 1959), pp. 76–111.

Paton, A. 'The botany of Croome Court', *Transactions of the Worcestershire Archaeological Society*, vol. 6, 3rd series (1978), pp. 71–73.

Rowell, C. 'Portraits of "Dr Burton's Commoners" at Winchester College: one signed and dated (1737) by Isaac Whood (1689–1752)', *The British Art Journal*, vol. XIV, no. 1 (Spring 2013), pp. 3–17.

Savill, R. 'The 6th Earl of Coventry's purchases of Sèvres porcelain in Paris and London in the 1760s', *The French Porcelain Society Journal*, vol. 5 (2015), pp. 134–60.

Stone, M., Hooper, A., Shaw, P. and Tanner, L. 'An eighteenth century obsession: the plant collection of the 6th Earl of Coventry at Croome Park, Worcestershire', *Garden History*, vol. 43, no. 1 (Summer 2015), pp. 74–125, and published by the National Trust (Croome, 2016).

Stroud, D. 'The architectural works of Lancelot Brown', *Country Life*, vol. 87 (6 and 13 January 1940).

Willis, P. 'Capability Brown's account with Drummond's Bank 1753–1783', *Architectural History*, vol. 27 (1984), pp. 382–91.

ONLINE SOURCES
http://www.historyofparliamentonline.org

UNPUBLISHED SOURCES
Beresford, C., *Croome Court: Historic Landscape Survey for the National Trust*, unpublished report on behalf of the National Trust, 1996.

Cooper, N. *Croome Court: The Seventeenth-Century House. A Discussion*, unpublished report on behalf of the National Trust, December 2010.

Dolan, A. 'Reassessing the aristocratic male consumer: the Sixth and Seventh Earls of Coventry and their clothes, 1759–1830', BA History dissertation, Royal Holloway, University of London, 2009.

Gordon, C. *Croome Court, Worcestershire: An Historical and Archaeological Survey*, unpublished report on behalf of the National Trust, 2010.

Gordon, C. *The Red Wing, Croome Court: An Interim Report on its Structural Evolution and Historic Uses*, unpublished report on behalf of the National Trust, 2012.

Hassall, C. *Initial Paint Analysis: Croome Court*, undertaken on behalf of the National Trust, July 2008.

Hawkes, H.W. 'Sanderson Miller of Radway 1716–1780: architect', dissertation submitted for the Diploma in Architecture, University of Cambridge, 1964.

Kay, S. *Croome Court Conservation Management and Maintenance Plan*, undertaken on behalf of the National Trust, 2012.

Laing, A. *Croome Court Pictures*, 2004.

Milne, J. *The Chinese Bridge at Croome Landscape Park*, unpublished archaeological report on behalf of the National Trust, May 2014.

Purcell, M. *Notes on the Book Collection at Croome Court*, 2011.

Rodwell, K.A. *The Red Wing, Further Observations on the Structural Sequence*, 2005.

Rowell, C. *Croome Court – Notes on the Furniture and Works of Art*, 2004.

Wilton-Ely, John. *Notes from Visit to Croome Court, 18 June 2010*.

Picture Credits

The watercolour illustrations of the south elevation of Croome Court, on the cover and pages 100 to 105, were commissioned from David Birtwhistle especially for this book.

Cover, pp. 100–5: © The Croome Heritage Trust/David Birtwhistle; frontispiece, pp. 50–1, 91, 127 (below), 130, 136, 178–9, 198: © Jack Nelson; pp. 6–7: WAAS 705:73 BA14450/250 Worcestershire Archive and Archaeology Service; pp. 8–9, 11, 56, 67, 99 (left), 110, 115, 129, 135, 166, 176: © Catherine Gordon; p. 17: © Sir John Soane's Museum, London, SM Adam volume 35/4. Photo: Ardon Bar-Hama; p. 19: © Archivist/Alamy Stock Photo; p. 21: NPG 6063 © National Portrait Gallery, London; p. 22: NG1018 © The National Gallery, London, Wynn Ellis Bequest, 1876; p. 23 (above): © Rod Edwards/Alamy Stock Photo; p. 23 (middle): © Bob Farndon; p. 23 (below): © Pat Tuson/Alamy Stock Photo; p. 25: © By kind permission of the Earl of Leicester and the Trustees of the Holkham estate; p. 26: © Jane Tregelles/Alamy Stock Photo; pp. 28, 32, 33 (left), 33 (middle), 33 (right), 34, 39, 42, 181, 183, 185, 188, 189, 190: © The Croome Estate Trust. Photo: Jack Nelson; p. 40: © Photo: SCALA, Florence 2017; p. 41: WAAS 705:73 BA14450/153, July 26 1796 from Clanfield, Worcestershire Archive and Archaeology Service; p. 44: © Image from Worcester City collection; p. 47: WAAS 705:73 BA14450/209/1(18a) Worcestershire Archive and Archaeology Service; pp. 52, 117, 172–3: © National Trust/David Birtwhistle; pp. 54 (left), 62, 120 (above): © Ric Tyler; pp. 54 (right), 57: WAAS 705:73 BA14450/453(iv) Worcestershire Archive and Archaeology Service; pp. 60, 66: Prattinton Collection © The Society of Antiquaries, London; pp. 61, 82, 99 (right), 113 (left), 113 (right), 119, 122, 123, 124, 148: © National Trust/Robert Thrift; pp. 63, 65, 71: © National Trust Images; pp. 73, 93: © Hagley Estate. Reproduced by kind permission of Viscount Cobham; p. 74: WAAS 705:73 BA14450/248 Worcestershire Archive and Archaeology Service; p. 83: NPG 6049 © National Portrait Gallery, London; pp. 84, 85: © National Trust Images/Andrew Butler; p. 87: 163329 © National Trust Images/Andrew Butler; p. 88: WAAS 705:73 BA14450/F62/7 Worcestershire Archive and Archaeology Service; p. 89: WAAS 705:73 BA14450/F62A/3w Worcestershire Archive and Archaeology Service; p. 92: © Swindon Borough Council; pp. 95, 108 (above), 108 (below), 109 (above), 109 (below): © National Trust/Foster Surveys/Ric Tyler; p. 116: © Nick Joyce Architects Ltd 2017; pp. 120 (below), 150, 151: © Country Life Picture Library; pp. 128 (above), 169: WAAS 899:192 BA2432/1 Worcestershire Archive and Archaeology Service; p. 133 (left): © National Trust/Christopher Warleigh-Lack; p. 133 (right): © National Trust Images/John Millar; p. 137: NPG 2953 © National Portrait Gallery, London; p. 141: SM Adam volume 29/138 © Sir John Soane's Museum, London. Photo: Ardon Bar-Hama; p. 142 (above): SM Adam volume 29/136 © Sir John Soane's Museum, London. Photo: Ardon Bar-Hama; p. 142 (middle): SM Adam volume 11/34 © Sir John Soane's Museum, London. Photo: Ardon Bar-Hama; p. 142 (below): SM Adam volume 11/34 11/36 © Sir John Soane's Museum, London. Photo: Ardon Bar-Hama; p. 144: SM Adam volume 50/15 50/16 © Sir John Soane's Museum, London. Photo: Ardon Bar-Hama; p. 145: SM Adam volume 50/10 © Sir John Soane's Museum, London. Photo: Ardon Bar-Hama; p. 149: SM Adam volume 17/73 © Sir John Soane's Museum, London. Photo: Ardon Bar-Hama; p. 154: SM Adam volume 50/12 © Sir John Soane's Museum, London. Photo: Ardon Bar-Hama; p. 155: SM Adam volume 17/152 © Sir John Soane's Museum, London. Photo: Ardon Bar-Hama; p. 156 (left): WAAS 705:73 BA 14450/F62/30a Worcestershire Archive and Archaeology Service; p. 156 (right): SM Adam volume 50/11 © Sir John Soane's Museum, London. Photo: Ardon Bar-Hama; p. 158 (left): SM Adam volume 7/144 © Sir John Soane's Museum, London. Photo: Ardon Bar-Hama; p. 158 (right): © Sarah Kay; p. 159: SM Adam volume 14/145 © Sir John Soane's Museum, London. Photo: Ardon Bar-Hama; p. 160: WAAS 899:192 BA2432/3 Worcestershire Archive and Archaeology Service; p. 161: SM Adam volume 19/146 © Sir John Soane's Museum, London. Photo: Ardon Bar-Hama; p. 163: SM Adam volume 51/84 © Sir John Soane's Museum, London. Photo: Ardon Bar-Hama; p. 174: D19320 © National Portrait Gallery, London; p. 184: SM Adam volume 6/177 © Sir John Soane's Museum, London. Photo: Ardon Bar-Hama; p. 186: © Gift of Samuel H. Kress Foundation, 1958; p. 187: © Digital image courtesy of the Getty's Open Content Program; p. 193: © Victoria and Albert Museum, London; p. 195: WAAS 705:73 BA14450/439/1(8) from G. Ferne, Worcestershire Archive and Archaeology Service; p. 196: © Katherine Alker

Index

Illustrations are denoted by the use of *italics*.
Book titles are entered under the author's name.